University of Wisconsin
Center for Southeast Asian Studies

Monograph Number 7

ANTHROPOLOGY GOES TO WAR

Center for Southeast Asian Studies
University of Wisconsin
Monograph Series

Publications Committee

ANTHROPOLOGY GOES TO WAR

PROFESSIONAL ETHICS &

COUNTERINSURGENCY IN THAILAND

by

Eric Wakin

University of Wisconsin
Center for Southeast Asian Studies
Monograph Number 7

1992

Cover Photo Credits:

Eric Wolf   AP/Wide World Photos

Thai Soldier   Kim Gooi, *Far Eastern Economic Review*

Lao Peasant fleeing   John Everingham
U.S. bombing of
Plain of Jars,
northern Laos, 1971

Margaret Mead   American Anthropological Association.

Library of Congress Card No. 91-74029

Published by the

Center for Southeast Asia Studies
University of Wisconsin-Madison
Madison, WI 53706
USA

Telephone: (608) 263-1755
FAX: (608) 262-2150

Table of Contents

List of Tables

List of Appendices

List of Acronyms

AAA	American Anthropological Association
AACT	Academic Advisory Council for Thailand
AAS	Association for Asian Studies
AFOSR	Air Force Office of Scientific Research
AID	Agency for International Development
ARD	Accelerated Rural Development (Thailand)
ARO	Army Research Office
ARPA	Advanced Research Projects Agency
BPP	Border Patrol Police (Thailand)
CAL	Cornell Aeronautics Laboratory
CD	Community Development (Thailand)
CI	Counterinsurgency
CIA	United States Central Intelligence Agency
CINFAC	Cultural Information Analysis Center, originally, the Counterinsurgency Information Analysis Center (part of CRESS)
COIN	Counterinsurgency
CPT	Communist Party of Thailand
CRESS	Center for Research in Social Systems (at American University)
CSOC	Communist Suppression Operations Command (Thailand)
CT	Communist terrorist
DDR&E	Director of Defense Research and Engineering
DOD	United States Department of Defense
DSB	Defense Science Board
FCRC	Federal Contract Research Center
FFRDC	Federally Funded Research and Development Center
IDA	Institute for Defense Analyses
ISA	Office of the Assistant Secretary (of Defense) for International Security Affairs
JCS	Joint Chiefs of Staff
MACT, MACTHAI	U.S. Military Assistance Command, Thailand
MOI	Ministry of the Interior (Thailand)
MRDC	Joint Thai-U.S. Military Research and Development Center
ODDR&E	Office of the Director of Defense Research and Engineering

ONR	Office of Naval Research
OPS	Office of Public Safety (U.S.)
OSRD	Office of Scientific Research and Development
PP	Provincial Police (Thailand)
Psy Ops	Psychological Operations
RAC	Research Analysis Corporation
RSSP	Rural Security Systems Program
RTG	Royal Thai Government
SA/CI	U.S. Special Assistant for Counterinsurgency
SEADAG	Southeast Asia Development Advisory Group SMC
SMC	Student Mobilization Committee to End the War in Vietnam
SORO	Special Operations Research Office (former name of CRESS)
SRI	Stanford Research Institute
TNPD	Thai National Police Department
USAID	U.S. Agency for International Development
USIS	United States Information Service
USOM	United States Operations Mission/Thailand (AID)
VSF	Village Security Force (Thailand)

Acknowledgements

The idea for this study was suggested to me by Ann Stoler at the University of Michigan during the course of a seminar on Anthropology and Colonialism. It subsequently developed into a Master's thesis in Southeast Asian Studies at the same university. Without the fellowship support and encouragement of all those affiliated with the Center for South and Southeast Asian Studies, I would not have been able to complete this project. Thanks to Victor Lieberman for his advice, Michael Cullinane for answering countless questions at all hours, Jan Opdyke for providing me with a place to write, and David Akin for Howlin' Wolf.

Gary Hawes read draft chapters of the thesis and suggested changes. Alfred W. McCoy's suggestions for revision rescued the first draft of the monograph.

David Givens of the American Anthropological Association answered queries and led me to the bound copies of many years' of *AAA Newsletters*. The staff of the National Anthropology Archives at the National Museum of Natural History of the Smithsonian Institution, Washington, D.C., helped me through the archives of the American Anthropological Association. Cathy Creek copied hundreds of pages for me. Mary Wolfskill and the staff of the Manuscripts Division of the United States Library of Congress helped me to find my way through the Margaret Mead papers.

A number of people were kind enough to respond to my requests for interviews with generous amounts of their time. A full list of these individuals appears at the end of the bibliography, but I would like to single out here David Aberle, Gerald Berreman, George Foster, Delmos Jones, Joseph Jorgensen, Herbert Phillips, and, especially, Eric R. Wolf. Professors Berreman, Jones, Phillips, and Wolf graciously allowed me access to published and unpublished documents in their possession.

I thank Joyce Burkhalter Flueckiger for her sedulous efforts to edit the manuscript into shape for publication. Finally, for sundry assistance and advice, thanks to Sidney Jones, Edward Leibowitz, Ina Schoenberg, and Ara Wilson.

While I received encouragement and suggestions from many, I take responsibility for the final product.

CHAPTER ONE

INTRODUCTION

The Native still needs help.... Shall we therefore mix politics with science? In one way, decidedly, "yes," because if knowledge gives foresight and foresight means power, it is a universal stultification of scientific results to insist that they can never be useful or used by those who have influence.... The truth is that science begins with applications.

—Bronislaw Malinowski, anthropologist, 1945

Thailand is a good place to study because there are things going on there that can be studied which are not going on elsewhere. It is like a laboratory.

—Jesse Orlansky, psychologist,
speaking at the Thailand Study Group, 1967

In late March 1970 the Student Mobilization Committee to End the War in Vietnam (SMC) sent selected anthropologists copies of a series of documents detailing extensive contacts between distinguished American academics and the U.S. Defense Department.[1] Among the recipients were two members of the newly formed Committee on Ethics of the American Anthropological Association (AAA)—its chair, Eric Wolf, and Joseph Jorgensen. The documents, which had been copied surreptitiously from the files of anthropologist Michael Moerman, suggested that a number of American social scientists had been doing contract and consultation work for the Defense Department. Most importantly, the documents also seemed to indicate that these social scientists were providing information that was being used in an ongoing U.S. counterinsurgency campaign in Thailand.

What might have remained a purely academic debate became public on April 2, when the SMC published extensive excerpts from the documents in its newspaper, the *Student Mobilizer*,[2] and distributed copies along with statements by Wolf and Jorgensen at the annual meeting of the Association for Asian Studies (AAS) in San Francisco. Distribution of the documents at this professional convention sparked public charges and countercharges.

Over the next year and a half, the debate focused on issues related to the government–social science nexus, such as the responsibility of a researcher to the people studied and to professional ethical standards, the relation of the social scientist to government policy formulation and implementation, and the role of U.S. policy in Southeast Asia. The denouement to the controversy came when a special AAA committee chaired by Margaret Mead concluded that the anthropologists named in the documents had not violated the Association's standards of professional ethics.[3] The report, in turn, was rejected by the Council of Fellows of the AAA,[4] leaving the Executive Board to state that the "[s]pecific problems posed by the events referred to as the 'Thailand Controversy' stand essentially unresolved."[5]

The issues raised at the time of the Thailand Controversy are re-examined in this monograph, which reviews the major documents of the controversy and the U.S. government's policy of harnessing academics for applied research. It is no great revelation to find that social scientists have worked directly for government agencies such as the Agency for International Development or have had ties to the government through funding bodies such as the Rand Corporation. The U.S. government stands among major powers that enlist the aid of social scientists to help them understand and manipulate less powerful states. The projection of power and influence by stronger states to achieve objectives favorable to themselves in weaker, often Third World, states may well have detrimental results for the weaker state. This projection of superpower policy in Southeast Asia in the 1960s and 1970s was responsible for the deaths of over one million people. But policy is not self-generating; it is devised by individuals. In the sideshow to the Vietnam War that was Thailand, counterinsurgency policy was evaluated and formulated with the help of U.S. social scientists.

Unlike Project Camelot, an earlier government-funded social science project focused on Latin America, the events examined in this monograph do not have a catchy name. In its examination of the activities, the American Anthropological Association tied them together under the rubric of the "Controversy Concerning Anthropological Activities in Relation to Thailand." An article in the April 2, 1970, *Student Mobilizer* described them as part of "a counterinsurgency program directed against the revolution in

Counterinsurgency
Research on Campus
EXPOSED

Thailand." On the same day the *Student Mobilizer* article appeared, the *Los Angeles Times* reported that "UCLA Advisors Work with AID Unit in Thailand, Mission Called Effective in Improving Conditions in Red–Periled Districts." And on April 6, 1970 the *San Francisco Chronicle* reported that the issue was "A Question of Scholarship and Politics."[6] When referring to the events themselves and the debate surrounding them, I will use the phrase "Thailand Controversy."

In many ways, events that took place in Thailand during the 1960s, including those related to the Indochina War, have receded into a realm of remote, obscure history for most Americans. The Vietnam War has always taken center stage, reducing the rest of Southeast Asia to a sideshow. Since American scholarship and collective consciousness are so organized, events such as the Thailand Controversy are played out in the shadow of the Vietnam War. Government-sponsored research in Thailand became controversial partially because it did come to light in the midst of the Vietnam War. Although our attention has since wandered, the focus on the U.S. role in Southeast Asia during those years brought to light broad ethical questions regarding the U.S. role in the Third World that are relevant today, in an era when the United States is involved in Central America, South America, and the Middle East. The role that academics play in these controversies remains essential.

Those who planned and directed the use of U.S. military and intelligence forces in Vietnam were aware of the region's "instability" and the possibility for conflict elsewhere. Early in the decade, the conflict between Pathet Lao and Royalist Lao forces in Laos had created the need for a U.S. covert operations base. Neighboring Thailand was an ideal site. Over the next decade, the U.S. military built a massive infrastructure in Thailand, both to support the war in Vietnam and to prepare for any eventualities that might arise within Thailand. While this buildup was taking place, U.S. policymakers became aware, through studies of what went wrong in Vietnam, of what would be needed for future counterinsurgency efforts in Thailand. Judging from their responses, Pentagon officials evidently felt that social science research, including anthropological data on minority groups, was essential in the event of a future struggle for Thailand.

There were several government, private, and academic organizations that sought to assemble research to aid the policymakers. In their recruitment and use of social scientists, these groups almost always either explicitly or implicitly let it be known that data was to be used for the purposes of counterinsurgency planning and operations.

One of the most important of these private organizations was the Institute for Defense Analyses (IDA). The IDA, which received most of its contracts through the Pentagon, had been created in 1956 as a weapons–research firm. By 1959 the IDA formally acknowledged the importance of the social sciences to military planning. The result was the creation of the Jason Division, which called together groups of social scientists on short notice to work on specific problems. The IDA annual report for 1966 noted that

> increased government attention to such problems as counter-insurgency, insurrection, and infiltration led to the suggestion that Jason members might be able to provide fresh insights into problems that are not entirely in the realm of physical science.[7]

The IDA's Jason Division sponsored a Thailand Study Group (TSG) during the summer of 1967 to consider the insurgency in Thailand and possible counterinsurgency techniques. Four anthropologists who had worked in Thailand were among the specialists invited to participate in the TSG—Michael Moerman of the University of California-Los Angeles (UCLA), Herbert Phillips of the University of California-Berkeley, Steven Piker of Swarthmore College, and Lauriston Sharp of Cornell University. Piker had been the most active among them in the antiwar movement and was publicly critical of the U.S. role in Southeast Asia. The others all later expressed reservations and/or criticism of U.S. policy in the region.

The Department of Defense's Advanced Research Projects Agency (ARPA) was another important research agency; it functioned as an arm of the Office of the Director of Defense Research and Engineering (ODDR&E). In Thailand, according to George Tanham (the U.S. Embassy's Special Assistant for Counterinsurgency),

> the ARPA field unit was informally recognized as the research arm of the United States Mission regarding internal security programs.[8]

ARPA established a field office in Thailand in 1961. The advantages of the Thai testing environment were described as being "similar to Vietnam's but nobody's shooting at you."[9]

ARPA funded numerous research projects in Thailand and hired consultants as needed, among them Herbert Phillips. Seymour Deitchman, former Special Assistant for Counterinsurgency at ODDR&E and then director of ARPA's worldwide counterinsurgency program, Project Agile, has written that Phillips

> became an ARPA consultant and ... over the course of the next two years [1967–68] was to provide much useful understanding of the background to the problems with which ARPA was involved in Thailand.[10]

Phillips, in turn, found this suggestion ludicrous and wrote Deitchman to assert that none of his recommendations was ever enacted or even seriously considered; and furthermore, one of the reasons he had worked as a consultant was to lessen the negative effects of the U.S. presence in Thailand while, at the same time, strengthening any positive effects.[11]

In December 1967 the American Institutes for Research (AIR), a private research firm located in Pittsburgh, proposed to do a study for ARPA entitled *Counterinsurgency in Thailand: The Impact of Economic, Social and Political Action Programs.*[12] The proposal received funding (probably through ARPA) in 1968 or early 1969. A group of social scientists then traveled to Thailand for meetings with ARPA staff, Thai National Police Department officers, AID officials, Special Assistant for Counterinsurgency Tanham and his staff, and USIS staff. Michael Moerman was one of the members of the AIR Advisory Panel who traveled to Thailand. Moerman later wrote an internal evaluation letter that was candidly critical of certain aspects of the AIR program, but not wholly unsupportive of its goals.[13]

In September of 1968 the U.S. Agency for International Development (AID) and the Regents of the University of California signed an amendment to an earlier contract that committed a group of scholars to work as advisors to AID programs "dealing with development and counterinsurgency problems" in Thailand.[14] They were to work through the Academic Advisory Council for Thailand (AACT), established by AID in September 1966. While the scholars may not have known about the UCLA-AID contract amendment, the goals of AID in Thailand were not secret—the AID mission in Thailand had always been primarily concerned with "security" issues. The largest single AID project in Thailand provided assistance to various units of the Thai National Police Department,[15] and in 1965 AID cited "counterinsurgency" as the first priority of its program in Thailand.[16]

Topics of discussion at AACT meetings included liaison activities with ARPA; co–opting the Southeast Asia Development Advisory Group (SEADAG), created by AID and the Asia Society, by having Lauriston Sharp installed on its executive committee; sponsoring graduate-student research; and "abandon[ing] its pretensions to be representative" of Thai scholars and "accept[ing] its role as basically a consultative body to AID."[17]

David Wilson, a political scientist at UCLA, went to Thailand as an AACT representative in 1968. The 1969 representative (possibly Wilson again) met with the U.S. Ambassador, Special Assistant for Counter-insurgency Tanham, AID staffers, ARPA researchers, and the chief advisor to the Thai National Police Department. In late 1968 and 1969, anthropologist Lauriston Sharp was the chairman of AACT and anthro-pologists Charles Keyes and Michael Moerman were also members.

That anthropologists and other social scientists joined such a committee or participated in a meeting is no cause for alarm. Many of the anthropologists argued that the best way to change a destructive U.S. government policy was to work within the government. However, ethical dilemmas were bound to arise when that government was engaged in war or preparing for war. The goals of the U.S. government were clear: to formulate effective counterinsurgency practices against the background of the Vietnam War.

Coincidentally, the American Anthropological Association (of which every major participant in the Thailand Controversy was a member) had begun steps towards establishing ethical standards for anthropologists at the same time that the Thailand Controversy events were taking place, but before they had become public knowledge. This interest in ethical standards came on the heels of disclosures about Project Camelot, the aborted U.S. Army social science research project proposed for Latin America.

The AAA Executive Board delegated well–respected anthropologist Ralph L. Beals with the task of investigating the question of anthropology and ethics. The Beals Report, known formally as the *Background Information on Problems of Anthropological Research and Ethics*[18] was published in the *AAA Newsletter* in January 1967. In April 1967 the Association announced that the Fellows of the AAA had voted overwhelming acceptance of the *Statement on Problems of Anthropological Research and Ethics* (Appendix B).[19] The *Statement* was a loose collection of pronouncements on freedom of research, sponsorship, and government service. While the *Statement* was not binding (there was not yet an ethics committee to enforce it even if it were), it did urge anthropologists to avoid "clandestine intelligence activities" and "constraint, deception, and secrecy." In March 1970 the newly formed Committee on Ethics, chaired by Eric Wolf, published a request in the *AAA Newsletter* for the submission of information regarding the problems of anthropological research and ethics, to be used to help formulate an ethical code for anthropologists.[20]

While the academy was working towards a more formal, codified view of ethical responsibility, the issue was thrown into public debate through the release by the SMC of the above-mentioned documents. In early 1970, one of Michael Moerman's graduate students, who was at the time working as his assistant, took without permission from one of his unlocked, private files a group of documents detailing contacts between American academics and government officials. The student copied the documents and sent the copies to the Student Mobilization Committee to End the War in Vietnam.[21] One of the SMC's platforms for opposing the war was its newspaper, the *Student Mobilizer*. To expose what the editors must have seen as an example of an immoral connection between academics and the military, the *Student Mobilizer* published extensive excerpts from the documents on April 2, 1970. Before that issue of the newspaper was distributed, the SMC sent or delivered copies of the documents to Eric Wolf and Joseph Jorgensen. Wolf and Jorgensen then issued a statement to the SMC, which the SMC publicized. It said, in part:

> ... these documents contradict in spirit and in letter the resolutions of the American Anthropological Association concerning clandestine and secret research, we feel that they raise the most serious issues for the scientific integrity of our profession.[22]

Wolf followed up, four days later, with private letters to Moerman, Phillips, Piker, and Sharp, indicating that he had received the documents and would raise the issue at the next AAA Ethics Committee meeting, which would

> deal with cases on as anonymous a basis as possible, in an effort to develop an approach to cases without penalizing any individuals.... I should like to invite you to make any statement to the [Ethics] Committee that you wish.[23]

Moerman, Phillips, and Sharp reacted with outrage to the Wolf letter, saying Wolf had already judged them guilty in his statement to the SMC and was now proposing, as the chairman of the AAA Ethics Committee, to deal impartially with the information in the Thailand Controversy documents. At this point, the question of ethics became twofold: Did the conduct of the anthropologists mentioned in the Thailand Controversy documents violate codified or uncodified ethical standards for academics? And did the conduct of Wolf and Jorgensen violate the ethical standards required of their positions on the Ethics Committee? It might have been argued that one of these ethical dilemmas involved activities that had potential for killing people; the other had potential for ruining people's reputations. Both are important, but it would be difficult to argue for parity.

The controversy aroused a depth and intensity of emotion not often evoked in other social science professions.[24] Through field research, anthropologists often develop close ties to "their village"; they often feel that they should in some way serve as advocates or even protectors of their village. Minimally, most anthropologists agree to an informal ethic stipulating that the research or activities of an anthropologist should not endanger the village. This position is enshrined in the Principles of Professional Responsibility of the AAA: "In research, anthropologists' paramount responsibility is to those they study."[25] The late Kathleen Gough Aberle articulated the ethic as follows:

> Scientists have special obligations, *as scientists*, because of their special knowledge and the power it confers. Anthropologists' special knowledge relates in part to the needs, sufferings, and aspirations of contemporary non–western peoples. Our special obligations include that of defending their welfare and internationally recognized rights. We must dissociate ourselves from the acts of governments that seek to destroy these peoples or to infringe on their rights. We must do so the more firmly when the offenders are our own governments, precisely *because* we are largely funded by our governments. If we fail, our non–western friends may justly suspect that we have abandoned our responsibilities in return for our grants and tax–exemptions [emphasis in original].[26]

While anthropologists are under a particular obligation to those they study during their fieldwork, they are at the same time employees of either their own government or of private universities. Further, American development agencies continually call on academics to serve as consultants for development, education, nutrition, and other projects. Thus, anthropologists often stand between the people they study and various funding agencies, universities, and governments. The position is one in which ethical dilemmas will develop. With or without a codified set of responsibilities, anthropologists must make choices. This monograph is about some of those choices.

NOTES

[1] The chief documents are:

Academic Advisory Council for Thailand. "People Seen on AACT Trip: November 10 to December 22 1970." [On the document "1970" has been crossed out and replaced with "1969 (?)"] n.d.

Academic Advisory Council for Thailand. "Meeting of the Academic Advisory Council for Thailand." 19 October 1968; 24, 25 January 1969; 10, 11 June 1969; and 23, 24 July 1969. [These appear to be summaries of the minutes of the meetings.]

Agency for International Development. "Amendment No. 3 to the Contract Between the United States of America and the Regents of the University of California." (PIO/T 493-190-3-60152-A1; PIO/T 493-000.2-3-90050). [1 September 1968.]

American Institutes for Research. *Counterinsurgency in Thailand: The Impact of Economic, Social, and Political Action Programs* (A Research and Development Proposal submitted to the Advanced Research Projects Agency). Pittsburgh, PA: American Institutes for Research, December 1967.

American Institutes for Research. "Advisory Panel Meeting, 30 June-4 July 1969, Agenda."

American Institutes for Research. "Trip Report: Visit to Amphoe Nong Han, Changwad Udon, 28 May-6 June 1969," and attached consultant's bill.

Institute for Defense Analyses. "The Thailand Study Group" [Minutes from a "Jason Summer Study" at Falmouth Intermediate School, Falmouth, Massachusetts] 20, 21, 22, 27 [?], 28, 29, 30 June; 3, 4, 5, 6, 7 July 1967.

[2] *The Student Mobilizer* 3, 4 (2 April 1970).

[3] William Davenport, David Olmsted, Margaret Mead, and Ruth Freed, *Report of the Ad Hoc Committee to Evaluate the Controversy Concerning Anthropological Activities in Relation to Thailand to the Executive Board*

of the American Anthropological Association (Washington, DC: American Anthropological Association, 27 September 1971).

4 *Newsletter of the American Anthropological Association* [hereafter *AAA Newsletter*] 13:1 (January 1972), 1.

5 Ibid., 13:2 (February 1972), 6.

6 Davenport, et al., *Controversy Concerning Anthropological Activities; Student Mobilizer* 3, 4 (2 April 1970), 3; Peter Braestrup, "Researchers Aid Thai Rebel Fight," *New York Times,* 20 March 1967; William Trombley, "UCLA Advisors Work with AID Unit in Thailand," *Los Angeles Times,* 2 April 1970; Jerry Carroll, "A Question of Scholarship and Politics," *San Francisco Chronicle*, 6 April 1970. See also Jeff Weiner, "Thailand Counterinsurgency," *UCLA Daily Bruin,* 6 April 1970. Three years earlier, in March 1967, the *New York Times* had announced "Researchers Aid Thai Rebel Fight, U.S. Defense Unit Develops Antiguerilla Devices."

7 Institute for Defense Analyses, *The Tenth Year: March 1965 through February 1966* (Washington, DC: Institute for Defense Analyses, n.d.), 15.

8 George K. Tanham, *Trial in Thailand* (New York: Crane, Russak, & Co., 1974), 126.

9 General Robert H. Weineke in "Weapons, Sought for Remote Wars," *New York Times*, 17 January 1964, quoted in Michael T. Klare, *War Without End: American Planning for the Next Vietnams* (New York: Alfred A. Knopf, 1972), 226.

10 Seymour J. Deitchman, *The Best–Laid Schemes: A Tale of Social Research and Bureaucracy* (Cambridge, MA: MIT Press, 1976), 303.

11 Herbert Phillips, letter to Seymour Deitchman, 24 September 1978. I am enjoined by Phillips from quoting this letter directly.

12 American Institutes for Research, *Counterinsurgency in Thailand:* (A research and development proposal submitted to the Advanced Research Projects Agency) (Pittsburgh, PA: American Institutes for Research, December 1967).

13 Michael Moerman, letter to Dr. Paul A. Schwarz, AIROSD/ARPA/ RDC–T, [American Institutes for Research, Office of the Secretary of

Defense, Advanced Research Projects Agency, Research and Development
Center, Thailand], 13 February 1970.

[14] Agency for International Development, "Amendment No. 3 to the
Contract Between the United States of American and the Regents of the
University of California," 1 September 1968 (mimeograph), 4. The original
contract was AID/fe-267 enacted on 6 September 1966.

[15] U.S. Congress, Committee on Government Operations, Foreign
Operations and Government Information Subcommittee, *Hearings on
Thailand and the Philippines* (John E. Moss, chairman), 16 June 1969
(mimeograph), 3.

[16] United States Operations Mission/Program Office, "USOM/Thailand
Goals and Projects," 26 November 1965, quoted in R. Sean Randolph, *The
United States and Thailand: Alliance Dynamics, 1950-1985* (Berkeley:
Institute of East Asian Studies, University of California, 1986), 96.

[17] Academic Advisory Council for Thailand, "Meeting of the AACT," 10-
11 June 1969, 8; 23-24 July 1969.

[18] American Anthropological Association [hereafter AAA], "Background
Information on Problems of Anthropological Research and Ethics,"*AAA
Newsletter* 8:1 (January 1967), 1–13.

[19] AAA "Statement on Problems of Anthropological Research and Ethics,"
n.p.: AAA, 1967.

[20] *AAA Newsletter* 11:3 (March 1970), 9–10. The call for submission was
worded as follows:

> The Ethics Committee of the American Anthropological
> Association has begun to build up a file of anonymous cases
> diagnostic of ethical conflicts resulting from the differential
> commitments of anthropologists to informants, sponsors, fellow
> professionals and representatives of agencies of government,
> whether of the United States or of host countries.
> We ask the Fellows and Members of the Association to
> acquaint us with the details of cases in which they have been
> involved, or which they have collected on their own. From such
> case material we hope to extract or to document general principles
> of the formulation of an ethical code for anthropologists. Any

communication you may wish to make to the ethics committee will remain completely confidential; we are interested in general information on cases, but not in the names of persons or specific localities involved.

Please keep in mind that the committee is not a judicial body, and cannot take sides in any dispute, nor adjudicate a particular set of issues. We are interested in the circumstances of any particular case only to the extent that they can help us draw up general guidelines for conduct by anthropologists.

21 Moerman, letter to George Foster, 24 April 1970; Phillips, letter to Gerald Berreman, 4 April 1970; Lauriston Sharp, letter to Eric Wolf, 17 April 1970; Wolf and Joseph Jorgensen, "Anthropology on the Warpath in Thailand," *New York Review of Books* (19 November 1970).

22 Wolf and Jorgensen, statement, 30 March 1970.

23 Wolf, letters to Moerman, Phillips, Piker, and Sharp, 3 April 1970.

24 In political science, with its often depersonalized, statistical research, this feeling is much less in evidence, perhaps because micro studies are not the primary method of inquiry and extended contact with the same individuals is the exception, rather than the norm. In the history of political science, there are numerous examples of academics who have been consultants to the military arms of the government with few controversial results—Samuel Huntington, Ithiel de Sola Pool, and Lucien Pye, for example.

25 AAA, "Principles of Professional Responsibility," 1971. The revised 1990 version of the Principles states, "Anthropologists' first responsibility is to those whose lives and cultures they study."

26 Kathleen Gough Aberle, letter, *AAA Newsletter* 8:6 (June 1967), 11.

CHAPTER TWO

THEORETICAL & HISTORICAL CONTEXT

> *Without question social science research is in a strong position to contribute useful knowledge in designing and developing internal security forces.*

—Lucien Pye, political scientist, 1963

> *It is often necessary for the United States, because of its great power, which ramifies politically, economically, and militarily through out the world, to involve itself in the affairs of small states. Such involvement represents a continuing effort to find an order for world affairs within which peace and justice may be found. This effort to find an order—an effort not necessarily well conceived, free of failure, nor lacking in the use of force and power—is the substance of American imperialism.*

—David Wilson, political scientist;
member of the Academic Advisory Council for Thailand, 1970

The documents and events that make up the Thailand Controversy emerged in a unique historical moment to which several major theoretical and historical issues contributed. Among them are the five examined in this chapter: (1) development/modernization theory; (2) colonial applied anthropology; (3) post World War II U.S. government interest in applied social science research; (4) Project Camelot, an example of the government–social science link that served as a dry run for the Thailand Controversy; and (5) the ethical guidelines of the American Anthropological Association developed at the time.

DEVELOPMENT/MODERNIZATION THEORY

In the years preceding and intersecting the Thailand Controversy, one theoretical approach to the developing world that was wielded with particular power and righteousness was development or modernization theory. Modernization thinkers of the late 1950s and 1960s believed that the uplifting characteristics of Western development could be transferred to the Third World through loans and development programs, while disorder could be kept to a minimum through political and military guidance, just as nineteenth-century European leaders though that their versions of progress would uplift the "uncivilized" peoples of the Empire.[1] Walt Whitman Rostow, Kennedy's principal advisor on Vietnam and Johnson's national security advisor, postulated a linear progression of "stages" that new nations could follow, leading them to development along Western lines.[2] Samuel Huntington, another major modernization theorist, emphasized the need for stability and order along the road to change.[3]

The conservative nature of development/modernization theory, with its emphasis on stability as a counterbalance to the rapid social and economic changes that result from development, strengthened its appeal to U.S. leaders during the 1960s,[4] to which Rostow's governmental service attests. Linear evolution as a positive progression quite "naturally" accepts the desirability of foreign aid, guidance, and, if necessary, intervention of varying degrees. Modernization theory was comfortable with the projection of U.S. power, as illustrated in the following excerpt from a book published in 1960 by Rostow:

> It is clear then that the optimum policy still open to the United States is ... actively to use the nation's real, if limited, margin of influence on the course of history ...[5]

Within this theory, whatever upsets the development process, beginning in the political arena, is seen to be destabilizing. In the case of Thailand, popular analyses included the following assumptions: the bureaucracy is stable and concerned with the rational pursuit of desired goals; the monarchy functions for "legitimizing the polity and stabilizing the nation"; and "political stability has rested largely on military power and the legitimizing aura of the king."[6]

The desire for some form of self–defined stability was important not only to the U.S., but also to the Thai construction of desired reality.

"Stability," "security," and "order" are concepts linked to upholding respect for the tripartite national ideology of nation–religion–king in such a way that those who threaten stability are also seen to be threatening the revered institutions of the state. People threatening the stability of the state (protesting students and striking workers, for example) are labeled "confusing," confusing to the very *order* of the nation.[7]

In general, both Thai and American government officials favored policies that reinforced the power of the state in order to maintain stability. One such policy was the centralization of power (such as bringing minority peoples under central government control) in order to enhance the ability of the bureaucracy to implement policy nationwide. This strategy became especially important in the Thai context in the 1960s, since the insurgency first took root in the northeast and northern regions of Thailand, often among indigenous peoples who were divided from the central government both by ethnicity and geography. Towards a goal of stability, policies opposing the communist subversion of the state were adopted, policies that also served to legitimate the extensive U.S. role in Southeast Asia.

Development/modernization theory was only one of numerous factors contributing to U.S. involvement in Southeast Asia, but its influence is demonstrated through the actions of many of the advisors to the U.S. government at the time. However well-intentioned individual social scientists who participated in research for the government may have been, and whatever individual good they may have accomplished, they were participating in policies that had developed, in part, in response to the development/modernization theory.

Three American scholars, associated with organizations that were advising the U.S. government in foreign policy, were among those who articulated aspects of development/modernization theory as it was applied in Southeast Asia. Samuel P. Huntington, then a professor of government and associate director of the Institute for War and Peace Studies at Columbia University, writing for the Special Studies Group of the Institute for Defense Analyses in 1961, wrote:

> To maintain effectively a "balance of instabilities" ... [t]he U.S. Government must be willing to act in a variety of ways to prevent a friendly or "neutral" state from falling into the hands of the Communists.... Resort to military action to bolster a friendly regime is a sign of political failure. In some cases, it may be

necessary for the United States to assist directly or indirectly in the overthrow of unfriendly regimes. In some of these instances, quick, decisive military actions at an early stage may be more conducive to stability than delayed or prolonged direct or indirect measures.[8]

Guy J. Pauker, then a professor of political science at the University of California writing for the Technical Military Planning Operation of the General Electric Company in 1958, articulated themes of intervention, stability, repression, organizational strength, military government, and opposition to "social confusion":

> ... unless American efforts are dramatically stepped up, Southeast Asia will be lost to the Free World within the next decade....
>
> Efforts to foster political stability and economic growth are desirable not only for humanitarian reasons but in pursuit of the national interest of the United States....
>
> The repressive apparatus of governments, in Burma, Thailand, Malaya, South Vietnam, and the Philippines seems currently adequate to contain Communist expansion. But if repression ceases, other political organizations may prove less efficient in open competition with Communist parties....
>
> What is most urgently needed in Southeast Asia today is organizational strength.... Communist successes are the result of superior organizational strength.... The remedy [for the Communist threat] is more likely to be found at the present level of development of Southeast Asia in the officers corps than among the politicians.
>
> There is of course a danger that the officer corps would succumb themselves to the temptations of corrupt practices or to the attraction of governing for their own exclusive benefit. But the present character of the officer corps in most of Southeast Asia permits the expectation that the positive aspects of military control would outweigh the negative ones.

Recent developments in Southeast Asia indicate that the hope for genuinely representative government is premature. The real choice is between some form of authoritarian regime under military control which would leave the future open for development in a democratic direction, or political disintegration, economic stagnation, and social confusion which would lead the peoples of Southeast Asia toward Communist totalitarianism.[9]

Finally, in 1970 David A. Wilson, former UCLA professor and executive secretary of the Academic Advisory Council for Thailand (AACT), wrote:

We cannot know the future, regardless of our hopes or our revulsion from its unknown threats. But it is the character of our age, in which the fragile web of civilization links the peoples of the world, that Americans seek to control this dark future and that we are doomed to grapple with its ambiguities.... We carry on this struggle in this country and abroad by policy and politics, by persuasion and force, by leadership and attraction, and by whatever moral means we can muster. We do so in order to create and preserve the forms of life that we value. To so struggle is to serve our interests....

It is often necessary for the United States, because of its great power, which ramifies politically, economically, and militarily through out the world, to involve itself in the affairs of small states. Such involvement represents a continuing effort to find an order for world affairs within which peace and justice may be found. This effort to find an order—an effort not necessarily well conceived, free of failure, nor lacking in the use of force and power—is the substance of American imperialism.[10]

The above excerpts demonstrate that the application of development/modernization paradigms was accepted among many advisors to the U.S. government. Such theorizing reinforced government objectives, while government objectives, in turn, reinforced the theories. A similar relationship will be found between colonial applied anthropology and government policy.

COLONIAL APPLIED ANTHROPOLOGY

Anthropology as a discipline with the primary concern of research is a relative newcomer. In the latter nineteenth and first half of the twentieth century, the discipline was closely associated with the European colonial enterprise. While describing the discipline as "a child of Western imperialism"[11] and anthropologists as handmaidens of imperialism is overly reductionist, a brief discussion of some of the early links between anthropology and the colonialist enterprise will be helpful in putting into perspective the Thailand Controversy and in understanding the collective knowledge of anthropologists at the time.

Anthropology was part of the training of colonial administrators in most European colonial states. Training programs that included anthropology were used by the Dutch at Leiden and Utrecht Universities (with research also done through the Colonial Institute in Amsterdam); by the French at *l'Ecole Coloniale*; by the British at Oxford, Cambridge, and the University of London; by the Americans through the Bureau of American Ethnology; and by the Australians at the University of Sydney.[12]

By the period between the world wars, the teaching of anthropology as an adjunct to colonial administration had been institutionalized. An important moment in the linkage between anthropology and colonial administrators in England has been traced to the latter 1920s with the founding of the International Institute of African Languages and Cultures (IAI).[13] Funding for the IAI came from universities, missionary societies, the Rockefeller and Carnegie foundations, and some colonial governments. The IAI was founded to improve the education of the colonized people, and it provided funds for colonial administrators to take academic courses at the London School of Economics. Selections from the 1934-35 course guide for "Lectures and Classes in Colonial Administration and Anthropology" of the London School of Economics included:

> In the Lent Term of the session 1932–33 the London School of Economics and Political Science inaugurated a special course on Colonial Administration, which was designed for persons interested in the problems of Colonial Administration, including those actually in contact with such problems, whether as administrators, educationalists or missionaries....

The course covers the anthropological, administrative, legal and economic aspects of Colonial Administration and includes comparative studies of the principle colonial systems.[14]

The teaching staff in "Colonial Studies and Anthropology" included J. Coatman, professor of "Imperial Economic Relations"; Lancelot Hogben, professor of social biology; Julius Lewin, barrister–at–law; and anthropologists Raymond W. Firth, Meyer Fortes, Lucy P. Mair, Bronislaw Malinowski, and Audrey I. Richards. The anthropologists taught "Cognate Lectures and Classes in Anthropology," but also offered a full range of courses that integrated anthropology and colonial administration, all of which were included in the twelve pound, twelve shilling program fee charged to students.[15]

What we today refer to as "applied anthropology" was the subject matter of many courses. Students who opted to pay on a per–course basis were charged three pounds to study the "practical applications of anthropology" in Malinowski's "Practical Anthropology," or one pound four shillings to study its "application to practical affairs" (among other subjects) in Firth's "Introduction to Anthropology."[16]

For two pounds, Malinowski and Coatman's "Anthropology and Administration" was

intended to bring together administrative officers from the colonial services as well as missionaries and students of anthropology, and to establish the importance of Anthropology for administration, as well as the value of practical interest in the theoretical study of native races.[17]

Finally, for one pound four shillings, there was Firth, Fortes, and Lewin's "Principles of Applied Anthropology," which is described in the course guide as follows:

The seminar will be concerned with the application of anthropology to problems of administration, education, economic development, and social reorganization in the simpler societies now coming under European control.[18]

The anthropologists teaching courses in colonial administration were not necessarily unabashed supporters of the colonial endeavor, but they present ambivalent opinions at best. Fortes, in a collection of Fabian essays on colonialism, describes a Janus–faced Western civilization that is expressed both in the form of the "naked exploitation of land and labour" and in the "benign forms of legitimate commerce, missions and government." Fortes concludes his essay with the assessment that it is the "historic role of the white man to propose, initiate, even impose new social forms, economic relations and cultural values."[19] Fortes's 1945 assessment of colonialism is strikingly similar to David Wilson's 1970 assessment of imperialism:

> It is often necessary for the United States, because of its great power ... to involve itself in the affairs of small states. Such involvement represents a continuing effort to find an order for world affairs within which peace and justice may be found.[20]

Rather than oppose the colonial endeavor, Malinowski justified a particular type of applied research. In 1945 he wrote:

> The Native still needs help.... Shall we therefore mix politics with science? In one way, decidedly, "yes," because if knowledge gives foresight and foresight means power, it is a universal stultification of scientific results to insist that they can never be useful or used by those who have influence.... The truth is that science begins with applications.[21]

Malinowski's view is a precursor to the later theories of development/ modernization. This is evident particularly in his chapter titled "Indirect Rule and Its Scientific Planning" in *Dynamics of Culture Change*,[22] in which he justifies applied research on the basis of the benefits that will accrue to the colonized people: "We do not need to underrate the value and necessity of African assimilation and progress."[23]

Clearly, anthropology was considered important by some administrators, but the degree to which the advice of anthropologists was taken into consideration varied greatly. In this respect, there is a similarity between the use of social science research to aid colonial expansion in Africa and social science research to plan counterinsurgency in Southeast Asia. While some social scientists were willing to do the research and some agencies of the government requested such work, there was not a universal acceptance by all bureaucrats that the contributions of social scientists would be useful. This dynamic continues to manifest itself in relationships within and between large institutions and bureaucracies and private consultants.[24]

In the United States in the 1960s, various policy statements called for an increase in the contributions of social scientists to government–sponsored research. For anthropologists and political scientists willing to cooperate in the enterprise, this meant studying the development process as it took place in countries where the U.S. had a strategic interest. It also meant helping the U.S. government to understand how "stability" could best be maintained in these countries.

U.S. GOVERNMENT INTEREST IN APPLIED SOCIAL SCIENCE RESEARCH

United States government interest in academic social science research did not begin with American involvement in the Vietnam War. During World War II, the civilian Office of Scientific Research and Development (OSRD) carried out military research for the government through association with major universities. At Yale University, the Rockefeller Foundation–funded Institute for International Studies worked with the Department of State on research projects, while the Institute of Human Relations and its Cross Cultural Survey collected anthropological data on Pacific Islanders for use, if needed, by the Army and Navy Departments. The records of the Cross Cultural Survey were duplicated as the Human Relations Area Files (HRAF) and distributed to twenty other universities and later, it was rumored, to CIA headquarters in Langley, Virginia. Following the war, the Armed Services Procurement Act of 1947 authorized the military services to use advertising and bidding to contract with industries and universities. The Office of Naval Research (ONR) also supported postwar social science research before the advent of the National Science Foundation.[25]

The Kennedy presidency is a historical watershed at which we can situate the beginning of a massive U.S. policy effort to channel social science and other research to contain the expanding "communist threat" by countering insurgency.[26] In his inaugural address, President Kennedy codified the new U.S. policy as one that would "pay any price, bear any burden, meet any hardship, support any friend, oppose any foe." The position of the Kennedy administration was to some degree a response to the Soviet Union's support of wars of national liberation and to the active guerilla wars in Laos, Vietnam, and elsewhere. Kennedy (and such administration figures as General Maxwell Taylor and Secretary of Defense Robert McNamara) was convinced that the U.S. was going to have to counter communism by countering insurgency. Among Kennedy's staff, Walt Rostow was a particularly enthusiastic booster for counterinsurgency and research and development programs in Southeast Asia. In a memorandum to the president, Rostow urged the use of "our unexploited counter–guerilla assets" in Vietnam, noting, "we are not saving them for the Junior Prom."[27]

The changes presaged by Kennedy's inauguration speech were reflected in various policy statements and studies that followed. The role of the social sciences as part of the commitment to countering insurgency was explained in 1966 by Seymour Deitchman, special assistant for counterinsurgency to the Office of the Director of Defense Research and Engineering, at congressional hearings on *Behavioral Sciences and the National Security* :

> The State Department, the Defense Department, and key agencies such as the CIA, AID [Agency for International Development], and USIA [United States Information Agency] have increasingly had to turn their attention to meeting this [communist] threat.... the Defense Department's missions in this area have been viewed as broader than the traditional mission of providing U.S. Armed Forces for the national defense....
>
> The Defense Department has therefore recognized that part of its research and development efforts to support counterinsurgency operations must be oriented towards the people ... and the DOD has called on the types of scientists—anthropologists, psychologists, sociologists, political scientists, economists—whose professional orientation to human behavior would enable them to make useful contributions in this area....[28]

An example of the opinions of social scientists themselves can be found in a report in excess of 250 pages produced under Office of Naval Research contract during Kennedy's tenure. In this report, *Social Science Research and National Security*, nine social scientists stressed the appeal among social scientists for government research contracts on counterinsurgency. One of the authors in the volume described the enemy's use of violence as follows:

[C]ommunism places no immediate normative prohibitions on political violence; on the contrary communism justifies and glorifies violence. In communist doctrines, of course, violence is purely instrumental to other ends; among communists, however, violence may well be valued in itself.[29]

In the same volume, Lucien Pye wrote:

It is, indeed, not impossible that this area [guerilla warfare and counter–subversion] may prove to be a more fruitful one for social scientists than many other aspects of military strategy. This is because the problems posed by such forms of warfare and violence are intimately related to questions about the social structure, culture, and behavior patterns of the populations involved in such conflicts. *Without question social science research is in a strong position to contribute useful knowledge in designing and developing internal security forces* [emphasis added].[30]

The policy recommendations that Pye suggested were enacted. A rapid increase in U.S. government interest in all types of research, including social science research, was immediately evident during the Kennedy presidency. Total federal obligations for research and development increased from approximately 8 billion dollars in 1960 to 15.3 billion dollars in 1964.[31] The Defense Department's share during this period rose from 5.8 to 7.3 billion.

The earliest years for which I have a breakdown of spending for behavioral and social science research within the Department of Defense research and development budget are 1966–1970.[32] Total Defense Department research and development funding from 1966–1970 was between 16 and 17 billion dollars per year; the amount allotted for behavioral and social science research during this same period was between 34 and 48 million dollars. The percentage then spent on counterinsurgency research would have to be extracted from the various categories that make up the totals. In other sources, a figure of 5.1 million is cited for 1964 ("nonhardware research that could be considered directly relevant to counterinsurgency"), while 8.6 million is the figure given for 1968.[33] Given the different methods of inclusion, scanty data, and varied figures, it is difficult to guess the full amount spent on counterinsurgency, although a figure of 6-10 million per year during the 1966–1970 period would not be overestimating the amount.

Even before the introduction of U.S. ground troops to Vietnam, the Defense Department had set up an organizational structure to centralize research. The Defense Reorganization Act of 1958 created the position of Director of Defense Research and Engineering (DDR&E). Under the DDR&E was a deputy for "science and technology," who handled basic and applied research programs;[34] a full-time social scientist was also assigned at various times to the ODDR&E. In addition, social scientists were attached to the Defense Department's Advanced Research Projects Agency (ARPA) and to each of the military services' research offices. These included the Office of the Assistant Secretary of Defense for International Security Affairs (ISA), the Army Research Office (ARO), Office of Naval Research (ONR), and the Air Force Office of Scientific Research (AFOSR).[35]

Affiliated with these Defense Department research agencies were those private organizations that existed as Federal Contract Research Centers (FCRC) or Federally Funded Research and Development Centers (FFRDC). These centers received at least 70 percent of their income from federal agencies (in this case DOD) and existed as

> organizational units associated with universities and colleges whose creation and operation are not primarily related to the main function of the administering universities and colleges.[36]

The most famous FCRC was probably the RAND Corporation, established by the Air Force in 1946. Other FCRCs included the Institute for Defense Analyses (IDA) and the Center for Research in Social Systems (CRESS), founded as the Special Operations Research Office (SORO) in 1956 and affiliated with American University until 1969. CRESS was composed of a Cultural Information Analysis Center (CINFAC—originally, the Counterinsurgency Information Analysis Center) and the Social Science Research Institute (SSRI). Both CINFAC and SSRI were responsible for counterinsurgency, psychological warfare, and military civic action studies.[37]

The FCRCs' affiliation with universities allowed them access to academic researchers. It was generally through these private corporations or agencies that the Defense Department was able to realize its goal of integrating Defense Department objectives and social science advice. Through this process, the provision of applied social science advice became institutionalized.

PROJECT CAMELOT:
A DRY RUN FOR CONTROVERSY

The Defense Department–sponsored social science research project that served most aptly as a dry–run for the Thailand Controversy was the aborted Project Camelot (1964–1965). Several social scientists mentioned in this monograph were concerned enough about its legacy to explicitly deny the comparison between their work for the government with regard to Thailand and the work that had been proposed for Project Camelot. The word "Camelot" served as a shibboleth for all that was to be avoided in social science involvement with government contracts.

Camelot was a project proposed by the Army Research Office, to be undertaken by its Federal Contract Research Center, the Special Operations Research Office (SORO) at American University.[38] It was a social science research project in the grand, generalizable tradition that researchers attempt to use to explain the world. ("Camelot will be characterized by an orientation which views a country and its problems as a complex social system.")[39] In this case, the object for study was internal war; the loci for study was to be largely in Latin America; and total research expenditure was to be between three and a half and four and a half million dollars spread over three to four years. Camelot has been described as the "most ambitious social science research project on record."[40]

According to SORO documents:

> Project CAMELOT is a study whose objective is to determine the feasibility of developing a general social systems model which would make it possible to predict *and influence* politically significant aspects of social change in the developing nations of the world....

> By way of background: Project CAMELOT is an outgrowth of the interplay of many factors and forces. Among these is the assignment in recent years of much additional emphasis to the U.S. Army's role in the overall U.S. policy of encouraging steady growth and change in the less developed countries of the world. The many programs of the U.S. Government directed toward this objective are often grouped under the sometimes misleading label of counterinsurgency (some pronounceable term standing for insurgency prophylaxis would be better). This places great

importance on positive actions designed to reduce the sources of disaffection which often give rise to more conspicuous and violent activities disruptive in nature. *The U.S. Army has an important mission in the positive and constructive aspects of nation building as well as a responsibility to assist friendly governments in dealing with active insurgency problems* [emphasis added].[41]

To downplay counterinsurgency ("insurgency prophylaxis," indeed) was somewhat duplicitous on the part of the Camelot staff, given that Camelot came about following a specific DDR&E directive that the Army

develop a plan for a coordinated program of applied behavioral and social science research in support of counterinsurgency and special warfare on behalf of the entire Department of Defense.[42]

SORO hired sociologist Rex Hopper to be the director of Camelot. Due to several poorly conceived contacts by Hopper and University of Pittsburgh anthropologist Hugo Nutini, a consultant to Project Camelot, the existence of the project became known in Chile. Hopper discussed Camelot with personal friends while in Chile; and in his travels to Chile, Nutini also discussed Camelot informally with a number of people. Hopper invited John Galtung, a Norwegian social scientist working for the United Nations, to participate in a Camelot planning conference in Washington, D.C. However, Galtung publicly balked at participating in a study on counter-insurgency sponsored by the U.S. Army.

Although Camelot was not a classified project and Chile was not one of its primary research sites, the research design caused an immediate outcry from American and Latin American social scientists, the State Department, and the press. This resulted in the cancellation of Camelot in July 1965. At least two other similar projects were also cancelled: Project Colony in Peru, in which an anthropologist was working for the DOD to assess the ability of the Peruvian army to help integrate the indigenous Indian population into the national society; and Project Simpatico in Colombia, in which an anthropologist and a psychologist were measuring villagers' attitudes toward the government, the army, and "the turbulent events in their society."[43]

In Project Camelot, the topics discussed in earlier in this chapter come together. The Camelot document states that the goal of the U.S. government was to "encourage steady growth and change in the less–developed countries." To do this, it called upon the aid of applied social science researchers. Their work would fit into the Defense Department's "coordinated program" of social science research in support of counter-insurgency. Because it so perfectly epitomizes social science "gone bad," references to Camelot appear repeatedly in the Thailand Controversy documents.

The cancelled Project Camelot raises important issues regarding what happens when academics conduct social science research for the government, issues immediately relevant to the Thailand Controversy. Some of these are: what types of research result from exclusive government sponsorship? What type of control is the government as funder able to exercise over projects? Are there ethical differences in choosing between different government funding sources—Department of Defense versus Department of State or Education, for example? Is it a valid to undertake research or consultations for the Defense Department in the hope that a better–educated military will do less harm than an uninformed one? Can social science research undertaken for the government lead to more progressive government policies? Do policymakers listen to the opinions of outside consultants, or are they merely meant to legitimize policies already decided upon?

ETHICAL GUIDELINES OF THE AMERICAN ANTHROPOLOGICAL ASSOCIATION

Revelations about Project Camelot became public in 1965 and jarred the American anthropological community into formally considering the involvement of anthropologists in counterinsurgency research. At the 1965 annual meeting of the American Anthropological Association (AAA), the Executive Board decided to appoint a committee to examine

> issues involving the relationship between anthropologists and the agencies, both governmental and private that sponsor their research. Among these issues are those of access to foreign areas, governmental clearance, professional ethics and our responsibilities toward colleagues at home and abroad, the peoples with whom we work, and the sponsoring agencies.[44]

In addition to the problem of being granted access to foreign countries for the purpose of conducting research, an Executive Board statement pointed to the following issues:

The integrity of the field worker himself. Is he attempting to serve the cause of basic science, or the mission–directed role of a government agency, or both? Are these reconcilable?

The jeopardy in which all civilian social science researchers working on purely scientific problems abroad may be placed through the actions of mission directed projects supported by the U.S. Defense and Intelligence agencies.[45]

Ralph Beals of UCLA was appointed to head the Committee on Research Problems and Ethics.[46] Beals and former AAA executive secretary Stephen Boggs testified before a Congressional Subcommittee on Government Research in June 1966, in which they discussed the dangers of academic researchers aiding governments:

To this day, people at the village and tribal level are frequently reluctant to disclose information to outside researchers because they fear reprisals from local or national governments.

The anthropologist does not want to become a party to any such use of the information which he gathers in confidence from trusting informants. He does not want to become the heir of the colonial administrator's legacy of mistrust. Nothing would more surely doom the opportunity of carrying out any kind of social science research abroad. To avoid this, an absolutely impassible barrier must be established between the intelligence agencies of the U.S. Government and the universities, private foundations, and international voluntary organizations engaged in research....

Serious difficulties have also arisen abroad because of the allegation, justified or not, that some ostensibly disinterested social science research is being conducted to serve the purposes of mission–oriented agencies of the United States Government.... In order to avoid these difficulties we recommend that Federal support for basic social science research in this country and abroad be channeled through agencies which do not have any other purpose than the support of basic scientific research and education. The National Science Foundation, the National Institutes of Health, and the Smithsonian Institution at present are the only agencies which meet this criterion.[47]

Beals's comments conclude that data gathered by researchers should not be used against those studied; anthropologists should not continue to carry the mantle of the colonial administrator; and that there should be a complete division between intelligence gathering agencies and researchers and even between "mission–oriented" agencies of the government.

In other parts of his testimony, however, Beals did not rule out the use of social science research by the government "to improve its operations and to make more informed policy decisions,"[48] while at the same time distinguishing policy formulation from intelligence gathering. Beals also suggested the appointment of anthropologists to staff positions within the government, where they could help to interpret data:

> Anthropologists should be in staff positions where they may have a choice in identifying problems susceptible to anthropological methods and in determining how anthropologists are to be used....

> ... operating agencies might well consider developing small offices dedicated to interpreting research findings and relating them to agency operating needs.[49]

Beals and Boggs seemed to believe that anthropologists in these positions would not be replicating the function of colonial administrators. The distinction becomes blurred in the ambiguous language. While on the one hand intelligence–gathering and mission–oriented research is ruled out, on the other hand, staff positions for anthropologists and agency operations are not. Anthropologists involved in the Thailand Controversy attempted to make a similar distinction in discussing their own roles.

The Committee on Research Problems and Ethics continued its research through 1966. Members interviewed anthropologists and government officials and distributed surveys in preparation for a report and statement on ethics to be submitted to the Fellows of the AAA. The January 1967 issue of the *AAA Newsletter* contained a report titled *Background Information on Problems of Anthropological Research and Ethics*, which was meant to provide background on the Beals Committee's research. The report, informally known as the Beals Report, contained the following prescient statement:

The Fellows [of the AAA] should recognize that although Camelot is dead under that name, in a sense it has only gone underground. Similar types of projects have been conducted and are being planned under different names and through other kinds of agencies.[50]

Following the receipt of *Background Information,* AAA Fellows were mailed the *Statement on Problems of Anthropological Research and Ethics* (Appendix B). The Fellows voted 92.5 percent in favor of approving the Statement and 7.5 percent against (by a vote of 729 to 59).[51] A vote for approval of the resolution carried no weight regarding enforcement of any provisions in the Statement. It did not mean that members had to abide by the contents of the Statement as, in fact, we shall see several chose not to. However, it was an indication that the Association was concerned enough about such activities to instigate a formal investigation and put forth a consensual public statement on the results.

In late 1968 the Association's Committee on Organization proposed the creation of an Ethics Committee.[52] An Ad–Hoc Committee on Ethics was formed and held its first meeting in January 1969. Its co-chairs were David Aberle (University of British Columbia) and David M. Schneider (University Chicago); other members were Richard Adams (University of Texas), Joseph Jorgensen (University of Michigan), William Shack (University of Illinois–Chicago Circle), and Eric Wolf (University of Michigan). [53] The Ad–Hoc Ethics Committee proposed the election of a standing Ethics Committee responsible to the AAA Fellows, rather than to the AAA Executive Board. It also proposed a series of controversial measures that met with serious opposition. These included the establishment of a system of registration for anthropologists, controlled by the Ethics Committee, and the creation of detailed, specific ethical standards for the Association. The AAA Executive Board rejected the Ethics Committee Report (and its proposals), but approved the call for the election of a standing Ethics Committee.[54]

The ethical values of anthropologists was not the only issue being raised at this time. The Association had also passed a resolution against warfare in late 1966, which stated that

... we condemn the use of napalm, chemical defoliants, harmful gases, bombing, the torture and killing of prisoners of war and political prisoners and the intentional or deliberate policies of genocide or forced transportation of population for the purpose of terminating their cultural and/or genetic heritages by anyone anywhere.

These methods of warfare deeply offend human nature. We ask that all governments put an end to their use at once and proceed as rapidly as possible to a peaceful settlement of the war in Vietnam.[55]

This "political" trend in AAA activities enraged some AAA members. The correspondence pages of the *AAA Newsletter* during the late 1960s contain numerous examples of the spirited and eloquent debate for and against the ethics committee, resolutions on political issues, the individual versus the organization, and other topics.

One camp felt that the "political" turn the AAA had been taking was subverting its "professional" nature. Robert Ehrich, who was later a member of the Ethics Committee that would respond to the Thailand Controversy, wrote that he had not joined the AAA for it to act as "a politically motivated activist organization to represent me on matters outside of legitimate professional anthropological concerns."[56] Other writers deplored attempts to "involve the Association in political controversy," which would "lead to ruinous dissension"[57] or would "compromise our scholarly independence."[58]

The opposing camp of anthropologists disputed the political–professional division as "a formalistic evasion"[59] and said that "anthropology is not and has never been a value free science."[60] David F. Aberle, later the liaison member between the AAA Executive Board and its Ethics Committee, noted that previous AAA resolutions on "humanitarian" issues had included "deploring" the proposed usage by the British military of an Australian desert populated by aborigines as a rocket testing range;[61] another writer pointed out that the AAA had protested the prosecution of American Indians for using peyote in their religious rights.[62]

The debate involved the larger issue of the distinction and proper relationship between the anthropologist as a scholar and as a citizen,[63] roles which had overlapped in a complementary way during the heyday of colonial anthropology. With later attempts at "value–free" science, anthropologists tried to separate the roles. But in the 1960s, as some anthropologists criticized U.S. policy, a controversy erupted over the way in which the roles were again overlapping.

Such a dispute is ultimately unresolvable, and neither side was placated by the steps taken by the AAA. Those opposed to the political steps wanted to see them completely abolished, while those in favor wanted to see more. It was in this climate of conflict that an election was held to form a Standing Committee on Ethics, which was created in September 1969. The Executive Board passed the following motion regarding the function of the newly formed Ethics Committee:

> The charge to the [Ethics] committee will be to consider the earlier report of the Interim (or Ad Hoc) Ethics Committee, the body of AAA resolutions concerning ethical matters ... and recommend to the [Executive] Board what its functions should be.[64]

Three members from the Ad Hoc Ethics Committee were carried over to the Standing Ethics Committee—Joseph Jorgensen, William Shack, and Eric Wolf (who was named chair). David Aberle, then a member of the Executive Board of the AAA, was appointed liaison member to the Committee; other members were Norman Chance (University of Connecticut), Robert Ehrich (Brooklyn College, CUNY), Wayne Suttles (Portland State University), Terence Turner (University of Chicago), Oswald Werner (Northwestern University), and Gerald Berreman (University of California–Berkeley).[65] The members of the Committee proceeded to pursue one of the goals of the Ad Hoc Committee—to establish ethical guidelines for anthropologists. As part of this process, the committee published the following request in the *AAA Newsletter*:

> The Ethics Committee of the American Anthropological Association has begun to build up a file of anonymous cases diagnostic of ethical conflicts resulting from the differential commitments of anthropologists to informant, sponsors, fellow professionals and representatives of agencies of government, whether of the United States or of host countries.
>
> We ask the Fellows and Members of the Association to acquaint us with the details of cases in which they have been involved, or which they have collected on their own. From such case material we hope to extract or to document general principles of the formulation of an ethical code for anthropologists. Any communication you may wish to make to the ethics committee

will remain completely confidential; we are interested in general information on cases, but not in the names of persons or specific localities involved.

Please keep in mind that the committee is not a judicial body, and cannot take sides in any dispute, nor adjudicate a particular set of issues. We are interested in the circumstances of any particular case only to the extent that they can help us draw up general guidelines for conduct by anthropologists.

If you with to make such material available, please write to Eric R. Wolf, AAA Ethics Committee....[66]

Shortly after this request appeared in the *AAA Newsletter*, the Student Mobilization Committee sent Wolf a series of documents detailing contacts between U.S. government officials and American social scientists, whose unifying thread seemed to be a concern with counterinsurgency planning and evaluation for Thailand.

NOTES

[1] See Ronald H. Chilcote, *Theories of Comparative Politics: The Search for a Paradigm* (Boulder, Colorado: Westview Press, 1981), 271–346, and Chilcote, *Theories of Development and Underdevelopment* (Boulder, Colorado: Westview Press, 1984) for a more extensive overview and summary of theories of modernization and development and its critics.

[2] Walt W. Rostow, *The Stages of Economic Growth: A Non–Communist Manifesto* (Cambridge: Cambridge University Press, 1960).

[3] Samuel P. Huntington, "Political Development and Political Decay," *World Politics* 17 (April 1965), 386–430, and *Political Order in Changing Societies* (New Haven: Yale University Press, 1968).

[4] Although this type of thinking is somewhat timebound and a product of first–world scholarship, there are modern exceptions. See Likhit Dhiravegin, *Postwar Thai Politics* (Bangkok: Faculty of Political Science, Thammasat University, 1986), 715:

> ... when an investigation of the evolutionary process of the present system is undertaken, it would appear that such a system has inevitably emerged from a process which is both natural and probably desirable....

[5] Walt W. Rostow, *The United States in the World Arena: An Essay in Recent History* (New York: Harper and Brothers, 1960), 438.

[6] William J. Siffen, *The Thai Bureaucracy: Institutional Change and Development* (Honolulu: East–West Center Press, 1966), 244–245; Fred W. Riggs, *Thailand: The Modernization of a Bureaucratic Polity* (Honolulu: East–West Center Press, 1966), 108; Frank C. Darling, *Thailand: New Challenges and the Struggle for a Political and Economic "Take–Off"* (New York: American–Asian Educational Exchange, 1969), 32.

[7] The relevant Thai words are *sathienraphap* (stability), *khwam mankhong* (security), *khwam riap roi* (order), and *woon wai* (confusion). See David Morell and Chai-anan Samudavanija, *Political Conflict in Thailand:*

Reform, Reaction, and Revolution (Cambridge, MA: Oelgeschlager, Gunn & Hain, 1981), 29–31.

[8] Samuel P. Huntington, *Instability at the Non–Strategic Level of Conflict* (Special Studies Group, Study Memorandum Number 2) (Washington, DC: Institute for Defense Analyses, 6 October 1961), v–vi.

[9] Guy J. Pauker, *Southeast Asia as a Problem Area in the Next Decade* [Tempo Report RM 58 TMP–34] (Santa Barbara, California: Technical Military Planning Operation, General Electric Company, 31 December 1958) 11, 2, 8, and [last three paragraphs] 15.

[10] David Wilson, *The United States and the Future of Thailand* (New York and London: Praeger Publishers, 1970), 4, 163–164.

[11] Kathleen Gough, "Anthropology and Imperialism," *Monthly Review* (April 1968), 12.

[12] Felix M. Keesing, "Applied Anthropology in Colonial Administration," *Science of Man* (1945), 375–378.

[13] Stephan Feuchtwang, "The Colonial Formation of British Social Anthropology," in *Anthropology and the Colonial Encounter*, ed. Talal Asad (New York: Humanities Press, 1973), 82–83. Subsequent information on the IAI is from this source.

[14] London School of Economics and Political Science, *Lectures and Classes in Colonial Administration and Anthropology* (London: University of London, 1934–35), 3.

[15] Ibid. (1934–35), 5; (1938–39), 5.

[16] Ibid. (1936–37), 7; (1938–39), 7.

[17] Ibid. (1934–35), 8.

[18] Ibid. (1938–39), 7.

[19] Meyer Fortes, "An Anthropologist's Point of View," in *Fabian Colonial Essays*, ed. Rita Hinden (London: George Allen and Unwin, 1945), 224, 234.

20 Wilson, *The United States and the Future of Thailand*, 163–164.

21 Bronislaw Malinowski, *Dynamics of Culture Change: An Inquiry into Race Relations in Africa* (New Haven: Yale University Press, 1945), 4–5.

22 As noted by Feuchtwang, "Colonial Formation," 91.

23 Malinowski, *Dynamics of Culture Change*, 160.

24 On the importance of the relationship between the "professional administrator" and the "professional anthropologist," see The Right Honorable Lord Hailey, "The Role of Anthropology in Colonial Development," *Man* 5 (1944), 10–16.

On the conflict between policy and application, between European capital city planning and local colonial administrator skepticism, and between government funder and anthropologist in service, see Richard Brown, "Passages in the Life of a White Anthropologist: Max Gluckman in Northern Rhodesia," *Journal of African History* 20 (1979), 525–541.

Similar conflicts in the 1960s United States at the Office of the Director of Defense Research and Engineering (ODDR&E) are traced in Seymour J. Deitchman, *The Best–Laid Schemes: A Tale of Social Research and Bureaucracy* (Cambridge, MA: MIT Press, 1976).

25 For the OSRD and Procurement Act: Jonathan Feldman, *Universities in the Business of Repression: The Academic–Military–Industrial Complex and Central America* (Boston: South End Press, 1989), 148 and 150. For Yale organizations and HRAF: Robin W. Winks, *Cloak & Gown: Scholars in the Secret War, 1939–1961* (New York: William Morrow and Co., 1987). For the ONR: Ralph L. Beals, *Politics of Social Research: An Inquiry into the Ethics and Responsibilities of Social Scientists* (Chicago: Aldine Publishing Company, 1969), 101.

26 For discussion of the Kennedy administration as a watershed, see Douglas S. Blaufarb, *The Counterinsurgency Era: U.S. Doctrine and Performance 1950 to the Present* (New York: Free Press, 1977), especially Chapter Three, "The Kennedy Crucible," 52–88; Deitchman, *Best–Laid Schemes*, especially Chapter One, "Antecedents," 1–17; and Michael T. Klare, *War Without End: American Planning for the Next Vietnams* (New York: Alfred A. Knopf, 1970), especially Chapter One, "From Deterrence to

Counterinsurgency—The Kennedy Response to Wars of National
Liberation," 31–55.

[27] "Memorandum to the President from WWR[ostow]," 29 March 1961,
quoted in George McT. Kahin, *Intervention: How America Became Involved
in Vietnam* (Garden City, NY: Anchor Books, 1987), 131. In other
memoranda, Rostow urged (on July 5, 1961) "a guerilla *deterrence* operation
in Thailand's northeast" and (on April 12, 1961)

> The sending to Viet–Nam of a research and development and
> military hardware team which would explore ... which of the
> various techniques and gadgets now available or being explored
> might be relevant and useful in the Vietnam operation.

Both memoranda appear in New York Times, *The Pentagon Papers*
(Toronto; New York: Bantam Books, 1971), 95, 119.

[28] Statement of Seymour Deitchman, speaking as special assistant for
counterinsurgency, Office of the Director of Defense Research and
Engineering (United States Congress. House of Representatives), *Behavioral
Sciences and the National Security*. Report No. 4 Together with Part IX of
the Hearings on Winning the Cold War: The U.S. Ideological Offensive by
the Subcommittee on International Organizations and Movements (Dante B.
Fascell, Chairman) of the Committee on Foreign Affairs (Washington, DC:
U.S. Government Printing Office, 1966), 71–72.

[29] Harry Eckstein, "Internal War; The Problem of Anticipation," in *Social
Science Research and National Security*, ed. Ithiel de Sola Pool, et. al. A
report prepared by the Research Group in Psychology and the Social
Sciences, under Office of Naval Research Contract Nonr 1354(18), Task
Number NR 170–379 (Washington, DC: Smithsonian Institution, 5 March
1963), 106.

Names of the contributors to this report and their affiliations at the time
are given below. At the time of their comments, eight of the nine
contributors had been participants in the social science–government nexus as
employees of the Defense Department, its federal contract research centers,
or other agencies concerned with defense issues at the time of their
comments).

Ansley J. Coale: professor of economics at Princeton; consultant to the
President's Scientific Advisory Committee (which advises the Defense

Science Board (DSB) and the Rand Corporation. The DSB had been established in 1956 to advise the Secretary of Defense:

> Through its membership of distinguished men representing industry, government and the *academic world*, the Defense Science Board serves as the connecting link between the Office of the Director of Defense Research and Engineering [ODDR&E] and the scientific and technical community of the United States [emphasis added] (U.S. Department of Defense, ODDR&E, *Organization and Purpose of the Defense Science Board* [Washington DC, 1968], quoted in Klare, *War Without End*, 83. See Also U.S. Congress, *Behavioral Sciences and the National Security*, 187–191.)

W. Phillips Davison: senior research fellow at the Council on Foreign Relations; former staff member of the Social Science Department of the Rand Corporations; former consultant to the Operations Research Office and the DOD.

Ithiel de Sola Pool: professor of political science at MIT; chairman of the Research Board of the Simulmatics Corporation [Simulmatics had some problems with "financial management" of DOD supplied funds in Vietnam (Deitchman, *Best–Laid Schemes*, 312–313)]; member of the Air Force Scientific Advisory Board and the Advisory Board of the Naval Ordnance Test Station at China Lake; former member of the Steering Group of the Advisory Panel on Psychology and the Social Sciences of the ODDR&E.

Harry Eckstein: professor of political science at Princeton; later a consultant to Project Camelot.

Klaus Knorr: professor of economics at Princeton; consultant to DOD, IDA, Rand; member of the National Planning Association on Security through Arms Control.

Vincent V. McRae: at the Office of Science and Technology on leave from the Research Analysis Corporation.

Lucien W. Pye: professor of political science at MIT; member of the Advisory Committee to the Director of AID.

Thomas C. Schelling: professor of economics at Harvard; member of the Air Force Scientific Advisory Board; former consultant to DOD, State, and Arms Control and Disarmament Agency; later a consultant to Project Camelot.

Wilbur Schramm: professor of international communications at Stanford University; former member of the DSB; consultant to the State Department, USIA, and the Ford Foundation.

[30] Lucien W. Pye, "Military Development in the New Countries," in *Social Science Research and National Security*, ed. de Sola Pool et. al., 155.

[31] Unless independently footnoted, figures on research and development funding are from Klare, *War Without End*, 372–373. See also U.S. Congress, *Behavioral Sciences and the National Security*, 97.

[32] See Klare, *War Without End*, 372-373, for a table providing dollar expenditures for "Department of Defense Obligations for Behavioral and Social Science Research," 1966-1970.

[33] Deitchman, *Best–Laid Schemes,* 69; Beals, *Politics of Social Research,* 88.

[34] Deitchman, *Best–Laid Schemes,* 48–49.

[35] Ibid., 53-54. According to Deitchman, during the first years of his tenure, these social scientists were Lynn Baker and Kenneth Archer in the ARO; Richard Trumbell and Luigi Petrullo in the ONI; Charles Hutchinson in the AFOSR; and J. C. R. Licklider and Lee Huff at ARPA.

[36] Klare, *War Without End*, 75 (quoting the National Science Foundation).

[37] Information on the FFRCs and SORO is from Klare, *War Without End*, 76–81; and U.S. Congress, *Behavioral Sciences and the National Security*, especially the testimony of Theodore Vallance, director of SORO and Lt. General William Dick, chief of research and development, Department of the Army.

[38] General historical information regarding Camelot is taken from: Beals, *Politics of Social Research*, 4-11; Deitchman, *Best-Laid Schemes*, 139-189; Irving L. Horowitz, *The Rise and Fall of Project Camelot: Studies in the Relationship between Social Science and Practical Politics* (Cambridge, MA: MIT Press, 1967), 3-67; Klare, *War Without End*, 92-101; U.S. Congress, *Behavioral Sciences and the National Security*, passim.

39 Project Camelot, "Working Paper," 5 December 1964. Reprinted in Horowitz, *Rise and Fall of Project Camelot,* 53.

40 Klare, *War Without End,* 95

41 Description released by SORO on 4 December 1964. Reprinted in Horowitz, *The Rise and Fall of Project Camelot,* 47–49.

42 Statement of Lieutenant General W.W. Dick, Jr., Chief of Research and Development, Department of the Army, in U.S. Congress, *Behavioral Sciences and the National Security,* 30.

43 Deitchman, *Best–Laid Schemes,* 184–188.

44 *AAA Newsletter* 6:10 (December 1965), 1.

45 Ibid., 3.

46 Ibid., 7:2 (February 1966), 1.

47 Ibid., 7:7 (September 1966), 3, 4.

48 Ibid., 4.

49 Ibid., 5.

50 Ibid., 8:1 (January 1967), 5–6.

51 Ibid., 8:4 (April 1967), 1.

52 Ibid., 9:7 (September 1968), 3.

53 Ibid., 10:9 (November 1969), 9–10; AAA, *Annual Report 1969 and Directory* (The Bulletins of the American Anthropological Association) (Washington, DC: AAA, 1969), 21.

54 *AAA Newsletter* 10:4 (April 1969), "Report of the [Ad Hoc] Ethics Committee," 3–6; Ibid., 10:6 (June 1969), "Ethics Report Corrected," 1.

55 Ibid., 7:10 (December 1966), 2.

56 Robert W. Ehrich, letter, *AAA Newsletter* 8:2 (February 1967), 7.

57 John P. Gillin, George P. Murdock, Alexander Spoehr, letter, *AAA Newsletter* 8:2 (February 1967), 7–8.

58 Clark E. Cunningham, letter, *AAA Newsletter* 8:4 (April 1967), 10.

59 Henry Rosenfeld, letter, *AAA Newsletter* 8:4 (April 1967), 9.

60 Charles Leslie, letter, *AAA Newsletter* 8:5 (May 1967), 6.

61 David F. Aberle, letter, *AAA Newsletter* 8:5 (May 1967), 7.

62 Stephen P. Dunn, letter, *AAA Newsletter* 8:6 (June 1967), 9. Some other arguments favoring an engaged role for anthropologists include the following:

> Ehrich's letter and that of the Pittsburgh individuals [see note 57] reveal a fundamental misunderstanding of the nature of agitation and opinion–formation in a democratic society. We have in this country a well–established tradition of political participation by groups of all sorts, professional and other. I think it is well understood that positions taken collectively by such groups do not necessarily bind individual members.

> Finally, the danger of internal dissension referred to must, I think be considered a lesser evil in comparison with acquiescence, or the appearance of acquiescence in the present course of affairs in Vietnam. It makes little sense for us as an organization to issue heated protests on—relatively—secondary matters such as operation Camelot (which, embarrassing and distasteful as it may have been, has not yet to my knowledge killed or maimed anyone), while remaining silent about the unspeakable horrors committed daily in Vietnam in the names of all of us.... I would be appalled to find that by becoming a social scientist (rather than, say, a physician, an engineer, or a plumber) I had forfeited my right to speak out in my professional capacity when I felt my own cultural values threatened [Dunn, citation above]....

Those who claim that the AAA is not principally a political association are correct, but this does not mean that the Council should divorce itself from any expression of political opinion. If, for example, the systematic extermination of the American Indians or of Negroes were undertaken as official U.S. policy, one might hope that the anthropological community would feel called upon to express some concern and even outrage. The notion that since we are scientists we should not bring to bear on political issues the prestige and weight of our national organization is both irresponsible and naive. Advocates of such a position as well as members of the Association who attempted (and to a certain degree succeeded in) castration of the resolution [to condemn warfare in Vietnam] by amendment, are unpleasantly reminiscent of the "good" German scientists during the 1930s who hoped to keep their profession distinct from its political and social matrix.... [Sally R. Binford, Lewis R. Binford, letter, *AAA Newsletter* 8:6 (June 1967), 9].

A science of man lacking any concern for the preservation and improvement of human nature could only be a joke in bad taste.... To remain silent is to deny the value of science in the solution of human problems. To speak is to shoulder the burdens of Archimedes, Galileo, Darwin, and Oppenheimer.... [Alan R. Beals, letter, *AAA Newsletter* 8:6 (June 1967), 9].

[Regarding] the grounds of the separation of the roles of professional anthropologist and private individual. This reminds me of the anti-Nazi scientist in Germany who, just before his execution for opposition to Hitler's racists policies, was perplexed about whether he was being shot as a professional scientist belonging to a scientific body, or as a private individual [Charles C. Brant, letter, *AAA Newsletter* 10:5 (May 1969), 4].

63 This point is raised in Charles Leslie, letter, *AAA Newsletter* 8:5 (May 1967), 6.

64 *AAA Newsletter* 10:9 (November 1969), 9-10.

65 Gerald D. Berreman, "Ethics Versus 'Realism' in Anthropology" in *Ethics and the Profession of Anthropology: Dialogue for a New Era*, ed. Carolyn Fluehr-Lobban (Philadelphia: University of Pennsylvania Press, 1991), 43.

66 *AAA Newsletter* 11:3 (March 1970), 9-10.

CHAPTER THREE

IDA & THAILAND STUDY GROUP

Intellectual exercise is indispensable to survival and victory—
applied jointly with force or substituting for it.

—Statement on the inside cover of the first Institute for Defense
Analyses annual report, 1956–57

The question is how to get the Soc. Sci. community to infiltrate
the police and intelligence group and let them obtain the
information.

—C. Farrar, USAID official,
speaking at the Thailand Study Group, 1967

In the summer of 1967, two years after the cancellation of Project
Camelot, the Institute for Defense Analyses (IDA), a Defense Department
Federal Contract Research Center, convened a three–week "Summer Study"
under the title "The Thailand Study Group."[1] The Summer Study was held
under the aegis of IDA's Jason Division, which called together researchers
on short notice to work on problems of interest to the Defense Department.

Summer Study participants included social scientists and U.S.
government officials from the Defense Department, AID, and other agencies.
In addition to other social scientists, anthropologists Michael Moerman,
Herbert Phillips, Steven Piker, and Lauriston Sharp attended the summer
study. The June 19 to July 6 sessions have been described variously as "a
secret review of counterinsurgency research in Thailand"; an undertaking "to
explore policy questions" and "to learn what was known to Americans about
Thai society, and to assess the impact of American aid and policy on Thai
society"; and as an attempt "to explore the usefulness of creating a 'SS'
[social science] Jason."[2]

The minutes of IDA's Thailand Study Group are replete with
discussions about the advisability of setting up a social science Jason to

mirror the physical science Jason already in existence. The social scientists present also freely contributed opinions and recommendations to a dialogue that included such topics as insurgency and counterinsurgency tactics, U.S. policy objectives in Thailand, the nature of U.S.-Thai relations, and the problems of rural government.

Participants in the Thailand Study Group were aware that further consulting fees would follow the creation of a social science Jason, with benefits accruing to both the U.S. government and themselves. While discussing the advantages of this, there were frank exchanges as to whom IDA served and what function Thailand would have in all of this. As one social scientist put it: "Thailand is a good place to study because there are things going on there that can be studied which are not going on elsewhere. *It is like a laboratory* [emphasis added]."[3]

The contents of the minutes of the Thailand Study Group have been questioned by several participants, and their criticism will be addressed in the discussion of the minutes that follows. However, they remain the only extant remnant of what was said at the meetings. Before delving into the minutes, it is necessary to understand the activities and goals of the groups and corporations, such as the IDA and its Jason Division, that sponsored defense–related social science research on Southeast Asia. Tracing the history of an institute such as the IDA yields important information on the ideology, goals, and connections that helped to place IDA in the government–social science nexus. The IDA is an integral part of the academic–military complex and serves to unite the needs of academics (for research, funding, and prestige) with those of the Defense Department (for help in carrying out U.S. policy in Southeast Asia).

INSTITUTE FOR DEFENSE ANALYSES (IDA)

Founding

The IDA was incorporated in 1956 in response to a request made the previous year by the secretary of defense and the joint chiefs of staff to channel advice and research to the Department of Defense. IDA's first annual report states that the "nonprofit corporation" is

> an association of universities formed to promote, in the field of Defense studies, a more effective relationship between national security and scientific learning.[4]

A later statement of purpose describes IDA as

> an independent scientific advisory corporation on national security matters.... The basic objective of IDA is to provide an independent and objective source of studies, analyses, and advice for the Federal Government and, in particular, for the Department of Defense.[5]

IDA's five founding member institutions were California Institute of Technology, Case Institute of Technology, Massachusetts Institute of Technology, Stanford University, and Tulane University. By 1969 IDA's member institutions had grown to twelve. Harlan Hatcher, as president of the University of Michigan, joined the board of trustees in 1958, and the university became a member of IDA in 1959. Hatcher was replaced on the board by University of Michigan president Robben Fleming in 1968. Grayson Kirk, president of Columbia University joined the board of directors in 1959, and the university became an IDA member in the same year.[6] One can only speculate to what degree these men and their universities, described as "good companions in important labors" who "sponsored" IDA "as a public service," subscribed to the maxim on the reverse side of the cover of the first annual report: "Intellectual exercise is indispensable to survival and victory—applied jointly with force or substituting for it."[7]

At its inception IDA was issued start–up capital of $500,000 by the Ford Foundation. Dr. James A. Perkins, vice–president of the Carnegie Corporation joined IDA's board of trustees in 1958 and a grant (of $12,500) from Carnegie came in January 1960 to support studies on game theory and disarmament.[8] IDA began with a full-time professional staff of 59 in 1956 and had reached a total staff of 597 (278 professional and 319 support personnel) by 1969, not including people on special contracts or summer study. In addition to universities, IDA members came from and returned to government positions in the military branches, ambassador corps, presidential staff, NASA, the Department of Health, Education, and Welfare, and specific advisory agencies of the DOD that would call on IDA for further service.[9]

The first five annual reports each begin with a pithy narrative that unites the goals of IDA with a classical or ancient reference point. These include Noah ("to the extent that our efforts affect the survival of people, we sail in common cause with our common ancestor"), Hercules ("force is a necessary element when bargaining with the fates on the lots they may offer"), King David ("we salute the ancient King, finding ourselves with the same objectives in mind as had he"), and Saint Patrick ("a man of peace, who nevertheless kept a shillelagh handy at all times").[10] (The parable used in the IDA 1958-1959 report is reproduced as Appendix C.)

The primary purpose of IDA in its early stage was weapons research, through contracts granted to its various divisions by the Defense Department. But even in the year of its founding, studies outside the purview of the physical sciences were endorsed, including those in the fields of "psychology, history, political science, and others."[11] With the addition of Columbia University and the University of Michigan as member institutions in 1959, IDA's broader focus was stated even more explicitly:

> Our new Members are strong in the humanities and social sciences as well as in the physical sciences and engineering. The Institute thus increases its capability across the spectrum of talents needed by the government, while at the same time enlarging the section of the academic community afforded an increased, direct opportunity to absorb to advantage the wisdom that derives empirically from intimate contact with real and present problems.[12]

The goal was to have a two-directional flow of ideas, but the forum for this exchange was narrowly defined. As a funding agency, IDA directed its members to study certain "real" problems that were of interest to the Defense Department. This is explicitly stated in IDA's desire to "feed back to the country through educational channels a heightened awareness of the real problems of preserving the national integrity."[13]

Divisions and Research

IDA was composed of different divisions, of which the Jason Division was one. Although each had functionally specific tasks, information was shared between them. Originally, the majority of research centered on technology for strategic weaponry and related topics, such as missiles, nuclear weapons, satellites, communications, and mathematics. With the commitment of U.S. ground troops to the Vietnam War came an added emphasis on applied tactical weaponry, insurgency issues, and economic studies. At the same time, in the mid– to latter 1960s, IDA branched out into consulting on domestic issues, such as poverty and transportation. It is no coincidence that stepped–up research on domestic issues took place as IDA redefined the meaning of national security and campus criticism of the corporation increased. Partially in response to this external criticism, IDA instituted a total restructuring of its divisions in 1967, which included the formation of several new divisions, including the Office of Urban Research in the following year.

The introduction of new divisions was explained as follows:

> [S]ome of the most significant and pressing problems facing the Government are those on the domestic scene.... It became evident that our corporate charter should be broadened to acknowledge our readiness to apply IDA's capabilities to problems falling outside a conventional definition of national security.[14]

The types of research that IDA conducted with regard to Southeast Asia varied widely; discerning exactly what each division did is difficult because much of the research remains classified. As the 1966 annual report notes, descriptions "may sometimes be tantalizingly vague."[15]

The Weapons Systems Evaluation Division (WSEG) was IDA's first and largest division. Its primary focus was on the physical, engineering, and mathematical elements of warfare. It conducted studies

> related to current land and air operations in Southeast Asia.... The Southeast Asia studies are expected to affect significantly the future limited–war capabilities of U.S. military forces."[16]

Following the 1967 restructuring, the Science and Technology Division and Systems Evaluation Division were formed and seem to have taken over many of the functions of WSEG. Studies associated with Southeast Asia included those on advanced sensors, the M–16 rifle, combatting infiltration of ground troops, political aspects of recurring violence, evaluation of social science research in Vietnam, and subversion warfare. Publications included "Pacification in Vietnam: A Survey" and "A Study of Considerations in Introducing New Weapons Into Southeast Asia." [17]

The Economic and Political Studies Division (EPSD) produced studies on Southeast Asia, on weapons and tactics in counterinsurgency, and on guerilla war.[18] But EPSD also branched out into domestic politics in the mid–1960s, producing studies such as "Poverty and Labor Force Participation" and "The Structural Change Hypothesis for Employment Among Youth, the Aged, and Minorities: A Critical Analysis." It also conducted a study for the Office of Economic Opportunity (OEO) that allegedly led to an OEO review program and to the evaluation of antipoverty programs.[19] In the field of education, an EPSD economist "drew on his experience in defense work" to produce a "program budgeting system for American colleges and universities."[20]

The International and Social Studies Division also produced a mix of studies on domestic and foreign problems. One study was

> made for the Joint Chiefs of Staff on the potential threat of insurgency to a key Asian country, and the ability of that country —in terms of its cultural, political, economic, and military vulnerabilities and resources—to deal with this insurgency.[21]

But another was done for the Department of Housing and Urban Development on low–cost housing "towards a means of facilitating exploitation of new technology and economies of scale."[22]

The above examples illustrate that the interest of IDA was directed towards both the war in Southeast Asia and potential national security problems at home. Those academics who worked on aspects of poverty in the U.S. may not have worked on the advantages of air–sown mines along the Ho Chi Minh trail; but for IDA, the amalgamation of research topics functioned as an attempt to lure back any academics who had been frightened away by campus protests. IDA noted this problem in its 1968 annual report:

> There has always been, however, a strong reluctance on the part of universities to engage in classified research except in times of major national emergency. This reluctance has increased in recent years and extends also to an unwillingness to engage in studies which may be used in politically controversial decisions.[23]

Public criticism on campuses of defense-related work was of such concern to IDA that by 1969 IDA had formally disassociated itself from the sponsorship of its twelve universities (while keeping individual members as trustees and continuing to have academics among its professional staff). The combination of distancing itself from universities and moving towards topics of domestic urgency was a calculated move for self–preservation, as the annual report for 1969 indicates:

> We believe this new arrangement will maintain an appropriate relationship between IDA and the university world, but will

eliminate those features that had become matters of campus contention....

Work for civilian agencies on some of the most important problems facing the nation will provide a challenge to staff members and prospective staff members who might be reluctant to commit themselves solely to defense problems.[24]

Jason Division

The Jason division of IDA was established in 1959 with a part–time group of about twenty academic members. The group was to work on selected problems for two or three weekends per month and four to six weeks in the summer, at Defense Department expense. This method of meeting would allow minimum interruption of the participants' normal academic schedules.[25] The first group consisted of mostly physicists, but this, like all other aspects of IDA studies, evolved with the needs of the Defense Department and of IDA itself.

The rapid deployment capabilities of Jason were duly noted:

The [Jason] Division as a whole can be very useful in "fire fighting," not only for the intellectual power but also the speed with which it can attack a problem, having acquired background through previous exposure and requiring very little orientation.[26]

With government interest in brush-fire insurgency in Southeast Asia on the rise, it was only fitting that IDA put its firefighters on the job. The 1966 annual report states:

Increased government attention to such problems as counterinsurgency, insurrection, and infiltration led to the suggestion that Jason members might be able to provide fresh insights into problems that are not entirely in the realm of physical science. It is too soon to determine the long term value of this work, but present indications are that ... the undertaking is worthwhile and may broaden.[27]

Jason rose to the task, mixing technology and social science. In addition to studies of North Vietnamese Army logistics, the division published "Explosively Produced Flechettes" and "Air Sown Mines for

Specialized Purposes," both limited to official use or classified, as were all internal IDA publications.[28]

In 1966, a Jason member stated his opposition to the bombing war over North Vietnam after calculating the costs of losses in American airmen and planes versus the benefits of killing Vietnamese. Jason proposed, instead, an anti–infiltration barrier across the demilitarized zone that would use air–sown mines, sensors, and specifically targeted bombing raids.[29] The individual functions of each division came together in this project. The Jason Division conducted its own research on mines and used that on sensors, night vision devices, and communications produced by other divisions to create an interdiction plan.

THAILAND STUDY GROUP

Formation

Given the history of IDA's research activities, its sponsorship of a "study group" to discuss Thailand was a logical development. The Defense Department wanted to jump on suppressing the nascent insurgency of the Communist Party of Thailand, which in 1965 had engaged in combat with the Thai government for the first time, before the Thai political and military situation deteriorated. According to Steven Piker, an anthropologist in attendance at the Thailand Study Group:

> The Jason Division of IDA was (so I was informed by the anthropologist who invited me to attend) [most likely Michael Moerman] undertaking an evaluation of the effects of American programs in Thailand on the Thai nation and society generally.[30]

From the point of view of IDA and Defense Department officials, such an evaluation could be used to better tailor American programs to the task of counterinsurgency.

According to Herbert Phillips, the Thailand Study Group owed its inception to the chance meeting of anthropologist Michael Moerman and physicist Murray Gell–Mann on an airplane.[31] Phillips says that Moerman and Gell–Mann, who was involved with the IDA, were coincidentally seated next to each other and started talking. In the course of discussing each other's interests, Gell–Mann became interested in the idea of a meeting to discuss the cooperation between scholars and the government.

In a letter to the *AAA Newsletter*, Moerman recounted the formation of the Study Group as follows:

In 1967, a representative of Jason, a group of physical scientists who consult for the government, asked me to help arrange a summer seminar on US policy to Thailand in which representatives of government agencies would brief and listen to a floating group of social scientists specializing in Thailand. Jason's purpose was to experiment with the possibility of adding a social science component. This interest in Thailand was an accidental compromise, but I (along with the co–organizer) felt that the social scientists could alert the government to the dangers of directing its aid, "Occupant, Thailand," with no knowledge or concern for how that aid benefitted some kinds of persons and consequently deprived other—frequently better—ones. The conference failed on both grounds. Jason decided, wisely I feel, that it would be a mistake to add a social science component. I learned that every single American agency that spoke to us took counterinsurgency as its main policy rationale. They were therefore unconcerned with the harm their programs might be doing the Thai people. I was unwilling to consult for the government, and so ceased in September 1967.[32]

Phillips said he was attracted to the idea of a Thailand Study Group because, as a scholar, "I had a fascination with Thai peasants in revolution." He said, "All I knew was that Gell–Mann had worked out a contract to see what could be contributed to insurgency in Thailand." When he got to the meeting, he found he had to "overcome bizarre governmental views" and "ignorance," and "most of the participants knew nothing about Thailand and could have been talking about Mars."

With regard to the accuracy of the minutes, Phillips said, "[I] had very relevant criticisms of the U.S. government. I couldn't believe this was the record of all important questions."[33] Moerman later wrote, "The so–called minutes ... are notes taken by an IDA representative which the other participants specifically rejected as minutes because of their gross inaccuracy."[34] Steven Piker said that he could not tell how accurate the minutes were, but that most of the "meetings focused on areas in which sponsored counterinsurgency programs were most active."[35] This corresponds with Moerman's letter to the *AAA Newsletter*, that the

TABLE 3.1: PARTICIPANTS IN THE INSTITUTE FOR DEFENSE ANALYSES' THAILAND STUDY GROUP: JUNE–JULY 1967[36]

NAME	AFFILIATION
J. E. Barmack	City University of New York, psychologist
James E. Cross	Secretary of the Institute for Defense Analyses
Seymour Deitchman	Director of Project Agile for the Advanced Research Projects Agency (ARPA)
G. Farrar	AID, "responsibility for all of AID planning"
J. Fitzgerald	"in ISA [Office of the Assistant Secretary of Defense for International Security Affairs] concerned with policy planning on V.N. [Vietnam]—assistant for COIN [counterinsurgency] planning"
P. Franklin	ARPA
Murray Gell–Mann	California Institute of Technology, physicist, conference organizer
Robert Gomer	University of Chicago, chemist
James Hoath	United States Operations Mission/Thailand (AID), chief of Research and Evaluation Division
Howard Kaufman	Cornell Aeronautics Laboratory
Louis Lomax	author of *Thailand: The War That Is, The War That Will Be*
Millard F. Long	University of Chicago, economist
Michael Moerman	UCLA, anthropologist
Jesse Orlansky	Founder of Dunlap and Associates, a behavioral research firm; psychologist
Herbert Phillips	University of California-Berkeley, anthropologist
Steven Piker	Swarthmore College, anthropologist
Gary Quinn	ARPA
Lauriston Sharp	Cornell University, anthropologist

NAME	AFFILIATION
General Maxwell Taylor	President of IDA as of 1966
M. Ladd Thomas	Northern Illinois University, political scientist

Other individuals present at the conference were two people whose affiliation was identified only as "Jason" (Henry W. Kendall and Louis Mayer), at least two who seem to be government officials judging from their statements at the Summer Study (L. Carter, Carl Nelson), and W. Bell, P. Gyorgy, Robinette Kirk ("works for Mr. Lomax"), Don Marshall; H. Moskowitz, W. Stark (apparently connected with ARPA), S. York, and S. Young.

---

representatives of "every American agency" who spoke to the group "took counterinsurgency as [their] main policy rationale." While the minutes may be incomplete or inaccurate in some ways, according to the criticism of some of the engaged parties, they do reflect basic attitudes of various representatives of government agencies.

Participants

Although it is difficult to reconstruct the structure of the meetings from the minutes, it appears that they often began with a guest presenting research findings or a report on ongoing activities. This was followed by discussion of the presentation and related topics. Discussion was not limited to the presentations, although they often seemed to be a starter for discussion. Piker remembers there being perhaps twelve to fifteen people in the room at one time.[37]

According to the minutes, anthropologists Moerman and Phillips were present every day, Piker from June 28-30,[38] and Sharp from July 3-5.[39] Piker recalls being paid about $75 dollars per day.[40] In addition to these four social scientists, a wide array of other academics and government officials were present at the Summer Study (see Table 3.1). Knowledge of affiliations is particularly useful in assessing the function of Jason in general and of the Thailand Study Group in particular.

Government participants seem to have been chosen carefully to reflect a cross section of U.S. government agencies concerned with counter-insurgency research. Agency representatives candidly articulated both the specific goals of their agencies and the larger American goal in Thailand, suggesting ways in which social scientists could help in policy formulation and implementation.

Governmental Mandates to Study Group

The social scientists attending the Thailand Study Group were presented with clear policy statements about the function and goals of IDA and Jason by the non–academic participants representing IDA, the Assistant Secretary of Defense for Internal Security Affairs (ISA), the Defense Department's Advance Research Projects Agency (ARPA), and USAID.

A reasonable summation of the needs of the U.S. government was given at the end of the Summer Study by General Maxwell Taylor:

> Looking back at my Vietnam experience the most serious problem was getting basic data soon enough.... To correct this situation in Thailand would be a major contribution. You need people who are students of Thailand, ethnology, etc. We don't get enough people who have that kind of background.... We would like methodical surveys, frequently repeated to get trend data....
>
> It is important to identify the problems that our government should be doing. Some countries should achieve a certain level of turbulence and development before we spend time on them, e.g., Africa.
>
> Selectivity in further involvement militarily will be important.
>
> What are our interests in those areas? What is the state of development? Should we and how, participate in the development?...
>
> I hope you can find a way of setting up a structure in IDA which would draw in the services we need to get this job done.[41]

J. Fitzgerald, the ISA representative, told the group that ISA was concerned with bases, arms sales, and counterinsurgency. He advised the social scientists present on how best to sell their product—research:

> Is there an insurgency? In Thailand I would want to know what they are doing? What do they think they are doing? Who are they? What support are they getting? from where? Why would we want to support them?...

> Why do you break it [units of analysis] up by geographic areas rather than by problems, e.g., counterinsurgency? *This would have customer appeal....*

> There are a lot of people in government who are interested in violence and development.... I think you are hung up on a regional focus. The DOD is interested in development or in violence or other functions or problems [emphasis added].[42]

At one point, physicist Gell–Mann seemed unclear as to exactly what it was Fitzgerald wanted. He was told that it was "tools," not "indices" :

> [Fitzgerald:] We need SS information to let us know whether we should get into any particular COIN [counterinsurgency]. [Secretary of Defense] McNamara thinks there is a relationship between security and state of development. The relationship is probably curvilinear.

> [Gell–Mann:] Are you asking from the SS community a dialogue and indices?

> [Fitzgerald:] *I want tools* [emphasis added].[43]

Gary Quinn, an ARPA representative, expressed interest in having social scientists join his unit of the Defense Department ("We need more social scientists at ARPA.") and stressed the policy angle:

> There is a need for more effective communication between the policy maker and the academic community. Part of the problem is the reduction of information to essentials of interest to the policy maker.[44]

It would have been impossible to listen to a list of what ARPA envisioned in Thailand from Seymour Deitchman, director of Project Agile, and still mistake the goals:

> What we want to have done in Thailand with 150–250 professionals is:
>
> 1) A systematic approach to COIN [counterinsurgency] with unique data to show the policy planner how and why to do things better.
>
> 2) To learn how to control the border.
>
> 3) How to use limited police and military resources in an integrated way.
>
> 4) How to use Psy. Ops. [Psychological Operations] in a way which is based on villager perception of needs.
>
> 5) How to contribute to economic development by planning and evaluation, e.g. the Strategic Hamlet idea in VN was adopted on a big scale before we knew whether it worked. It flopped on a big scale.[45]

C. Farrar of USAID weighed in with what AID thought would be a useful function for social scientists working with the police and intelligence services:

> We ought to sensitize the Thais to the need for this kind of information [attitudinal and behavioral indices] and encourage them to get it. The question is how to get the Soc. Sci. community to infiltrate the police and intelligence group and let them obtain the information.[46]

These are not the circuitous statements on counterinsurgency that were often made publicly or were presented in previously examined documents. They are blunt, direct, and from varied quarters—the nonprofit corporation serving the Defense Department, various Defense Department offices, and even the United States agency that is concerned with international development—USAID. Even within the framework of setting up a social science Jason, as we shall see below, the discussions often centered around the function of social scientists in helping the government to formulate, evaluate, and *implement* counterinsurgency policy. Comparisons were made with Vietnam and U.S. military policy there; the key was to use applied research to prevent the U.S. from "losing" Thailand.

Creation of a Social Science Jason

The original Jason model for physical scientists, now being adapted for social scientists, was explained early at the conference: "It has permanent part–time physical scientists who work on *problems of choice from a list of government problems* [emphasis added]."[47] Later, the broader, but still overlapping, appeal of social science research was explained:

> [Deitchman:] The customer for Physical Science Jason is the DOD [Department of Defense]. Who would be requesting a SS Jason project?

> [Gell–Mann:] DOD, AID, State.[48]

And, of course, there was always the ability to link U.S. policy with the future of the discipline:

> [Deitchman:] It is important to get anthropological and sociological information on areas of U.S. interest such as South America. A S.S. Jason can help effect it.

> [Sharp:] It is also important to keep the growth of the discipline moving.[49]

Keeping in mind the history of government-social science nexus discussed in Chapter One, it is apparent that some of the social scientists in attendance at the Thailand Study Group were both being asked and were themselves volunteering to aid the U.S. government in policy implementation of a specific type. There were bound to be conflicts and problems inherent in such an arrangement linking social scientists to counterinsurgency policy. These ethical issues were on the minds of some participants, but it did not prevent them from offering advice regarding counterinsurgency operations in Thailand.

One of the consequences of doing research for IDA's Jason or any other corporation under contract to the Defense Department is that the researcher almost invariably must use classified data, which makes publication problematic. A 1965 IDA Consultant Security Briefing made this decidedly clear:

> All papers generated by you, including both classified and unclassified, that have been prepared in connection with your consultancy to IDA should be submitted to IDA for approval prior to publication and distribution.[50]

It is unclear if the Summer Study Participants were given this or a similar security briefing, although the problems inherent in working for the government were discussed. At an early meeting, the group as a whole discussed the conflicts inherent in working for Jason and/or the U.S. government and then trying to publish:

> An argument against a Jason S.S. group is that the work and reputation of a Jason physical scientist is not jeopardized by involvement on classified issues whereas this may not be true of the S.S. Access to classified information would put an unwanted brake on the freedom to write in cognate areas.[51]

Other concerns were in evidence at the Summer Study. Michael Moerman noted that the interests of the government were not "isomorphic with" those of academic disciplines.[52] Further problems in recruiting social scientists to the government cause were also discussed, including the low caliber of personnel attracted to government work, poorly trained military personnel who functioned as supervisors, and "the priority of 'ethical' values."[53] (It is interesting that the notetaker surrounded the word "ethics" with quotation marks, as though it were something unusual or difficult to define.)

Fears of a repetition of the Project Camelot fiasco were expressed and assuaged. "[Stark:] We are afraid of Congress, a Camelot repetition...."[54] The group cited "The Vietnam War, Camelot, and the incompatibility of classified research with the university mission ..." as "deterrents" to attracting social scientists to government work.[55] Phillips said, "Everybody is worried about Camelot, but it is not applicable to Thai."[56]

The fear of a "Camelot fiasco" refers to the public scrutiny and subsequent cancellation of Camelot, but not to its existence as a research project. Camelot was an applied social science project whose intent was to aid the United States in encouraging stable growth in the developing countries. As such, Camelot was directly relevant to the discussions at the Thailand Study Group about the roles of social scientists.

A fear of the effect of the statements of ethics made by the American Anthropological Association was also raised:

> [Marshall:] He cited the position of the U. Pa. and the American Anthropological Association condemning classified and CIA or military work on campus. The AAA believes that undercover work subverts the acceptance of all anthropological researchers in foreign countries.[57]

Finally, the general corrupting influence of work in service to the government was discussed by the group:

> A real concern was that involvement in government work was corrupting. To the extent that political scientists are concerned with the legitimacy of power and the maintenance of order, they have been corrupted by their culture.[58]

Phrases such as "legitimacy of power" and "maintenance of order" dovetail with concerns for "stability" that are common in development/modernization theory; and the stability of the Thai government was a U.S. goal in Thailand.

A plethora of remedies for the crises of conscience or pocketbooks that social scientists might face during their dealings with the government were suggested over the course of the Summer Study. These included increasing salaries; focusing on domestic issues as well as foreign ones (this corresponds with IDA's broadening its scope of mission as evidenced in the excerpts from annual reports in the first part of this chapter); giving the opportunity to look at subjects not of immediate interest to the government (Moerman); stressing the appeals of Jason: "congenial group, money, interesting problems—like the existence of Thai communists" (Gell–Mann); patriotic motives: "the desire to help the country, an obligation of service" (Orlansky); and, of course, "There is an appeal of "being able to influence government policy" (Farrar).[59] Moerman's suggestion can be seen as a way to interest the government in funding other projects—those not concentrated on counterinsurgency. Such suggestions, while noble, fell on deaf ears among government participants at the conference.

The most remarkable remedies to the lack of attraction of social scientists to government service reflect the idea that anthropologists might replicate some of the functions of their predecessors in the colonial service. It does not appear that the first of the following excerpts was suggested by an anthropologist, although it appeared on a list of "remedial measures" that had been culled from a discussion by some of the participants:

> Support a university program of training administrative anthro-pologists as were developed by the British and French.[60]

> [Deitchman:] It would be useful in State, AID and ISA to get an area scholar to come into the desk officer's spot and learn bureaucracy, function for a few years, and then leave.[61]

The social scientists in attendance at this Summer Study had varying responses to suggestions that they participate more closely in the government's counterinsurgency policy. AID official Farrar noted, "There are people who will not work for the government because of its policies, but we do get to the others."[62] If one accepts the validity of the following excerpts, they may be read as indications that Moerman, Phillips, and Sharp might have considered being part of "the others." But the three all said later that they had also been trying to push the government's interest away from counterinsurgency and towards a middle ground This was a tricky line to tread, particularly in such counterinsurgency-obsessed times.

> Moerman advocated that social scientists have greater access to classified information and play a greater role in deciding the kinds of information which should be collected....[63]

> [Farrar:] AID has tried giving SSs access to classified data to pull together. But it didn't work.

> [Phillips:] I would want to work on some problems if I could get an unclassified paper out of it.

> [Sharp:] I would be willing to assist AID in analyzing its data....[64]

[Phillips:] Most of the SS is concerned only about the truth. The things which have been stressed are how do you get an agency to buy the outcome.[65]

Social Scientists and Counterinsurgency

The overall U.S. policy favoring counterinsurgency, as opposed to democratization, was best–stated by Carl Nelson, whose specific position in the government, unfortunately, is not clear from the minutes:

The main objective is to strengthen the Thai government and society and motivate them to recognize the threats from outside its borders, and to avoid the use of our troops to contain the spread of communist influence in this area. *The democratization of the central government is not the immediate problem. The containment of communist aggression as we face it in V.N. is the immediate objective.* Hopefully the experience in V.N. will convince them that wars of liberation won't work. Our strengthening policy is not in terms of personalities but in terms of stable governments capable of resisting externally supported insurgency [emphasis added].[66]

Moerman, Phillips, and Sharp offered notions of democracy that can be read as being similar to those of Nelson. Some of the following remarks have an air of innocent brainstorming; how government planners would have used a particular research question or opinion, however, is uncertain:

[Moerman, from a list of proposed questions for discussion:] Does democratization weaken respect for authority more than it strengthens the economy and polity of Thailand?...[67]

[Moerman:] One argument for democratization is to get the villager to share in the responsibility for the failure of some programs....[68]

[Moerman, on a possible future Thai political system:] Couldn't we have ward politics at the village level?

[Gell–Mann:] How would the ward politicians be rewarded?

[Moerman:] Through the dispensation of goodies which give him status and power....[69]

[Phillips:] You want political participation [by villagers], not necessarily the right to vote....[70]

[Sharp:] It is important that people believe that somebody cares— the corruption doesn't matter as long as they see things are being done.[71]

Moerman summarized the issues relating to the insurgency as follows:

There are three problems:
  1) Isolating and/or destroying
  2) Strengthen governments.
  3) Advancing economic development.

They don't have to be done in the same place and at the same time, nor by the Thai government.[72]

Nelson followed his policy statement with a list of "elements which are pressing for democratization of the present structure." These included members of the Western–trained elite, journalists, and intellectuals.[73] Now if the concern was not with the introduction of democracy, but instead with the maintenance of stability, into what category would go those who pressed for democracy? Could they not be seen as a threat to stability and might they not need to be isolated and/or destroyed?

There is evidence in later Thai history that this, indeed, happened. In October 1973, after several years of anti–government opposition activity, a Thai democracy movement that included, but was by no means limited to, the strata that make up Nelson's elements, succeeded in forcing out the military rulers. Thai politics entered a phase of much broader participation. This interlude, which lasted until October 1976, was probably the most "democratic" period in twentieth-century Thailand until the latter 1980s. But while it was a progressive period, it was also one of extralegal repression of people labeled as "communists," with farm and labor organizers, student leaders, journalists and academics often targeted. The 1976 coup that ended this democratic period was precipitated by a bloody police, army, and paramilitary unit assault on the campus of a Bangkok university in which scores of protesting students were killed, by means that included burning alive and lynching.[74]

I am not concluding that any of the anthropologists, or even Nelson, would support the liquidation of government opponents. However, I suggest that the kind of reasoning that supports nebulous stability while democracy remains on the back burner is a misfocused intellectual effort, and that U.S. policy in Thailand had manifestly bad consequences for Thais because of this focus. The emphasis on maintaining alleged Thai stability is also evidence of a peculiar labeling process. From 1932, the date of the coup that overthrew the absolute monarchy, until 1973, Thailand had had twelve different prime ministers (an average of 3.3 years per person), eight successful coups, and many more attempted coups—more a picture of instability than one of stability in need of support.[75]

Discussion of Insurgent Activities

Discussion of the tactics and activities of the Communist Party of Thailand (CPT) is prominent in the minutes of the Thailand Study Group, with social scientists contributing actively. "Much of the second week of the Thai Study Group was spent discussing the insurgency in Thailand," a working paper states.[76] The following exchange demonstrates both the research concerns of individual social scientists and the needs of government agencies:

> [Piker:] As a SS I want to know the outcome of the interrogation of captured insurgents to find out their motivation.
>
> I would like to know how often the various Thai agencies are actually visiting the villages and what they are actually doing.

> [Moerman:] We don't know what the specific patterns of appeals by the C.T. [communist terrorists] are.
>
> We would like evidence on whether style is more important than substance in the COIN programs.

> [Young:] What is the analysis of the village power structure? Who are the village elite? How permanent and pervasive is the *nakleng* [tough guy/gangster] organization?

[Quinn:] RAC [Research Analysis Corporation, an Army FCRC] is going to try to get samples of the C.T. propaganda and harangues.

[Thomas:] What is the reaction of the villages to the C.T. and the effect of programs?

[Stark:] We have a critical shortage of researchers.

[Phillips:] We can train them quickly and cheaply.

[Thomas:] You can't trust the reports of Thai investigators.

[Stark:] We are doing research in depth and are also looking for indices.

[Fitzgerald:] We want to know what kinds of COIN do we get involved in.

[Stark:] Advice to a foreign government could become running the government. Where do you pass the line?

[Fitzgerald:] The most successful advisory program we have had was in post–war Japan. Of course we had control. We don't control V.N. or Thailand.[77]

Agency officials constantly focused the discussion on their counterinsurgency needs, while social scientists stressed their research needs. Each group may have been trying to get the other's needs to overlap with its own. Thus, social scientists wanted a government less obsessed with counterinsurgency and more with topics of academic interest; agency officials wanted social scientists who would shade their academic research interests over into counterinsurgency objectives. Where the objectives of the two groups did overlap, ethical dilemmas arose. In other discussions, government participants also brought up the insurgency in terms of the Chinese role, motivation, recruitment, the lack of data on what the communists say, and their effect on villages.[78]

U.S. and Thai responses to Communist Party of Thailand appeals were also discussed at the Summer Study. Deitchman summed up the intent of counterinsurgency policy with a medical metaphor: "You want to create a condition where the uncommitted neutral people could be immunized against the C.T."[79] To create this condition, one needed to know villagers' attitudes and the effectiveness of the current counterinsurgency policy. Policies discussed included the Thai government's 0910 counterinsurgency policy (essentially a military–police combat operation that included short–term development projects in villages), the transfer of primary school administration to Ministry of the Interior control so the Ministry could "identify and dispose of subversive teachers more effectively, and the advantages of hiring police versus arming villagers."[80]

The most disturbing comments made by participants were about potential counterinsurgency programs that might involve negative stimuli, starvation, and spying:

[Gell–Mann:] Can we find out what effect increasing police density or ear cutting or other negatives have on villagers' attitudes?...[81]

[Farrar] You have clear evidence of Thai overreaction—e.g. restricting the flow of rice from the villagers. But it isn't necessarily wrong, you listen to the complaints but you haven't listened to the police. Resources control was done in Malaya by the British when most people thought it was wrong but it proved to be right....[82]

[Moerman:] You need area information and indices and then translate them into programs. The indices and area information can come from low level people. The scarce commodity is the translator. He needs community intelligence. You can bug people or plant spies.[83]

The group as a whole did succeed in formulating some recommendations for counterinsurgency policy. They agreed that sweep operations do more harm than good; that village defense forces need to be created and supported as "an armed, uniformed, paid militia"; and that development should be withheld from "red" areas. Further, perhaps in the interests of continuing its consultancy, the group concluded that more study was needed about villager–official interaction and about the motivation of extant organizations.[84] In the working paper "Insurgency in Thailand," an interesting suggestion for overcoming Thai citizens' reliance on the government was suggested:

It is possible that government accountability provides material for insurgency (e.g., officials can cure disease, but are too corrupt or unjust to try). This phenomenon, assuming its existence, may result in part from government promises and admissions of past failures. If this is its cause, and if the result is politically dangerous, then government messages should be modified accordingly.[85]

An earlier comment on research topics by Phillips touched on the need for the above type of study: "A good IDA study is where do the Thai place blame for undesirable events?"[86]

Opposition to U.S. Policy

General Maxwell Taylor asked the participants to comment on U.S. policy in Thailand. The response at other times may have been firmer, but to Taylor the reply was middling:

[Taylor:] Did you look at all of our programs?

[Moerman:] Yes, but we found that practically all programs are concentrated on COIN or COIN related activities.

[Taylor:] Is this a good thing?

[Gell–Mann:] We don't know and we don't have the data to find out.[87]

The only record of a participant criticizing the overall affects of U.S. policy at the conference, rather than offering constructive criticism to improve the policy, is Louis Lomax, who spoke as follows: "I oppose American policy in V.N.—the whole thing. What we are doing in Thailand is worse. It will be more disastrous."[88] This *does not* mean that no one else spoke out against U.S. policy at the Thailand Summer Study, merely that there is no record of it in the minutes. From correspondence subsequent to the Summer Study and a from recent interview with the author, it is clear that Piker strongly opposed the U.S. war effort and was a member of a vocal group of scholars opposed to the war.[89] Sharp and Phillips, in recent interviews with the author, also expressed opposition to the U.S. role.[90] Moerman declined to be interviewed, but some idea of his views can be found in his letter to the *AAA Newsletter* quoted above.[91] The primary motivation of Moerman, Phillips, and Sharp was to influence policy from the inside, rather than from the outside. That they all became disillusioned when the majority of their ideas were not accepted is some indication of the lack of value government officials put on consulting that did not validate their counterinsurgency–obsessed views.

Phillips, apparently without any intended irony or reference to the Study Group, made the following statement about the insurgents:

> The N.E. [Northeastern region of Thailand] C.T. do research by discussion, the outcomes of which legitimize what is going on. The majority of the research doesn't get to the top officials but if it does it may be suppressed it if doesn't tie in with their views or interests.[92]

If one were to substitute "Jason social scientists" for "communist terrorists" in the above excerpt, the sentence could reflect easily back onto the Study Group. Here was a group of social scientists doing "research by discussion" on the insurgency. Agency officials were hoping it would legitimize the U.S. role in Thailand; research that did not correspond to the views of the American leaders would be suppressed or ignored.

No further Jason summer studies on Thailand took place, and one can only speculate to what degree government planners used any of the information discussed at Falmouth in 1967.

NOTES

[1] Institute for Defense Analyses, "The Thailand Study Group" [Minutes from a "Jason Summer Study" at Falmouth Intermediate School, Falmouth, Massachusetts], 20, 21, 22, 27 [?], 28, 29, 30 June; 3, 4, 5, 6, 7 July 1967.
   It is unclear whether the minutes that appear under each particular date refer to that date or the previous day (for example, the minutes labeled "June 20" actually correspond to the proceedings on 19 June, but those labeled "June 30" seem to correspond to 30 June). To avoid confusion, dates cited in the endnotes conform to the dates cited at the beginning of each day's minutes (thus, the June 20 label is used). The minutes cited as "27 June" in the endnotes are marked "June 27?".

[2] Klare, *War Without End*, 84; Deitchman, *Best–Laid Schemes*, 304–305; Eric R. Wolf and Joseph G. Jorgensen, "Anthropology on the Warpath in Thailand," *New York Review of Books*, 19 November 1970, 27; concurring with (and preceding) Wolf and Jorgensen is also Allen Myers, "Scholars Join with US Gov't for Purposes of Counterinsurgency," *Student Mobilizer* 3:4 (2 April 1970), 8.

[3] Psychologist Jesse Orlansky speaking at IDA, "Thailand Study Group," 4 July 1967, 6.

[4] IDA, *Annual Report* [for 1956–57] (Washington, DC: IDA, n.d.), 1.

[5] IDA, *Report on the Activities Ending February 28, 1967* (Arlington, Virginia: Institute for Defense Analyses, n.d.), 6.

[6] IDA, *Annual Report III* [for 1958–59], 14; *Fourth Annual Report* [for 1959–60], 3, 18; *Annual Report 1968*, 34.

[7] IDA, *Fourth Annual Report* [for 1959–60], 3; *Report on the Activities Ending February 28, 1967*, 7; *Annual Report* [for 1956–57].

[8] IDA, *Annual Report* [for 1956–57], 8; *Annual Report III* [for 1958–59], 14; *Fourth Annual Report* [for 1959–60], 15.

[9] IDA, *Annual Report II* [for 1957–58], 4; *Annual Report 1969*, 42, 44; *Report on the Activities Ending February 28, 1967*, 30.

[10] IDA, *Annual Report II* [for 1957–58], on reverse of cover [r.o.c]; *Annual Report III* [for 1958–59], 3; *Fourth Annual Report* [for 1959–60], r.o.c.; *Annual Report Number Five* [for 1960–61], r.o.c.

[11] IDA, *Annual Report* [for 1956–57], 4.

[12] IDA, *Fourth Annual Report* [for 1959–60], 4.

[13] Ibid.

[14] IDA, *Annual Report 1968*, 9–11.

[15] IDA, *The Tenth Year: March 1965 through February 1966*, 7.

[16] IDA, *Report on the Activities Ending February 28, 1967*, 13.

[17] IDA, *Annual Report 1968*, 18–19, 53, 58; *Annual Report 1969*, 16.

[18] IDA, *Activities of the Institute for Defense Analyses 1961–1964*, 19–20; *Report on the Activities Ending February 28, 1967*, 23. EPSD's acting director later published a book that was an outgrowth of an IDA study: James E. Cross, *Conflict in the Shadows: The Nature and Politics of Guerilla War* (Garden City, NY: Doubleday, 1963).

[19] IDA, *Report on the Activities Ending February 28, 1967*, 23–24; *The Tenth Year*, 17.

[20] IDA, *The Tenth Year*, 17.

[21] IDA, *Annual Report 1968*, 24.

[22] Ibid., 29.

[23] Ibid., 8.

[24] IDA, *Annual Report 1969*, 9, 10.

25 IDA, *Fourth Annual Report*, 11–12.

26 IDA, *Annual Report Number Five* [for 1960–61], 9.

27 IDA, *The Tenth Year*, 15.

28 IDA, *Report on the Activities Ending February 28, 1967*, 24; *Annual Report 1968*, 62.

29 Frank Baldwin, "The Jason Project: Academic Freedom and Moral Responsibility," *Bulletin of Concerned Asian Scholars* 5:3 (November 1973): 2–12; Klare, *War Without End*, 181–185; and New York Times, *Pentagon Papers*, 502–509.

30 Steven Piker, letter to Eric Wolf, 6 April 1970.

31 Herbert Phillips, telephone interview with author, 1 May 1991.

32 Michael Moerman, letter to the editor, *AAA Newsletter* 12:1 (January 1971), 9–11.

33 Phillips, interview, 1 May 1991.

34 Moerman, letter to the editor, *AAA Newsletter* 12:1 (January 1971), 9–11.

35 Piker, telephone interview with author, 5 April 1991.

36 Sources for the affiliations of participants:

Barmack: Deitchman, *Best–Laid Schemes*, 279.

Cross: IDA, *Annual Report 1968*, 65. Cross is also the author of *Conflict in the Shadows* (see this chapter, note 18).

Deitchman: Deitchman, *Best–Laid Schemes*, 45–6, 290. In addition to directing Project Agile, Deitchman was a member of IDA in 1960 and was Special Assistant for Counterinsurgency Programs at ODDR&E in 1963. Keep in mind that Agile was described in 1968 by the Director of Defense Research and Engineering, John S. Foster, Jr., as:

A broad program in applied research and development through which ARPA examines problems of multiservice and multi–government interest and application in the fields of counter-insurgency and limited conflict (quoted in Klare, *War Without End*, 215.)

Farrar: IDA, "Thailand Study Group," 3 July 1967, 1, 5 July 1967, 2.

Fitzgerald: Ibid., 29 June 1967, 1. ISA is under the Assistant Secretary of Defense and is "responsible for reviewing the international implications of military affairs, and for coordinating Defense with State Department activities" (Deitchman, *Best–Laid Schemes*, 49).

Franklin: Ibid., 28 June 1967, 10.

Gell–Mann: Myers, "Scholars Join with US Gov't...."; *Student Mobilizer*, 7.

Gomer: Ibid.

Hoath: Ibid.

Kaufman: IDA, "Thailand Study Group," 27 June 1967, 1; Klare, *War Without End*, 174; Deitchman, *The Best–Laid Schemes*, 309. (In 1964 Cornell Aeronautics Laboratory shared with the University of Michigan a $3–4 million ARPA grant to study infrared reconnaissance technology in Southeast Asia.)

Kendall: IDA, "Thailand Study Group," 6 July 1967, 1.

Kirk: Ibid.

Lomax: Louis Lomax, *Thailand: The War That Is, The War That Will Be* (New York: Vintage Books, 1967).

Long: Myer, "Scholars Join with US Gov't...., 7.

Mayer: IDA, "Thailand Summer Study," 6 July 1967 [afternoon], 1.

Orlansky: Deitchman, *Best–Laid Schemes*, 54.

Quinn: IDA, "Thailand Study Group," 30 June 1967 [afternoon], 1.

Stark: Ibid., 28 June 1967, 10.

Taylor: IDA, *The Tenth Year*, 30.

Thomas: Myers, "Scholars Join with US Gov't....," 5.

[37] Ibid.

[38] By Piker's own count, he was present for five days (Piker, letter to Wolf, 6 April 1970).

[39] Sharp recalls being present at only one day's meetings, and perhaps being in Falmouth one day and two nights (Lauriston Sharp, telephone interview with author, 29 April 1991).

[40] Piker, interview, 5 April 1991.

[41] IDA, "Thailand Study Group," July 6, 1967 [afternoon], 7-8.

[42] Ibid., 30 June 1967, 4, 9, 10. The persistent subtext of social scientists "selling" a product to policymakers is also demonstrated in IDA, "Thailand Study Group," 30 June 1967 [afternoon], 9; and 3 July 1967, 10.

[43] Ibid., 30 June 1967, 5.

Fitzgerald also had something interesting to say about semantics: "The policy planning staff [of ISA?] is dropping the name 'counterinsurgency' because it is reactive. It is now called 'Counter–Subversive Aggression'" (IDA, "Thailand Summer Study," 4). Compare this with the SORO statement on Project Camelot (Chapter One) pleading for a phrase to cover "insurgency prophylaxis," which "places great importance on positive actions designed to reduce the sources of disaffection...."

[44] IDA, "Thailand Study Group," 30 June 1967 [afternoon], 7, 9.

[45] Ibid., 4 July 1967, 1. The importance of Deitchman's point (4), psychological operations, to Thailand had been recognized earlier, as the objectives from the following research project on "Effective Communication by Americans with Thai" indicate:

The research committee, very realistically appraising the current competitive international situation listed 10 objectives for the

American communicator in Thailand. These are, briefly, as follows: promote good will toward the United States, promote expectation of success for the United States and its friends, encourage cooperation with the United States, show importance of developing new energy sources, arouse hostility toward Chinese Communists, discredit the Communists, show appreciation for Thai accomplishments, convince of non–interference by the United States in internal affairs of Thailand, instill hope for the future, and strengthen common ideals for Thai and Americans.

(Imogene E. Okes, "Effective Communication by Americans with Thai," *Journalism Quarterly 38 (1961): 347–341* in *The Art and Science of Psychological Operations: Case Studies of Military Applications* (Department of the Army pamphlet No.525–527, 2 vols.) (Department of the Army [n.p.: Headquarters, Department of the Army, 1976], Prepared by the American Institutes for Research [AIR], Washington, DC., under Army contract), 591.

See also U.S. Information Agency, "Attitudes, Communications and Communist Propaganda: Factors in Insurgency in Southeast Asia—1962" in *Psychological Operations*, Department of the Army (n.p: U.S. Information Agency, 1962), 553–572.

[46] IDA, "Thailand Study Group," 3 July 1967, 5.

[47] Ibid., 21 June 1967, 1. The government list would no doubt concentrate on "problems of preserving the national integrity" (IDA, *Fourth Annual Report* [for 1959–60], 4).

[48] Ibid., 3 July, 1967 [afternoon], 8.

[49] Ibid., 4 July 1967, 6.

[50] IDA, "Consultant Security Briefing" (Arlington, VA: IDA, October 1965), 5.

[51] IDA, "Thailand Study Group," 21 June 1967, 1.

[52] Ibid., 28 June 1967 [afternoon], 11.

[53] Ibid., 27 June 1967, 2.

[54] Ibid., 28 June 1967 [afternoon], 10.

55 Ibid., 20 June 1967, 1.

56 Ibid., 5 July 1967, 7.

57 Ibid., 27 June, 1967, 1–2. My copy of this day's minutes is poorly reproduced and some of Marshall's comments do not appear on it. However, the complete version was reproduced from another copy in Myers, "Scholars Join with US Gov't..," 8.

58 Ibid., 21 June 1967, 1.

59 Ibid., 27 June 1967, 2; 21 June, 2; 30 June [afternoon], 8; 5 July, 3, 4.

60 Ibid., 27 June 1967, 2.

61 Ibid., 4 July 1967, 6.

62 Ibid., 3 July 1967 [afternoon], 11.

63 Ibid., 20 June 1967, 1.

64 Ibid., 5 July 1967, 3.

65 Ibid., 3 July 1967 [afternoon], 11.

66 Ibid., 22 June 1967, 2.

67 Ibid., 20 June 1967, 2.

68 Ibid., 29 June 1967, 5.

69 Ibid., 3 July 1967, 7.

70 Ibid., 6 July 1967, 4.

71 Ibid., 3 July 1967, 4.

72 Ibid., 3 July 1967, 3.

73 Ibid., 22 June 1967, 2. In agreement with part of Nelson's contention, a Thai social scientist has found that the Thai educational system tends to reinforce "traditional political culture" among elites, including authoritarian political attitudes and dislike of criticism (Thinapan Nakata, *The Problems of Democracy in Thailand: A Study of Political Culture and Socialization of College Students* [Bangkok: Praepittaya International, 1975]).

74 Information on farm, labor, and student groups and the rightist reaction to them can be found in Morell and Chai–anan, *Political Conflict in Thailand*. On the political structure of Thai society and the 1970 period, see John L. S. Girling, *Thailand: Society and Politics* (Ithaca: Cornell University Press, 1981), 119–230. On the coup, see Benedict Anderson, "Withdrawal Symptoms: Social and Cultural Aspects of the October 6 Coup," *Bulletin of Concerned Asian Scholars* 9:3 (July–September 1977), 13–29; Marian Mallet, "Causes and Consequences of the October '76 Coup," *Journal of Contemporary Asia* 8:1 (1976), 80–103; Puey Ungphakorn, "Violence and the Military Coup in Thailand," *Bulletin of Concerned Asian Scholars* 9:3 (July–September 1977), 4–12; and the gruesome photographs in Watanachay Winitjakul, ed., *Samut Phap Duan Tula* [October Photograph Notebook] (Bangkok: National Student Union of Thailand, Thammasat University, 1988).

75 Benedict R. O'G. Anderson, "Studies of the Thai State: The State of Thai Studies" in *The Study of Thailand: Analyses of Knowledge, Approaches, and Prospects in Anthropology, Art History, Economics, History, and Political Science*, ed. Eliazer B. Ayal (Athens, Ohio: Ohio University Center for International Studies, Southeast Asia Program, 1978), 216.

76 IDA, "Insurgency in Thailand" [apparently a working paper from the Thailand Study Group], 3 July 1967, 1.

77 IDA, "Thailand Study Group," 30 June 1967, 4–5.

78 Ibid., 22 June 1967, 4; 29 June 1967, 8, 9; 4 July 1967, 2.

79 Ibid., 3 July 1967, 1.

80 Ibid., 22 June 1967, 1; 22 June, 4; 28 June [afternoon], 3. "0910" is named after the Buddhist calendar years 2509–2510, or 1966–1967 on the Christian calendar. See Kanok Wongtrangan, *Change and Persistence in Thai Counter–Insurgency Policy* (Bangkok: Institute of Security and

International Studies, Chulalongkorn University, September 1983), 6–7 and George K. Tanham, *Trial in Thailand* (New York: Crane, Russak & Co., 1974), 86–87.

81 IDA, "Thailand Study Group," 3 July 1967, 4.

82 Ibid., 5 July 1967, 5.

83 Ibid., 4 July 1967, 3.

84 These conclusions are found in IDA, "Insurgency in Thailand."

85 IDA, "Insurgency in Thailand," 7.

86 IDA, "Thailand Study Group," 29 June 1967, 6.

87 Ibid., 6 July 1967, [afternoon], 6.

88 Ibid., 4.

89 Piker, letter to Wolf, 6 April 1970; Piker, interview, 5 April 1991.

90 Sharp, interview, 29 April 1991; Phillips, interview, 1 May 1991.

91 Moerman, letter to the editor, *AAA Newsletter* 12:1 (January 1971), 9–11.

92 IDA, "Thailand Study Group," 3 July 1967, 2.

CHAPTER FOUR

ARPA & AIR IN THAILAND

It is [ARPA's Project] Agile's primary thesis that remote area warfare is controlled in a major way by the environment in which the warfare occurs, by the sociological and anthropological characteristics of the people involved in the war, and by the nature of the conflict itself.

—Dr. R. L. Sproul, director of the Defense Department's Advanced Research Projects Agency, testifying before U.S. Congress, 1965

Any social scientists who has been in Thailand for a week knows about the role that ARPA—with its annual budget of 5–12 million dollars—plays in subverting the purpose and direction of social science research in that country.

—Herbert Phillips, letter to the members of the American Anthropological Association Committee on Ethics, May 1970

In December 1967, six months after the conclusion of the Institute for Defense Analyses' Thailand Study Group, the American Institutes for Research (AIR), another private corporation, submitted a research and development proposal to the Defense Department. AIR proposed to assess the "Impact of Economic, Social, and Political Action Programs" on counterinsurgency in Thailand.[1] As an aid in "designing preventative counterinsurgency measures," the objectives of the AIR project were to:

1) devise reliable and valid techniques for determining the specific effects of counterinsurgency programs in Thailand;

2) apply these techniques to ongoing action programs to generate feedback data useful both in the formulation of broad programming

strategies and in the design of the specific mechanics of program implementation;

3) assist the Royal Thai Government in establishing an indigenous capability for the continuing application and refinement of these techniques; and

4) pave the way for the generalization of the methodology to other programs in other countries. [2]

Unlike the Thailand Summer Study, which apparently was not repeated, the AIR proposal did, in fact, result in an active and ongoing research project in Thailand. Social scientists were recruited as consultants, and the project took shape under the Defense Department's Advanced Research Projects Agency (ARPA), as can be determined from a 1969 agenda for an advisory panel meeting, a trip report, and other documents. [3]

ADVANCED RESEARCH PROJECTS AGENCY (ARPA)

History

ARPA was established in early 1958 as a unit of the Defense Department to help the nascent U.S. space program. Now known as DARPA (for *Defense* ARPA), it is a part of the Office of the Director of Defense Research and Engineering (ODDR&E). The creation of ARPA was part of an institutional reaction to the Soviet Union's launch of Sputnik, [4] which jarred United States policymakers into the realization that research and development spending would have to be vastly increased if the U.S. was to keep up with the USSR. ARPA was immediately offered technical advisory support by the Institute for Defense Analyses, which established its own Advanced Research Projects Division to formalize this support. [5] In 1960 (by which time ARPA was satisfactorily running) this IDA division underwent a name change, and the "extremely close collaboration with the government personnel at ARPA," as the IDA describes it, was reversed. [6] That is, the mentor (IDA) came to work for its student (ARPA).

After the U.S. space program got underway, ARPA broadened its scope to become a general Defense Department agency for research and development, which became more important as the U.S. military commitment to Southeast Asia increased. [7] For example, according to 1963

Congressional testimony by ARPA's director, Dr. J. P. Ruina, ARPA's Project Agile (see below) was responsible for the initial application of defoliants in Vietnam long before Agent Orange became known to the Vietnamese and American public.[8] Before Congress in 1963, Dr. Ruina described ARPA as

> an integral part of the Office of the Director of Defense Research and Engineering.... ARPA is a line agency which directs projects assigned either by the Secretary of Defense or by the Director of Defense Research and Engineering.[9]

ARPA in Thailand

ARPA established a field office in Thailand in 1961, which continued to operate until 1972.[10] A spokesman described the advantage of the Thai testing environment to be that it was "similar to Vietnam's but nobody's shooting at you."[11] From 1961 to 1964 ARPA concentrated on technology applications for "remote area conflict" and counterinsurgency, but by 1965 its emphasis on the "soft" sciences had increased markedly. By 1966 ARPA operations were decidedly focused on counterinsurgency research.[12] (See Table 4.1 for a selected list of ARPA projects in Thailand.) Later, this focus was articulated during Congressional hearings, when ARPA's objectives in Thailand were stated to be:

> 1) Working with the pertinent Thai researchers on a project to describe and design the most effective RTG [Royal Thai Government] measures to counter the insurgent threat;
>
> 2) Research counterinsurgency topics in response to ad hoc requests generated by the U.S. mission;
>
> 3) Help develop Thai Ministry of Defense capability to define, manage and perform military research, development, testing, and evaluation.[13]

There are varying estimates of the number of staff that were employed at ARPA's Thailand office. One estimate for the 1969–1970 year is of a 500-member staff and a $10 million dollar budget, but George Tanham U.S. Special Assistant for Counterinsurgency to the American ambassador to Thailand, cites a staff complement of 200 as a maximum.[14] The majority

TABLE 4.1: SELECTED ARPA/MRDC RESEARCH PROJECTS IN THAILAND[15]

PROJECT	AUTHORS	DATE
Observations on Mobile Development Unit–2 Operations	Lee W. Huff	June 1963
Mobile Development Unit Follow–Up	Lee W. Huff	Nov. 1964
Village Security Pilot Study, Northeast Thailand	D. J. Blakeslee L. W. Huff R. W. Kickert	May 1965
Low–Altitude Visual Search for Individual Human Targets: Further Field Testing in Southeast Asia	D. J. Blakeslee	June 1965
Survival Manual for Thailand and Adjacent Areas. Annex. Edible and Poisonous Plants and Animals	Tem Smitinand Wilbur R. Scheible	April 1966
Ethnography of the Akah	Robert W. Kickert* (Austrian anthropologist)	in progress, March 1966
Examination of Popularly Held Images: Prerequisites to Political Integration of the Thai–Islam	M. Ladd Thomas* (political scientist, Northern Illinois University)	in progress, March 1966
Social Structure and Shifting Agriculture in a Meo Community	George A. Binney*	in progress, March 1966
A Social Anthropological Study of Yao People in Thailand	Peter K. Kandre*	in progress, March 1966
Concept of Insurgency Conflict in Thailand; Logistical and Transportation Studies	Research Analysis Corporation**	in progress, March 1966
[A research program on the basis of] Analysis of Regional Conflict; Surveillance; Communication; Insurgent Logistics; Population Control; Contingency Allocation; Counterinsurgency Operations of Indigenous Naval Forces	Stanford Research Institute**	in progress, March 1966

PROJECT	AUTHORS	DATE
Thailand Village Radio Study	James L. Woods Percy W. Collom Termpoon Kovatana Robert W. Kickert Jerrold Milsted	Jan. 1967
Vegetation Analysis of Pran Buri Defoliation Test Area I	——	——

* ARPA staff member or individual contractee.
** ARPA contractee.

---

of the staff were members of private civilian research groups under contract to ARPA. These included American Institutes for Research, Research Analysis Corporation, Cornell Aeronautics Laboratory, and Stanford Research Institute.[16]

The ARPA field unit was known as the ARPA Research and Development Center, but its research was conducted under the auspices of the Joint Thai/U.S. Military Research and Development Center (MRDC).[17] Although MRDC was officially a joint undertaking, most of its research was "primarily American both in concept and execution."[18] The connection between ARPA, as an arm of the Defense Department, private contractors, and the American Embassy was very close. According to Tanham "[T]he ARPA field unit was informally recognized as the research arm of the United States Mission regarding internal security programs."[19]

ARPA'S Project Agile

An integral part of ARPA's worldwide operation was its Project Agile, which operated out of the ARPA Thailand office as well as in Iran, Korea, and Vietnam.[20] Congressional testimony by Dr. R. L. Sproul, director of ARPA in 1969, described the objectives of Agile as follows:

It provides friendly nations of the developing areas with better ways of organizing their own resources to counter insurgent threats. The major portion of the program continues to focus on Southeast Asia, including closely integrated support of the war in Vietnam.[21]

Agile used a "systems" approach to join together various agencies and activities to accomplish

the immensely complicated task of welding weapons and politics, mobility and social development, communications and economic progress into effective instruments for counterinsurgency.... Scenes of present and incipient conflict afford the opportunity to learn with scientific precision whether given combinations of resources have the expected effect....[22]

Agile's systems R&D is intended to provide a basis of knowledge, techniques and technology from which to draw "blueprints" for deterring insurgency in its early stages.[23]

"Scenes of present and incipient conflict" no doubt refer to Vietnam and Thailand.

ARPA's technical research projects included studies on communications, magnetic sensors for tracking trail and waterways traffic, combat rations, and equipment, as well as the production of a map of Thai highways suitable for emergency aircraft landings and maps of trail networks. Social science research under ARPA produced handbooks on the "hill tribes" (ethnic minorities within Thailand) and counterinsurgency manuals; other studies included the capabilities of the Border Patrol Police, political integration, and village leadership. ARPA even sent an American scholar to advise in the formation of a behavioral science division of the Thai National Research Council.[24] This broad range of projects demonstrates ARPA's linkage of technology with social science research.

The Role of Social Scientists

ARPA recognized early the contribution that social scientists could make to the U.S. counterinsurgency effort in Thailand and elsewhere. In a statement describing Project Agile in 1965, Sproul testified that:

It is Agile's primary thesis that remote area warfare is controlled in a major way by the environment in which the warfare occurs, *by the sociological and anthropological characteristics of the people involved in the war*, and by the nature of the conflict itself [emphasis added].[25]

The type of environmental, sociological, and anthropological data that Sproul described could best be collected by social scientists. In 1965, about a year after the above testimony was given, ARPA completed and published a massive pilot study of village security in Thailand, conducted by political scientist Lee W. Huff, anthropologist R. W. Kickert, and others.[26] The four–page questionnaire (later revised to five pages, reproduced as Appendix D) for the study includes requests for the exact map coordinates of the village, names of all officials, occupations of residents, descriptions of the "defense perimeter," and location of all roads, buildings, and communication equipment.[27] The Stanford Research Institute (SRI) was later given a contract to compile a "village data base" on *all* Thai villages using the information in this pilot study as a base. SRI's project, Village Information System (VIST), was not completed before ARPA funding for it ran out.[28]

While acknowledging the need to accumulate such data as an aid to possible future conflict, ARPA officials were also keenly aware of the criticism that would be forthcoming if they continued to promote ARPA's role as a collector of "social science" data. For ARPA's functions to be discussed in Congressional appropriations hearings would be acceptable, but a public hearing would be another matter. Therefore, following the intense scrutiny of the government–social science nexus that arose with Project Camelot, ARPA underwent a transition. Seymour Deitchman, who took over as director of Project Agile in 1966, described the change as one of "reshaping ARPA's program of social research on insurgency problems."[29] This "reshaping" included dropping any identifying label that announced a "social science research" program, classifying much of the Agile research, and limiting all work to that which was useful to the Defense Department.[30] This would "minimize the possibility of embarrassment" and would prevent scrutiny by members of the press, while assuring that researchers and research were "*instruments* of policy and not *makers* of policy" [emphasis in original].[31]

In spite of these efforts, ARPA activities still came under criticism. In 1966, an ARPA project called the Rural Security Systems Program (RSSP) became known in social science circles. The goal of the program was to "assist the Royal Thai Government and the U.S. Mission in Thailand in their efforts to suppress the growing Communist insurgency in that country's northeast provinces."[32] The RSSP's methodology was similar to the general methodology of ARPA and Project Agile: to gather data on geography, "way of life," and attitudes toward the government; to compile files on insurgent activities and government responses; and to analyze the effectiveness of government responses "to plan future CI [counter-insurgency] programs." The program was a first for Agile, according to Congressional testimony:

> This program will mark the first time that R&D has been given a
> major role in supporting a counterinsurgency in a comprehensive
> way, from the earliest stages of the conflict.[33]

Anthropologists Meet Project Agile Director

Director's Account

Several social scientists responded vocally to the RSSP program. Anthropologists Charles Keyes (University of Washington), Michael Moerman (UCLA), Herbert Phillips (University of California-Berkeley), and Lauriston Sharp (Cornell) wrote to Seymour Deitchman, then director of Project Agile, requesting information on RSSP, citing its Project Camelot–like implications.[34] ARPA's stated objectives in Thailand were very similar to those of Camelot in Latin and South America.

At Deitchman's invitation, the four anthropologists met with him in Washington on January 5, 1967.[35] According to Deitchman's account of the meeting, the four anthropologists were concerned that RSSP was going to involve hundreds of social scientists descending on Thailand. They were told that this was not the case. However, they were also told that it *was* designed to "resolve the problems of insurgency" and to study how development might prevent insurgency. According to Deitchman, the anthropologists were worried about the pressure being exerted by the U.S. on Thailand for development. Some time after the meeting, Deitchman says, word reached him that Peter Kunstadter, another anthropologist then working in Thailand, was worried that a large ARPA social science project in his area would interfere with his research.

At the conclusion of his meeting with the four anthropologists, Deitchman gives the following account of their support or noninterference with ARPA's objectives (which varies with the accounts of the anthropologists):

> I then asked whether, since they were among the recognized American experts on Thai culture and history, they would be willing to help us do a better job by helping in the research. The responses varied. One said that if the work were later to be criticized, he would not want to be associated with it but would rather be free to join the critics (although he later sent us a copy, which was very helpful, of his yet–to–be–published Ph.D. thesis on life in Thai village society). Others promised benevolent neutrality.
>
> But one of the group decided that it was time to "put my money where my mouth is," and to help if he agreed with our objectives. This was Dr. Herbert Phillips of the University of California (Berkeley), who became an ARPA consultant and who in the course of the next two years was to provide much useful understanding of the background to the problems with which ARPA was involved in Thailand.[36]

According to Deitchman, that makes one paid consultant (Phillips); one who does not wish to be associated with ARPA *if* ARPA will later come under criticism, but who then sends a copy of his dissertation to help out (probably Moerman);[37] and two for "benevolent neutrality" (probably Keyes and Sharp). No one voiced opposition to the program on the basis of its explicit intent to help the U.S. and Thai counterinsurgency effort.

Deitchman also writes that

> as late as 1968 one anthropologist, who had earlier been concerned that he not come under attack by his colleagues for undertaking counterinsurgency research, nevertheless indicated his willingness to accept ARPA support for an overseas linguistic study he had in mind.[38]

Deitchman is probably referring to Moerman, who did receive funding in 1968 through the Air Force Office of Scientific Research by way of an

ARPA contract (ARPA itself does not grant funds but provides them through agreements with other agencies),[39] to prepare a report that analyzed Lue conversation.[40] The Lue (or Lu) are an ethnic minority residing in northern Thailand.

In his book *Best-Laid Schemes*, Deitchman's account of the meeting is a scant three pages long. The exact words he used to describe the RSSP to the visiting anthropologists cannot be known. According to his account, Deitchman stressed the interest of the Defense Department in understanding the effects of modernization on Thais. That he also discussed its objectives with regard to the insurgency is clear, because his account corresponds with a memorandum issued by Moerman and Keyes some time after the meeting.[41]

The stated objective of RSSP, like those of ARPA, were "reshaped" over time. The Congressional testimony describes RSSP as providing "a major role in supporting a counterinsurgency"; the objective is downgraded in Deitchman's account of his meeting with the anthropologists to helping "resolve the problems of insurgency"; and, finally, ends up in the Moerman/Keyes memo as proposing to "study 'rural security.'"

Moerman/Keyes's Account

Sometime between January and March 1967, Moerman and Keyes, writing for the group that met with Deitchman, issued a memorandum to "AACT [Academic Advisory Council for Thailand] members and [the] ad hoc committee on ARPA Northeastern Thailand Project," explaining their understanding of RSSP. They begin by being "worried that the ARPA scheme might be another 'Camelot',"[42] but then provide reassurance:

> Insofar as the social science component is concerned, the major objective is to study "rural security" in northeastern Thailand. The first efforts will be directed towards compiling an inventory on the locations and characteristics of the villages in an area of the project's interest. This information will be used to place in perspective subsequent knowledge about changes (including "security incidents") and the impact of government programs—both Thai and American—which occur in the villages of the area.[43]

One primary concern stated by Moerman and Keyes in the memo corresponds with Deitchman's account. In their two-and-a-half page memo, the authors state or allude to no less than three times that the number of researchers will not be as large as they had imagined. They describe the project as though the collection of specific data on villages and villagers was intended to be similar to a census rather than part of a counterinsurgency program.

To counteract the "danger that the project might become too purely military," the authors suggest the training of Thai personnel to eventually take over the project.[44] Their argument here is that "without Thai participation the project (and, by implication, American social science) is open to the accusation of intellectual colonialism...."[45] This is a strange assertion on two counts. First, the phrase "too purely military" implies that a "somewhat military" project might be acceptable. Second, Thais conducting an American project under American direction are hardly independent from "intellectual colonialism."

At the conclusion of the memorandum, the authors give a circuitous imprimatur ("benevolent neutrality" in action?) to the project:

> Although the anticipated project is not the sort in which academic field workers usually participate, its scale and importance make it one of which all doing fieldwork in Thailand will have to take account. In addition, the size and complexity of programs of directed culture change in northeastern Thailand, ARPA's desire for accurate knowledge and ARPA's refusal to commit itself in advance to a single technique for social science research all will impinge upon and contribute to intellectual inquiries about the nature of Thai society and culture.[46]

Phillips's Account

Herbert Phillips later took exception with Deitchman's characterization of his role as an ARPA consultant. Phillips said that he was a member of the Scientific Advisory Group to ARPA in 1967 and 1968. During a two–year period, Phillips said he devoted six weeks to this consulting work. Although he does not remember his rate of pay, he notes that he was issued an identification card that gave him the assimilated rank of major general. This was arrived at by multiplying his daily consulting rate by 365 days per year. "The whole thing was bizarre," he said.[47]

In a 1978 rejoinder to Deitchman, Phillips disputed Deitchman's assertion that he had agreed to help ARPA "if he agreed with our objectives." He wrote that he had had no idea what ARPA's objectives were and had joined for a variety of reasons. These included a desire to know exactly what ARPA was doing in Thailand; a concern about the effects of ARPA on Thai social science; a desire for a greater awareness about the insurgency; a desire to lessen the negative consequences of the U.S. presence in Thailand, while accentuating its positive effects; and lastly, for the extra income provided to consultants. In spite of his work as a consultant, Phillips asserted that none of his recommendations to the Scientific Advisory Group or to the Military Research and Development Center was enacted or even seriously considered. At the end of his two-year association with ARPA, Phillips said he came to the realization that ARPA's work in Thailand was detrimental and insupportable.[48]

Phillips later wrote to Margaret Mead that because of his experience with ARPA, he probably knew more about U.S. government counter-insurgency research in Thailand than almost any other anthropologist.[49]

Media Account and Phillips's Response

Rather than stepping gingerly around the controversial aspects of ARPA's goals as the Moerman/Keyes memorandum did, a March 1967 article in the *New York Times* sensationally announced that "Researchers Aid Thai Rebel Fight, U.S. Defense Unit Develops Antiguerilla Devices."[50] The article stated that in Thailand there were

> 157 anthropologists, engineers, ordnance specialists and other researchers. They are part of Project Agile, the Pentagon's world-wide counterinsurgency research program.[51]

This article, in turn, elicited a critical response from a group of six graduate students in the Department of Anthropology at the University of Chicago. The graduate students sent a clipping of the article and a letter to Herbert Phillips at the University of California-Berkeley,[52] saying they were referred to Phillips by two anthropology professors who knew he was "familiar with anthropology in Thailand." The six requested information from Phillips on research in Thailand, referring specifically to the Beals report on anthropological ethics, writing:

> ... the article raises serious questions of scientific ethics, concerning the relation of the anthropologist to his informants and to his government's foreign policy. The issues include with what kinds of government funds (if any) and under what organizational

sponsorship may anthropologists legitimately pursue research. Also in question is the use made of the results of the research, whether those results should be made secret and whether they should be used to form military strategy, possibly directed against the very people studied.[53]

The graduate students pointed out some of the key issues overlooked in the Moerman/Keyes memorandum. One such issue was that the data gathered was clearly going to be used to help design military strategy, which, if used, would be used against the people from which the data was collected.

What follows is a discussion of Phillips's May 1 response to the students, written before he became an ARPA consultant.[54] (I am obliged to paraphrase the letter since Phillips has enjoined me from quoting it directly.) Phillips wrote to the students that his information on ARPA was drawn from talks with the ARPA Thailand director and staff and from the meeting with Deitchman in Washington. He stated that while ARPA's foci in Thailand did not have anything to do with anthropology, ARPA officials were nonetheless concerned with the possible negative effects that their projects might have on other research in Thailand. He wrote that ARPA staffers were particularly concerned that their research not become another Project Camelot and were prepared to prevent this.

In spite of Phillips's assertions, the reshaping of ARPA goals following Project Camelot indicated that its officials were concerned with the *public* perception of their mission. They were worried that attendant publicity might lead to criticism that would force the cancellation of their operation. Apparently, they were *not* worried that the *goals* of their operation mirrored those of Project Camelot because, quite frankly, as a social science project using a systems approach whose intention was to influence policy in a foreign country, it already *was* a Project Camelot.

Another point in Phillips's response concerned the number of real (as opposed to pseudo) anthropologists who were working for ARPA in Thailand at the time.[55] He came up with a figure of two real and eight pseudo-anthropologists, with the explanation that the latter were actually trained in physics, public administration, or systems analysis. He posited that ARPA had given these researchers the title of "anthropologists" in order to give them more credibility. Phillips wrote that he was upset by this usage, but that there was probably little that could be done by outsiders to change this practice. He assumed that ARPA would claim the necessity to use such a title because of its widely understood meaning.

Phillips's dismissal of the pseudo-anthropologists and his concern with establishing the precise number of anthropologists misses the point that the existence of *any* anthropologists assisting in counterinsurgency projects must raise ethical questions. The AAA *Statement on Problems of Anthropological Research and Ethics* (unbinding, but approved one month before Phillips wrote his response to the graduate students) speaks directly to this issue:

> The international reputation of anthropology has been damaged by the activities of unqualified individuals who have falsely claimed to be anthropologists, or who have pretended to be engaged in anthropological research while in fact pursuing other ends.... Academic institutions and individual members of the academic community, including students, should scrupulously avoid both involvement in clandestine intelligence activities and the use of the name of anthropology, or the title of anthropologist, as a cover for intelligence activities.[56]

Whether or not he agreed with the sentiment in the *Statement*, Phillips responded as though he were unaware of its existence.

Phillips wrote that one of the two genuine anthropologists at work for ARPA in Thailand may have been enjoined from publishing some of his research data because it concerned ARPA projects. He went on to say that, in all other ways, this anthropologist felt that ARPA had not inhibited him from his ethnographic work. Further, while this anthropologist had no control over ARPA's use of his research, neither did other anthropologists, *not* working for ARPA, whose work was in the public domain. Phillips compared the position of this ARPA anthropologist to that of Gerald Hickey, who, while working for the Rand Corporation in Vietnam, was still able to produce good scholarship. Ultimately, Phillips wrote, such work for ARPA or Rand was an individual choice that did not reflect poorly on the profession of anthropology. Nevertheless, Phillips added that he opposed such a position for himself, his students, and his colleagues.[57]

By citing Hickey's well–respected work, Phillips attempted to demonstrate that even researchers employed by the government could produce excellent scholarship. However, surely ARPA counterinsurgency research projects are not the same as personally chosen research projects.

Who chooses the research questions? To what uses does the Defense Department put such scholarship?[58] Finally, it is confusing for Phillips to have vigorously opposed such an intellectual position for himself, only a short while before consenting to work as a consultant to ARPA following his meeting with Deitchman in Washington.

Phillips concluded his letter to the graduate students by justifying ARPA activities in Thailand in two ways. The first was that ARPA did nothing without the approval of the Thai government. This justification hardly answers the charges satisfactorily since the Thai government, just like the American, was capable of giving approval to projects whose sole objective was to aid in a counterinsurgency effort that may have resulted in harm to people. The second was Phillips's assertion that whatever ARPA was doing in Thailand, it was not secretive or similar to CIA activities. ARPA researchers, Phillips wrote, were simply trying to gather descriptive materials on Thai society.[59]

But why did ARPA want this data? ARPA was gathering descriptive materials on Thai society to counter insurgency. The questions asked in the village security pilot study (discussed above) are clear examples of preparation for the possibility of war. The contract of the Stanford Research Institute to compile data on all Thai villages is another example. And, although Phillips was apparently unaware of it, the CIA *was* funding and directing the intelligence division of the Thai National Police Department to conduct the same types of surveys that ARPA was funding, explicitly to locate communists and communist sympathizers among villagers.[60]

Furthermore, the U.S. government was also funding two programs in northeast Thailand known as Census Aspiration Cadre (or Census Operation Teams) and People's Action Teams, which had been adopted from CIA projects in Vietnam. A former CIA agent who served in Thailand during the 1960s described the methodology of these programs:

> The census takers were trained in census taking and supposedly could determine the political leanings of villagers by saying they were there to listen to problems and grievances against the government. Census cadres sent frequent reports to their headquarters naming villagers as either pro–government or pro–communist.[61]

Although Phillips was most likely unaware of all of the details, there were things both decidedly secretive and CIA–like about ARPA activities in Thailand.

Phillips concluded his letter with the assertion that there was little that scholars could do to affect ARPA short of practicing applied anthropology or becoming advisors to ARPA. Such a position, Phillips wrote, involved both professional and moral dilemmas, but also more responsibility than simply criticizing ARPA from the outside.[62]

Phillips's conclusion allowed him to take a position seemingly contrary to his earlier position of being opposed to the position of the ARPA–employed anthropologist. In a manner similar to the ambivalent Moerman/Keyes memorandum, the Phillips letter closed by advocating working for ARPA in order to change the way it works. The letter was written on May 1; in June Phillips attended the IDA's Thailand Study Group with Moerman and Sharp. In the end, Phillips chose to serve as an advisor to ARPA on matters of anthropology, as an applied anthropologist, with the position's attendant professional and moral dilemmas. That he eventually saw ARPA's activities as negative and detrimental is admirable. That he thought he could have an effect on the deleterious ARPA activities while working for them reminds me of a comment by Eric Wolf in a recent interview: "The capacity of human beings to delude themselves is great."[63]

Reinforced with a history of ARPA activities in Thailand, we may now turn to the specific AIR project as it was carried out.

AMERICAN INSTITUTES FOR RESEARCH (AIR)

Domestic and International Applications

Seymour Deitchman, the director of ARPA's Project Agile, has written about the private corporations that assisted ARPA in Thailand in his book on social science research and bureaucracy, *The Best–Laid Schemes*. According to him, there were

> ... one or two sources of first rate talent ... such as the American
> Institutes for Research, specializing in social science research of the
> quantitative character we were looking for.[64]

The Pittsburgh–based AIR corporation brought the "first rate talent" of its researchers to bear in designing and then implementing the study *Counter-insurgency in Thailand: The Impact of Economic, Social, and Political*

Action Programs.[65] The thorough manner in which the objectives of the $1.2 million proposal[66] were enacted can be traced by examining two later documents. The first is a report on a trip to Thailand, taken by a group of consultants in May and June 1969, who filed the report a year and a half later. The second is the schedule of an advisory panel meeting (of which Michael Moerman was a member) that took place in June and July 1969.[67] In these two documents, it is clear that the AIR proposal was funded through ARPA and contributed toward the counterinsurgency effort in Thailand.

The overall goal of the project was to aid in "designing preventative counterinsurgency measures" for Thailand. However, there was also the desire to formulate generalizable conclusions and methodological advances for application to other countries as well, including the U.S.[68] The author or authors of the 1967 proposal are not credited, but the language in the AIR proposal is clear:

During the past twenty years it has become clear that we must complement our awesome capabilities in conventional warfare with an equally sophisticated capability for dealing with the threats of insurgency and subversion; and, in the development of this capability, the social science aspects have lagged far behind the military and engineering components. To close the gap, techniques for obtaining meaningful feedback on social impact are clearly essential. And, since it has been the same methodological problem that has most hampered social action programs in the United States, the potential spin–off benefits of the proposed project are also exciting.[69]

For the authors of the AIR proposal, counterinsurgency problems abroad and subversion problems at home were linked in a way reminiscent of the domestic applications recognized by the IDA in its annual reports. The "exciting" domestic spin–off was restated more explicitly at the conclusion of the AIR proposal:

The potential applicability of the findings in the United States will also receive special attention. In many of our key domestic programs, especially those directed at disadvantaged sub–cultures, the methodological problems are highly similar to those described in this proposal; and the application of the Thai findings at home constitutes a potentially most significant project contribution.[70]

Policy Contributions of Social Scientists

The AIR proposal echoes both Deitchman's description of the "reshaped" ARPA and its function as an advisor to policymakers and statements made at the Thailand Study Group on the policy-advisor roles that could be filled by consultants—planning proceeds with the help of evaluators:

> The task of the planner is, first, to try to predict which of the many potentially important conditions are most instrumental in shaping public response [to insurgent pressure]; and, then, to try to predict which of the many alternative programming approaches will be most effective in bringing about the desired changes in these conditions. The task of the evaluator is to provide the planner with feedback on the accuracy of his predictions, so that increasingly effective programs can be projected.[71]

According to the AIR proposal, the conflict between a government and insurgent forces may involve three types of operations by the opposing sides. These are to make "inputs" to the local population to gain their support (including "threats, promises, ideological appeals, and tangible benefits"); to reduce "competing inputs" ("cutting communication lines, assassinating key spokesmen"); and to neutralize the successes of the opposing side (usually with "military confrontation").[72] The proposal recognizes that social scientists have specific roles to play in such conflicts:

> The social scientist can make significant contributions to the design of all three types of operations. But it is in the first area— that of designing programs to win or strengthen public support— that he is expected to take the lead and it is with this area that we are chiefly concerned. What kinds of economic, social, and political action are most effective in building national unity and in reducing vulnerability to insurgent appeal?[73]

> A wide variety of the measurement techniques of psychology, sociology, anthropology, and other behavioral disciplines will be applied to the search for a solution.[74]

The proposal is couched in the "scientific" language of inputs, disposing conditions, and stimuli and responses. One type of stimulus that may be studied, as used by either the government or the insurgent forces, is food. The following excerpt is reminiscent of comments on withholding food from intransigent villages made by USAID official Farrar during the Thailand Study Group:

> The offer of food in exchange for certain services affords a convenient example. If this has in the past been a strong stimulus, it can probably be weakened by increasing local agricultural production. *If it has been a weak or neutral stimulus, it can probably be strengthened by burning the crops* [emphasis added].[75]

Crop destruction had been studied as a counterinsurgency technique by the Research Analysis Corporation, a U.S. Army Federal Contract Research Center in a study titled "Economic–Crop Destruction as a Cold War/ Counterinsurgency Weapon."[76] There is no reason to doubt that the AIR project, when completed, would yield data on the effectiveness of such crop destruction for the U.S. and Thai counterinsurgency effort.

AIR proposed that social scientists participate in their project by reviewing the "reports and documents pertaining to the insurgency in at least Thailand and Vietnam," interviewing both U.S. and Thai officials responsible for counterinsurgency operations and insurgents, and making "structured and detailed observations in a sample of communities."[77] In another incarnation, this is the same set of procedures undertaken to produce dissertations in the social sciences.

Attention was paid in the proposal to the interaction of Thai and American researchers—a concern of the four anthropologists who met with Deitchman at ARPA headquarters in Washington in early in 1967. Professional interaction between Thais and Americans would "enrich the personnel resources on which the Royal Thai Government will be able to draw for future assistance on counterinsurgency and other important national needs."[78] But AIR was realistic. Just as Special Assistant for Counter-insurgency Tanham reminded us that ARPA was the operational arm of the U.S. embassy's research program in counterinsurgency, the AIR proposal stated that

> During the project's developmental stages, it would seem appropriate to limit the scope of program evaluation to activities in

which U.S. agencies play a vital role, and to view the project organizationally as an extension of the agencies involved. Attaching it in the first instance to the American Embassy would ideally reflect its inter–agency orientation.[79]

The result was that Thai researchers would participate—but in an evaluation of American programs conducted out of the U.S. embassy. This hardly escapes the label of "intellectual colonialism."

Preliminary Trip Report

The AIR proposal to ARPA eventually became an ARPA operating project in Thailand. Documents do not indicate on what date research began in Thailand, but a report summarizing a trip from late May to early June 1969, prepared by AIR representatives, is available. All persons mentioned in the report (see Table 4.2 below) were affiliated with the Thai Department of Community Development (CD), particularly its Research and Evaluation Division, the United States Operations Mission/Thailand, or with AIR.

AIR developed contacts with the Thai Department of Community Development as a prelude to going forward with its project. The Department of Community Development had been created in 1962 as a link between the government and villagers. Its mission was to send workers to villages to assess needs and develop projects that utilized village labor to address these needs.[80] Thus, the CD Research and Evaluation Division was briefed on the AIR project and suggested that AIR members review and comment on a questionnaire that CD had prepared for a survey of regions (in which CD employees had worked for five years).[81] Meetings also took place between USOM advisors and AIR members, and USOM advisors King and Doughty were "very pleased to learn that AIR would be able to assist the [CD] Research and Evaluation Division."[82]

Visits to villages were made by AIR members Bhakdi, Krug, and Murray. The observations noted by them are rather uninformative, such as:

[Krug and Bhakdi:] Villages differ. If the village, rather than the villager is the primary unit for analysis (as had always seemed probable) there will be variance.[83]

TABLE 4.2: PERSONS MENTIONED IN MAY–JUNE 1969 AIR TRIP REPORT[84]

NAME	AFFILIATION
S. P. Bhakdi	represented American Institutes for Research (AIR)
Charas	Thai Department of Community Development (CD), Research and Evaluation Division
C. H. Doughty	United States Operations Mission Thailand (USOM/T), Community Development Advisor
James Hoath	USOM/T, Research Director
Travis King	USOM/T, Community Development Advisor
Robert E. Krug	Associate Director of AIR International, psychologist
D. A. Morell	represented AIR
C. A. Murray	represented AIR
Phairat	CD, Research and Evaluation Division
Preecha	CD, probably Research and Evaluation Division
Sai Hutacharern	Director General of CD
Suwit	Director, CD Research and Evaluation Division

The trip report concludes with a review of the interview technique and the questionnaire that was being used to gather data and some suggestions for improvement.[85] The Agenda for the Advisory Panel Meeting, which took place one month later, yields more interesting information.

AIR Advisory Panel Meeting

The AIR proposal, *Counterinsurgency in Thailand,* had called for the placement of at least six professional staff members in Thailand and suggested this number should include one psychologist, one anthropologist, and one political scientist.[86] It also proposed the formation of an advisory board, as follows:

> The Advisory Board should consist of high–level personnel drawn from the staff of ARPA and other interested agencies of the Department of Defense, and of eminent specialists with relevant interests and experience drawn from the professional community at large. It is planned that a total of seven specialists will form the at-large contingent, to be jointly selected by ARPA and AIR.[87]

In the proposal, AIR suggested four individuals (Harvard professor of government John Montgomery, Northern Illinois University professor of political science M. Ladd Thomas, and two AIR executives) to fill a majority of the seven positions on the advisory "board."[88] Three of the proposed names appear as members of the actual advisory "panel" in the "Advisory Panel Meeting" document. Other panel members were UCLA professor of anthropology Michael Moerman, Harvard's John Montgomery, two AIR executives, a probable USOM advisor, and two others. M. Ladd Thomas, who attended the IDA's Thailand Study Group in June 1967, does not appear as an actual panel member, although his name was one of the four originally proposed. (See Table 4.3 below for participants in the Advisory Panel meetings.) The Panel members were paid $150 per day plus expenses, judging by Moerman's statement of expenses/bill.[89]

The Advisory Panel meetings brought together a disparate grouping of people. Moerman, Montgomery, and others met with American commanding general of Military Assistance Command, Thailand (mentioned by title only in the "Advisory Panel Meeting" document), the Thai commanding general of the Joint–Thai U.S. Military Research and Development

TABLE 4.3: PARTICIPANTS IN AIR ADVISORY PANEL MEETINGS[90]

NAME	AFFILIATION
Philip Batson	"senior U.S. advisor to the Thai National Police Department"; chief of the Thailand office of U.S. Office of Public Safety, which directed the majority of U.S. assistance to foreign police and paramilitary units.
Bauer	Panel Member
S. P. Bhakdi	AIR
R. L. Cardwell	most likely on staff of U.S. Special Assistant for Counterinsurgency
Lt. Col. Chaichuey	Thai National Police Department (TNPD)
Maj. Gen. Chamras	TNPD
[Raymond?] Coffey	civic action advisor to the Border Patrol Police"; most likely Raymond Coffey of Development Consultants, Inc. (DEVCON), a CIA–front corporation
[Forest?] Cookson	probably economic advisor, USOM/T
Robert E. Krug	associate director of AIR International
MacMichael	ARPA researcher
Michael Moerman	UCLA anthropologist; panel member
John D. Montgomery	Harvard professor of government; panel member
D. L. Morell	AIR
C. A. Murray	AIR
Col. Phao	TNPD

NAME	AFFILIATION
Maj. Gen. Prakarn	TNPD
Maj. Gen. Prasart	commanding general of Joint Thai–U.S. Military Research and Development Center (MRDC), under whose aegis ARPA Thailand officially operated
Rowe	AIR senior consultant on international projects; panel member
P. A. Schwarz	Director of AIR International Division, degrees in mathematics and psychology
Sharp	ARPA researcher
Somchai	ARPA researcher
Maj. Gen. Surapon	TNPD
George K. Tanham	U. S. Special Assistant for Counterinsurgency
[S. Rains?] Wallace	most likely president of AIR, panel member
Webb	panel member
Terry Wood	USOM/T
Philip Worchel	professor at University of Texas; director of ARPA's Research and Development Center in Thailand
Lt. Gen. Yuan	TNPD

Center (MRDC), U.S. Special Assistant for counterinsurgency George Tanham, ARPA researchers, and AIR executives. Other panel members met with generals in the Thai National Police Department.

Participants in the Panel meeting were directed to study questions of counterinsurgency, as the document makes clear. The agenda takes Panel members through an organized review of the different aspects of the counterinsurgency programs of the Thai and U.S. governments. It asks them to reflect on the information and come up with ideas to better the program.

According to the meeting agenda,[91] the Panel was called together between June 30 and July 4, 1967 to work on the following three problems:

[1] indicators of CT insurgency in Village X,
[2] criteria for our current Community Development and Police assessment projects, and
[3] improvements in tentative SA/CI [U.S. Special Assistant for Counterinsurgency] information systems.[92]

The first day of the meeting was taken up with briefings on the current state of the insurgency and counterinsurgency activities. It included a lunch meeting with George Tanham, which would "... center on his expectations and wants re the AIR project [and] his substantive suggestions on the three Panel tasks...." This was followed by an "Overview of the insurgency by three members of the SA/CI staff ... [and] a brief description of the situation in the various regions...."[93]

The second day's meetings were also concerned with the insurgency. On Tuesday, the Panel went to the ARPA field office, which Tanham has described in his book as the informal research arm of the U.S. Embassy regarding internal security operations. Here they met the Thai general in command of the Joint Thai–U.S. Military Research and Development Center (MRDC) and Philip Worchel, chief of the ARPA Thailand office. The minutes indicate one-half hour spent with Major General Prasart and one hour with Worchel, during which the latter discussed "... ARPA's expectations and wants re the AIR project [and] his substantive suggestions for the conduct of the research."[94] The panel also met to "explore the dynamics of insurgent operations at the village level" with ARPA researchers and the USOM's Coffey. Later in the day, the panel split up and interviewed Thai district leaders on their role ... in CI [counterinsurgency], on their experiences re what works, on the indicators they use at the village levels as signs of progress or problems, on the respective advantages that the RTG [Royal Thai Government] and the CT [communist terrorists] have in gaining population support, etc.[95]

On Wednesday, the meeting topics moved to community development and police activities. Cookson, Moerman, Rowe, and Krug interviewed USIS staffers who were "working in sensitive areas," while Bauer, Montgomery, Murray, and Bhakdi interviewed community development supervisors on the following topics:

> villager reactions to mobile information teams and various psyops [psychological operations] approaches; what indicators and signs they have learned to look for in the villages and why they think each is important; any differences they have noted in villages that are under active CT pressure; the impact of CD [Community Development], Police, and other Government programs; and kinds of Government inputs that seem to get the best results, and the probable reasons; the kinds of inputs that seem to work best for the CT, and the probable reasons, etc.[96]

While the above-mentioned interviews were being conducted, Wallace, Webb, Schwarz, and Morell interviewed police advisor Batson to discuss "TNPD [Thai National Police Department] capabilities, role and interest in impact assessment."[97] Each of the three subgroups then met with "key officials" of the organizations at which they conducted their interviews.

The Panel was divided into two groups in the interest of helping them to think like either the government or the insurgents, as follows:

> It will be noted that the Panel has been split into a "Blue Team" ... (to be concerned with the criteria for government inputs) and a "Red Team" ... to be concerned mainly with indicators of CT activity.... Throughout the interviews, it is suggested that the Blue Team representative "think blue" and that the Red Team representative "think red" so that both topics will be covered in the questions put to the interviewees.[98]

Apparently, Panel members worked late into the night on Wednesday, as indicated by the festive note in the agenda addressed to spouses: "Wives of Panel members and staff free to have a night on the town while we are working."[99]

On Thursday began the attack on the final of the three problems that had been assigned, as the Panel members applied "their newly gained wisdom to a critique of the tentative SA/CI information system."[100] They also met with the American Commanding General of the Military Assistance Command, Thailand, and members of his staff "... to ask questions about relevant military inputs ... and to test the new ideas they have developed on these experienced individuals, to see which fly better than the others."[101] Similar discussions were then held with USOM officials, who would also "constitute an excellent sounding board for ideas of all types that have been developed."[102] The Panel then again met with Tanham to test their ideas, and a similar meeting was suggested with Worchel, although it is unclear from the agenda if it actually took place. Friday, July 4th ("Because this is a holiday, sports shirts are suggested")[103] was the summation day, with drafts on each of the three problems polished up and distributed by Blue Team, Red Team, and the entire group for the SA/CI information system.

A review of the Advisory Panel Meeting document reveals the thoroughness with which AIR and ARPA organizers planned the five days of meetings. Their pursuit of effective counterinsurgency practices brought together academics, intelligence officials, and generals in the best tradition of social science research in the service of government.

The feelings and opinions of of individual panel members are impossible to ascertain from the list of meetings. Michael Moerman later wrote to the *AAA Newsletter* that

> The AIR project was initially described to me as devoted to developing techniques by which the Thai government could evaluate the success of its own programs. By the second [Panel] meeting it became clear that some leading members of the AIR Thailand staff were seriously attempting a counterinsurgency justification for their work.[104]

Moerman appears to have been initially somewhat naive about AIR's goals. A consultant desiring more information might have asked, "What techniques for which type of programs?"

Later, Moerman did express a range of opinions about the AIR project in a letter to Schwarz (with copies sent to Montgomery, Rowe, and Wallace).[105] In the letter, Moerman discussed modernization and insurgent recruitment in light of information in the semiannual AIR reports. He also touched on some subtle theoretical issues not evident in the IDA or AIR data. Of governments, he wrote:

> I nevertheless take issue with the fundamental assumption that governments in general, or specifically the Thai government (even limiting it to those components of the Thai government which we support) has as its fundamental goal enlisting popular support. Governments want to remain in power. One of their devices for this is the enlistment of popular support. They can also permit or encourage popular apathy, insure the irrelevance or impotence of popular protest, or use suppression. All governments engage in some mixture of these strategies; this is one reason why I am slowly becoming more of an anarchist.[106]

Apparently, Moerman's growing anarchism did not surface before he joined the AIR Advisory Panel. In his letter, Moerman also criticized the Thai government:

> It takes only a brief visit to a Thai village to convince the observer of the stunning ineffectiveness of the Thai government in rural settings.... It seems to be only in the cities of Thailand—and in providing infrastructure—that the RTG can work with comparative effectiveness. Why don't we try to keep them there?[107]

Moerman further criticized the AIR program in light of its policy applications:

> I am still troubled by the extent to which the program has slipped toward policy making and advising.... may I suggest that you distinguish among the following, and avoid some of them: showing the Thai how to evaluate their own programs, evaluating those programs, proposing program modifications, proposing new programs, letting George [Tanham] know which RTG agencies are doing a good job of CI [counterinsurgency].[108]

Together, these statements indicate a remarkable skepticism and penetrating critique of government in general, and of the Thai government and the U.S. advisory role in particular. Moerman clearly did not subscribe to the distinction that Project Agile Director Deitchman made between policymaking and policy advising. For Deitchman, policymaking should be left to others, but policy advising and informing was the objective of ARPA in the post–Camelot restructured period. Which of the AIR activities Moerman would proscribe is unclear in his letter, but one assumes they are the policymaking programs, while programs of evaluation would be acceptable. After his wide-ranging and perceptive criticism, Moerman closed his letter with a decidedly positive assessment of AIR's ability to demonstrate the impact of different programs on each other:

> I think AIR is further along on being able to deliver the goods here than anyone else is. If the project succeeds at all, it should certainly succeed in this regard. This is a contribution of unique and immense value which you should not neglect to emphasize in selling the program and attempting to renew its support.[109]

It is clear that Moerman saw the positive aspect of the AIR program to be that of assisting specific community development activities, and that he was willing to separate this goal from the other counterinsurgency objectives of the various agencies involved. But the U.S. government was not willing to separate the two. Moerman wrote that when he could not change the focus from counterinsurgency, he resigned.[110]

Herein lay the problem. The government was constantly trying to link defense-related work with non–defense work. Thus, IDA consulted for the Office of Economic Opportunity and AIR hired individuals with experience evaluating non–defense related projects to administer defense–related projects. This is a relationship of which social scientists must remain continually aware and must question, as the events discussed in the next chapter make clear.

NOTES

1 American Institutes for Research [AIR], *Counterinsurgency in Thailand: The Impact of Economic, Social, and Political Action Programs* (A Research and development proposal submitted to the Advanced Research Projects Agency) (Pittsburgh, PA: American Institutes for Research, December 1967).

2 Ibid., ii.

3 AIR, "Advisory Panel Meeting, 30 June–4 July 1969, Agenda"; AIR, "Trip Report: Visit to Amphoe Nong Han, Changwad Udon, 28 May–6 June 1969."

4 Beals, *Politics of Social Research*, 108; Deitchman, *Best–Laid Schemes*, 49; United States Congress, House of Representatives, Committee on Appropriations, Subcommittee, *Department of Defense Appropriations for 1970, Hearings* (part 5), 91st Congress, 1st session (Washington, DC: U.S. Government Printing Office, 1969), 809. Hereafter these hearing are cited as simply *Defense Appropriations* with the appropriate year appended. Defense appropriations hearings take place during the year *before* the funds are used, thus the date of publication does not correspond to the year of funding use.

5 IDA, *Annual Report II* [for 1957–58], 7–8.

6 IDA, *Activities 1961–1964*, 10–11.

7 Deitchman, *Best–Laid Schemes*, 67. Cf. IDA, *Fourth Annual Report* [for 1959–60], 7:

> Thus ARPA, having satisfied the emergency requirements of the immediate post–Sputnik era, moves toward its planned position as the operating arm of the Office of the Director of Defense Research and Engineering, as advisor on research and development matters, in selection of areas for intensified effort, in providing enabling machinery for the acquisition of new knowledge, and in assessment in state of the art in various fields....

[8] U.S. Congress, *Defense Appropriations for 1963*, 121.

[9] Ibid., 108.

[10] R. Sean Randolph, *The United States and Thailand: Alliance Dynamics, 1950–1985* (Berkeley: Institute of East Asian Studies, University of California, 1986), 110; Tanham, *Trial in Thailand*, 125.

[11] General Robert H. Wienecke, in "Weapons Sought for Remote Wars," *New York Times*, 27 January 1964, quoted in Klare, *War Without End*, 226.

[12] U.S. Congress, *Defense Appropriations for 1966*, 530; Deitchman, *Best–Laid Schemes*, 68; Randolph, *United States and Thailand*, 111.

[13] U.S. Congress, Senate, Committee on Foreign Relations, *United States Security Agreements and Commitments Abroad, Hearings,* (part 3, Kingdom of Thailand) (Washington, DC: U.S. Government Printing Office, 1971), quoted in Randolph, *United States and Thailand,* 110.

[14] Randolph, *United States and Thailand*, 110; Tanham, *Trial in Thailand*, 25.

[15] Sources for Table 4.1. For the six projects listed as "in progress, March 1966": USOM, Research Division, "Current Research Projects in Thailand" ([Bangkok:] USOM, March 23, 1966). All others from a fragmentary (consisting of only pages 17, 18, 25, 27, 28, 32), untitled document listing unclassified MRDC projects with the following information: document number, title, author, date, number of pages, and description. I received this document courtesy of Gerald Berreman, who received it from MRDC.

[16] Randolph, *United States and Thailand*, 111.

[17] Tanham, *Trial in Thailand,* 125; Randolph, *United States and Thailand*, 110.

[18] Randolph, *The United States and Thailand*, 110.

[19] Tanham, *Trial in Thailand*, 126.

[20] Klare, *War Without End*, 218.

[21] U.S. Congress, *Defense Appropriations for 1969*, 590.

[22] U.S. Congress, *Defense Appropriations for 1966*, 530.

[23] U.S. Congress, *Defense Appropriations for 1969*, 590.

[24] For information on and examples of projects initiated by ARPA in Thailand, see Beals, *Politics of Social Research*, 105–106; Deitchman, *Best–Laid Schemes*, 69; Klare, *War Without End*, 226–236; Randolph, *United States and Thailand*, 112–113; and U.S. Congress, *Defense Appropriations*, for years 1961–1972.

ARPA was not the only agency directing the preparation of guidebooks on the "hill tribes." See, for example, United States Department of the Army, *Minority Groups in Thailand* (Ethnographic Study Series) [Department of the Army Pamphlet No. 550–107] (Washington, DC: Department of the Army, 1970), which was prepared by the Cultural Information Analysis Center (CINFAC) of the Center for Research in Social Systems (CRESS) of American University. This 1,100 page "pamphlet" includes such categories as "civic action considerations" and "paramilitary capabilities" along with ethnographic data for each minority group.

[25] U.S. Congress, *Defense Appropriations for 1965*, 134.

[26] D. J. Blakeslee, L. W. Huff and R. W. Kickert, *Village Security Pilot Study Northeast Thailand*, 3 vols. (Bangkok: Joint Thai–U.S. Military Research and Development Center, May 1965).

[27] Blakeslee, et. al., *Village Security Study*, 363–366.

[28] Klare, *War Without End*, 230; Randolph, *United States and Thailand*, 113.

[29] Deitchman, *Best–Laid Schemes*, 292.

[30] Ibid., 295.

[31] Ibid., 292–293.

32 U.S. Congress, *Defense Appropriations for 1968,* 175–176. All following information on RSSP in this paragraph is from this source.

33 Ibid., 176.

34 Deitchman, *Best–Laid Schemes,* 300.

35 Ibid., 301–303.

36 Ibid., 303.

37 Moerman's dissertation was "Farming in Ban Phaed: Technological Decisions and Their Consequences for the External Relations of a Thai–Lue Village," Yale University, 1964.

38 Deitchman, *Best–Laid Schemes,* 311.

39 Beals, *Politics of Social Research,* 106–107.

40 Moerman, "Analysis of Lue Conversation: Providing Accounts, Finding Breaches, Taking Sides," 12 August 1968. [This is a two–page abstract of the "unclassified" report of the same name on a form labeled "Document Control Data— R&D." The "contract or Grant No." is listed as "ARPA Order #836; AFOSR–66–1167; AFOSR–68–1428."]

41 Michael Moerman and Charles F. Keyes, Memo to AACT members and ad hoc committee on ARPA Northeastern Thailand Project, n.d. [but it must have been issued between January and March 1967], 1.

42 Ibid.

43 Ibid., 2.

44 Ibid.

45 Ibid., 2–3.

46 Ibid., 3.

47 Herbert Phillips, telephone interviews with author, 1 May 1991; 21 May 1991; Phillips, *Between the Tiger and the Crocodile: Scholarly Ethics and Government Research in Thailand,* unpublished manuscript, 40–41.

48 Phillips, letter to Deitchman, 24 September 1978. I am enjoined by Phillips from quoting this letter directly.

49 Phillips, letter to Mead, 24 April 1971. I am enjoined by Phillips from quoting this letter directly.

50 Peter Braestrup, "Researchers Aid Thai Rebel Fight," *New York Times,* 20 March 1967.

51 Ibid.

52 Paul Rabinow, et. al., letter to Dr. H[erbert]. Phillips, 24 April 1967.

53 Ibid.

54 Phillips, letter to William Rittenberg, et. al., 1 May 1967. I am enjoined by Phillips from quoting this letter directly.

55 Clark E. Cunningham, an anthropologist at Yale, also responded to the *New York Times* article. In a letter sent from Thailand, he wrote that there was only one "qualified anthropologist" who was an ARPA employee. He also cited a figure of two other qualified anthropologists "working on counterinsurgency" in Thailand. Cunningham's concern was with the *perception* of the number of anthropologists involved (which was one step removed from a concern over the actual number, and many steps removed from a concern with the ethical question of having *any* anthropologists employed by the Defense Department.) Cunningham wrote:

> Agencies may wish to hire anthropologists to explore this important problem [counterinsurgency], but it is severely detrimental to independent enquiry overseas if scholarly anthropologists are thought to be concentrating on political work of the kind which your article describes. In Thailand, contrary to the picture which you present, few anthropologists have been hired for such research, and the great majority of anthropologists are pursuing only scientific interests (Clark E. Cunningham, letter to the editor, *New York Times*, 16 May 1967. I am unaware if this letter was later published in the newspaper.).

[56] AAA, "Statement on Problems of Anthropological Research and Ethics," n.p.: AAA, 1967.

[57] Phillips, letter to Rittenberg, et. al., 1 May 1967.

[58] Cf. Cunningham:

> The present concern for "security" in Thailand is leading to a desire for "crash research" and expenditure in these terms, but in areas where "crash answers" are very difficult to obtain. I do not maintain that anthropologists should not engage in short–term research; that policy–oriented research is without value. However I feel that the various levels at which proper research should be conducted must be discussed, and both "urgency" and schedules (for anthropologists and policymakers) must be considered in other than academic and fiscal years (Clark E. Cunningham, "Urgent Research in Northern Thailand," *Bulletin of the International Committee on Urgent Anthropological and Ethnological Research* 8, 69).

[59] Phillips, letter to Rittenberg, et. al.

[60] Ralph W. McGehee, *Deadly Deceits: My 25 Years in the CIA* (New York: Sheridan Square Publications, 1983), 96–106; Lobe, *United States Assistance to the Thailand Police*, 153.

[61] McGehee, *Deadly Deceits*, 107.

[62] Phillips, letter to Rittenberg, et. al., 1 May 1967.

[63] Eric Wolf, telephone interview with author, 21 May 1991.

[64] Deitchman, *Best–Laid Schemes*, 320.

[65] AIR, *Counterinsurgency in Thailand*.

[66] Ibid., v.

[67] AIR, "Advisory Panel Meeting"; "Trip Report: Visit to Amphoe Nong Han, Changwad Udon, 28 May–6 June 1969."

---

[68] AIR, *Counterinsurgency in Thailand*, ii.

[69] Ibid.

[70] Ibid., 34.

[71] Ibid., iii.

[72] Ibid., 1.

[73] Ibid.

[74] Ibid., 26.

[75] Ibid., 7.

[76] NARMIC [National Action/Research on the Military Industrial Complex], *Weapons for Counterinsurgency* (Local Action/Research Guide No. 1) (Philadelphia: American Friends Service Committee, 15 January 1970), 30.

[77] AIR, *Counterinsurgency in Thailand*, 24–25.

[78] Ibid., 33.

[79] Ibid.

[80] Tanham, *Trial in Thailand*, 73–74.

[81] AIR, "Trip Report," 1.

[82] Ibid., 2.

[83] Ibid., 3.

[84] Information on affiliations of individuals mentioned in the Trip Report is from AIR, "Trip Report," 1–2; with the exception of Krug, for whom the source is AIR, *Counterinsurgency in Thailand*, 39. According to his AIR

biography, from 1964–1967 Krug held two positions with the U.S. government: Director of Research for the Peace Corps and Director of Plans and Evaluation for the Job Corps, Office of Economic Opportunity (OEO). "In the latter capacity he was responsible for the assessment of a variety of action programs directly relevant to the focus of the proposed research." The proposed research, interestingly enough, was to study *Counterinsurgency in Thailand*. A further point to remember is that the IDA conducted at least one study for the OEO on antipoverty programs in the mid–1960s (IDA, *The Tenth Year*, 17).

85 Ibid., 3–7.

86 AIR, *Counterinsurgency in Thailand,* 38, 36.

87 Ibid., 40.

88 Ibid., 41–42.

89 AIR, [Statement of Expenses/Bill from Michael Moerman], 5 July 1969.

90 The source for biographical information on participants is AIR, "Advisory Panel Meeting," 1–5, except for additional information on Batson, Cookson, and Coffey (source: Thomas Lobe, *United States National Security Policy and Aid to the Thailand Police* [Denver: University of Denver (Colorado Seminary), 1977], 80–81, 145–6); Montgomery, Rowe, Schwarz, and Wallace (source: AIR, *Counterinsurgency in Thailand,* 39, 41–42); and Worchel (sources: Deitchman, *Best–Laid Schemes,* 361; Tanham, *Trial in Thailand,* xiv).

91 Specific quotations are cited by page number, but general information is taken from AIR, "Advisory Panel Meeting," 1–5.

92 AIR, "Advisory Panel Meeting," 1.

93 Ibid.

94 Ibid.

95 Ibid., 2.

96 Ibid., 3.

97 Ibid.

98 Ibid., 4.

99 Ibid.

100 Ibid.

101 Ibid.

102 Ibid., 5.

103 Ibid.

104 Moerman, letter to the editor, *AAA Newsletter* 12:1 (January 1971), 9–11.

105 Moerman, letter to Dr. Paul A. Schwarz, AIROSD/ARPA/ RDC–T, [American Institutes for Research, Office of the Secretary of Defense, Advanced Research Projects Agency, Research and Development Center, Thailand], 13 February 1970.

106 Moerman, letter to Schwarz, 6.

107 Ibid., 8.

108 Ibid., 11–12.

109 Ibid., 12.

110 Moerman, letter to the editor, *AAA Newsletter* 12:1 (January 1971), 9–11.

CHAPTER FIVE

USAID, AACT & SEADAG—
PLANNING FOR INSURGENCY

Except for a modest amount of technical assistance projects, most of which we are gradually phasing out, our assistance in Thailand is concentrated on counterinsurgency activities; approximately 75% of our total effort is in this field.

—testimony of USAID officials before U.S. Congress, 1969

AID has established the Academic Advisory Council for Thailand (AACT), composed of social scientists with background specialization in Thailand to provide coordination between the academic community of Thai scholars and AID.

—USAID contract with UCLA, 1968

In September of 1968, the U.S. Agency for International Development (USAID) and the Regents of the University of California (UCLA) signed a unique agreement that committed a group of scholars to work as advisors to AID programs "dealing with development and counterinsurgency problems" in Thailand.[1] The group was known as the Academic Advisory Council for Thailand (AACT). The objective of the agreement was summarized as follows:

The overall objective of this contract is to make available the resources of the Contractor [UCLA], including personnel, to support and strengthen the operations of the U.S. aid program in Thailand, particularly with respect to the research activities undertaken by the Research Division of USOM Thailand [AID].[2]

The USAID–AACT arrangement was unique not simply because it called for a group of social scientists to advise an agency of the U.S.

government, but because it specifically identified the "services" to be directed towards counterinsurgency research. The interest of AID in defeating the Thai insurgency (not immediately apparent in the name of "international development") was explicitly stated by AID officials.

U.S. AGENCY FOR INTERNATIONAL DEVELOPMENT (USAID)

The overall philosophy driving the U.S. aid effort in Thailand during the 1960s was that a combination of civil, police, and military operations would be able to defeat the growing communist–led insurgency.[3] The functional role of the U.S. Agency for International Development (whose Thai office, established in 1954, was called the United States Operation Mission/Thailand, or USOM) within this doctrine was to provide a range of programs to train and supply units of the Thai police and to conduct community development and infrastructure–building operations. It was assumed that an increase in civic action programs would result in a decrease in poverty and thus in insurgent activities.[4] In this way, the USAID program was essentially a reactive effort in response to insurgent activities that were addressing village problems in northeast Thailand. The attention of AID to these problems was an attempt to assure village loyalty in order to achieve stability.[5]

USAID publications of this period document the agency's concern with "security" issues. A 1965 document explains:

Thailand is currently of enormous strategic importance in terms of U.S. national interests:

1. Thailand is located in the midst of the all–out struggle between Free World and Communist forces in Southeast Asia.

2. Thailand is formally committed to the side of the Free World despite its perilous location.

In this situation we seek to make this area less susceptible to Communist influence. We are persuading and assisting the Thais to establish programs and take measures which will develop the depressed areas, economically and socially, and to promote the abilities of rural peoples to help themselves increasingly. We hope thereby to lead rural peoples to identify themselves with their government and look to that government for support and guidance.[6]

By 1965 USAID cited "counterinsurgency" and "nation building" as the first and second priorities of its program in Thailand. AID projects were chosen on the criteria of meeting these goals.[7] Congressional testimony by an AID administrator in 1969 described USAID projects as being concentrated in three areas concerned with the insurgency—rural security, rural development, and government services:

> Except for a modest amount of technical assistance projects, most of which we are gradually phasing out, our assistance in Thailand is concentrated on counterinsurgency activities; approximately 75% of our total effort is in this field.[8]

A single–minded focus on the insurgency is also evident in an examination of USAID project budget submissions, in which almost every project is related to the effect it will have on security issues, counter-insurgency, or improving the socio-economic base of the northeast region.[9] For example, even the benefits of a "Potable Water" project are first related to building villager loyalty and defeating the insurgency and then to improving health standards:

> The major objective is to strengthen the capacity of the RTG [Royal Thai Government] to respond effectively to the most frequent requests of village people—for drinking water—and thus to provide a public service through which the people can identify themselves with their government. In the security sensitive areas this is a particularly effective vehicle for supporting counter-insurgency efforts of the RTG. Accomplishing this objective will make a major impact on the general health of rural communities, most rapidly in the North and Northeast.[10]

The focus of the USAID program was conditioned by growing U.S. involvement in Southeast Asia during the 1960s. Early in the decade, U.S. interest in the conflict in Laos necessitated the use of a friendly neighboring country for launching covert operations and for training mercenaries. By the middle of the decade, the Thai insurgents had declared the beginning of their armed struggle. Finally, a massive U.S. military infrastructure, particularly air bases, had been constructed in Thailand and needed to be protected. AID programs supplemented those already instituted by the CIA and the U.S. military, particularly where it was bureaucratically more feasible for a non–military or non–intelligence agency to do so.[11]

Rural Security

The largest single USAID project in Thailand in the 1960s provided assistance to various units of the Thai National Police Department (TNPD) to improve rural security.[12] The operation was conducted by the U.S. Office of Public Safety (OPS), which was created in 1962 to coordinate and centralize all U.S. assistance to foreign police departments; in Thailand it was organizationally a division of AID.[13] Between 1965 and 1968, 47 percent of all USOM aid to Thailand went to the TNPD and 80 percent of this aid was spent on materiel. Total police advisory and equipment aid during this period was almost $50 million.[14] OPS aid included counter-insurgency training and the provision of weapons, munitions, vehicles, and communications equipment.[15]

The primary recipient of OPS–AID aid was the Border Patrol Police (BPP) (created by the CIA in the early 1950s) and the Provincial Police.[16] The BPP was sufficiently equipped for paramilitary, intelligence gathering, development, and other operations. By the 1960s, the BPP had become a crucial unit for patrolling Thailand's porous borders with Laos and for attacking insurgents in border provinces; CIA operatives under OPS cover continued to train the BPP. An AID budget report described one project that aided the BPP—the "Remote Area Security" project—as follows:

> The primary objective of this project is to assist the Border Patrol Police (BPP) in the creation of a friendly, cooperative local population—firmly committed to Thailand and willing to support the RTG [Royal Thai Government] in identification, location, and elimination of subversives.... Specifically, this project aims at involving the remote villager in his own development in order to consume his latent energies with constructive activities easily assisted by these tradition–oriented peoples and readily appreciated as evidence of RTG concern for their well being.[17]

Social scientists made a significant theoretical contribution to "security" by endorsing the creation of non–police village defense forces. A June 1964 study for the Rand Corporation was produced by Herbert Phillips and David Wilson, funded through ARPA's Project Agile.[18] Its purpose was to address

> selected aspects of the politics, administration, social organization, and culture of rural Thailand that are closely related to the problem of maintaining and strengthening the country's internal security.[19]

Phillips and Wilson advocated the formation of a "village defense corps," to be made up of veterans, unemployed villagers, and youths. Their reasoning was: " ... just as the Communists might exploit the motivations and even the skills of these marginal groups, so might the Thai government."[20] There had been several experimental paramilitary defense forces in existence in Thailand since at least the early 1960s;[21] thus, the contribution of the research by Phillips and Wilson was not original in terms of specific local applications. Their innovation came in identifying the groups from which to recruit and in suggesting a nationwide force (although the People's Assistance Teams in Vietnam were something of a precedent). Phillips later rebuffed a suggestion that his study was instrumental in the formation of village defense forces:

> The fact is that this Village Security Force originates in a 1937 Thai law (promulgated when I was eight years old and before there was even a U.S. embassy in Thailand) and assumed its present form in 1954 (two years before I ever set foot on Thai soil).[22]

An attempt was made in Thailand several years later to consolidate the disparate village paramilitary units and create new ones under the name Village Security Force (VSF), but this failed due to intrabureaucratic conflicts.[23]

In the past decade, human rights groups have done extensive research on the dangers and problems created for civilian populations that are compelled to patrol, in support of the government, against guerilla forces.[24] As an integral part of counterinsurgency strategy, civil patrols—almost always mandatory—compel peasants to do the work of the army without adequate weapons or training. Those who do not participate are threatened and/or punished (often with the accusation that they must be guerrillas or guerilla sympathizers if they do not want to patrol); the purchase of arms and equipment is often borne by the patrollers themselves. Youths are forced to patrol in contravention of international law; and the amount of time spent patrolling takes farmers away from their fields or youths from school. Finally, and most seriously, patrollers must engage in combat with members of their own community; thus, they are caught between threatening, heavily armed soldiers and better-organized, armed guerrillas. Phillips and Wilson may not have been aware of these specific dangers in the absence of these contemporary studies, but their experience should have created an awareness of the general dangers.

A social scientist who believes that the insurgents and the government against which they fight both present dangerous options for the peasants stands between Scylla and Charybdis. The question that presents itself is whether it is better to stand aside or to try to influence government policy from the inside. Phillips later wrote about his overall involvement with the U.S. government and its programs in Thailand:

> In my own case curiosity, both professional and personal, about how the U.S. Government actually functioned in Thailand was at first probably as strong a motive as the possibility that I might be of assistance to Thai villagers. As the magnitude and portentous quality of U.S. activities in Thailand became increasingly obvious to me, so also did the latter motive, as well as did the simple patriotic motive of trying to influence what I considered to be in America's best interests in Thailand—to leave the Thai alone to resolve their own problems.[25]

Rural Development and Government Services

The second focus of USAID in Thailand was rural development, which was recognized by both Thais and Americans as useful in combating insurgency. Thai Prime Minister Thanom Kittikachorn gave a speech on "The Need for an Acceleration of Rural Development in Areas Threatened by Infiltration" in February 1965, in which he used the popular inoculation metaphor (a metaphor also favored by ARPA's Seymour Deitchman at IDA's Thailand Study Group in 1967):

> We could protect ourselves against this danger [the "instigation" of insurgency by "outsiders"] by building up our economic, social, and other strengths as we do against a disease by vaccination.[26]

USOM/Thailand's Accelerated Rural Development (ARD) project, created following discussions between USOM's Office of Rural Affairs and the Thai government, was designed to increase income in rural areas, strengthen the ties between villagers and the Thai government, and to increase "local self–government."[27] ARD projects would, in turn, lead villagers to identify with their government instead of with the insurgent forces. The ARD program was conceived as a development counter-insurgency program, and Thai provinces were targeted for projects on the basis of poverty and insurgent activity.[28] USOM documents confirm the loyalty–building and communist fighting objectives, with the goal of "stability," of the ARD program:

> The objectives of [ARD] are to increase the range and effectiveness of the Thai Government services in security sensitive rural areas in Northeast Thailand and to build popular loyalty and support for the Thai Government....[29]

> ... ARD programs were instituted to accelerate rural development as a means of meeting the Communist challenge. The ultimate objective of the program is to build a sound economic and social foundation for the people as a means of countering subversion and developing environmental conditions conducive to the maintenance of security and stability.[30]

Specific ARD projects included road building, dam and well construction, and medical team visits to remote villages. Other projects (such as improving the functioning of local governments in remote areas) were instituted by Thai Department of Community Development (CD) or by Mobile Development Units (MDU) under USOM/Thailand and U.S. military support, which combined intelligence gathering and community development.[31]

According to the Congressional testimony on Thailand, the third focus of USAID counterinsurgency efforts was government services and administration.[32] This included AID projects to train officials of the Thai Department of Local Administration; training villagers in "rudimentary self–government" and project planning techniques; and projects in civil service improvement, public administration, and management.[33]

The Thai agency created to coordinate all civilian, police, and military counterinsurgency operations in Thailand was the Communist Suppression Operations Command (CSOC), formed in 1965.[34] CSOC, directed by a Thai military officer, linked together the activities of the Border Patrol

Police, Accelerated Rural Development programs, the Department of Community Development, Mobile Development Units, and other organizations. As part of its commitment to the struggle against communism, CSOC even distributed to rural residents 65,000 bars of anti–communist soap provided by the American psychological warfare unit (7th PsyOps) in Thailand. Eight different slogans were printed on the soap at different layers so that as one washed off, new messages would appear. The slogans included "To remain a Thai one must be anti–communist" and "The government of His Majesty the King sends its good wishes to all the Thai people."[35]

RESEARCH DIVISION OF USOM

Social science research techniques were well integrated into USOM/ Thailand activities through its Research Division, later renamed Research and Evaluation Division (RED). Toshio Yatsushiro, a cultural anthropologist with the RED, noted in 1966 that

the dominant or majority group (e.g., the administrator or change agent) must respect ... and at best must understand the customs and values of the subordinate or minority group (e.g., the administered or client).... [I]n any change program, the change agent, who is in a far better position to initiate action than the client, must...

a) utilize to the optimum degree the resources available in the client's cultural background towards advancing the aims of the concerned action program and the general welfare of the client.

b) seriously examine his own cultural background with a view towards identifying and properly controlling those cultural factors that may be operating as obstacles or barriers to the achievement of desired ends.[36]

The "desired ends" were "change programs" that were to serve as barriers to communism while, in many cases, benefiting Thai peasants.

For example, a report in the following year on village attitudes about rural security in Northeastern Thailand notes the success of a Mobile Development Unit (MDU) road building program.[37] The colonel commanding a local MDU program was able to get villagers to construct a twenty kilometer road because he convinced the local abbot that the construction could be considered a major Buddhist merit–making activity. Thus, the dominant change agent (the colonel) was able to convince the subordinate administered people (the villagers) to undertake an "action program" (road building) by using the client's cultural background (his need to make merit). According to the colonel, "The people were most cooperative because they were building a 'road to Heaven.'"[38]

According to the report on rural security in Northeast Thailand, RED conducted numerous studies using anthropological research methodology, including resident participant observation, in–depth, open–ended interviews, gathering economic data, and so on. In addition, field researchers also gathered "other pertinent background data" on villages,[39] as Table 5.1 indicates.

To summarize, all AID activities in Thailand during the period 1965 through 1970 were related to the counterinsurgency effort of the U.S. and Thai governments. Some of these programs, such as the digging of wells or malaria eradication, were only indirectly involved in the suppression of insurgency; others, such as providing weapons to the BPP, directly contributed to the counterinsurgency effort. Nevertheless, all programs were predicated on the need to defeat the insurgency first and to benefit the population second.

FORMATION OF SOUTHEAST ASIA DEVELOPMENT ADVISORY GROUP (SEADAG)

In 1965 the Far East Bureau of USAID and the Asia Society formed the Southeast Asia Development Advisory Group (SEADAG). The members of SEADAG were social scientists and development program executives from universities, private foundations, and government agencies, notably AID.[40] The 1966/67 SEADAG directory describes SEADAG's objective as follows:

> The essential purpose of SEADAG is to help foster intelligent, mutually acceptable development in Southeast Asia. Through its activities it seeks to develop a broadened and deepened research program in the social sciences, thus strengthening U.S. competence for aiding Southeast Asian development.[41]

TABLE 5.1: SELECTED PUBLICATIONS OF THE UNITED STATES OPERATIONS MISSION/THAILAND, RESEARCH DIVISION, 1966–1968[42]

TITLE	DATE
Current Research Projects in Thailand [a brief summary of *all* officially sponsored or approved research projects underway in Thailand by ARPA, Research Analysis Corporation, Stanford Research Institute, National Research Council of Thailand, USOM, Ministry of the Interior, and CD]	23 March 1966
Village Organization and Leadership in Northeast Thailand [Toshio Yatsushiro]	May 1966
Economic and Social Benefits of Roads in the North and Northeast	18 July 1966
Election of a Phuyaiban [village leader] in a Highly Security–Sensitive Village in the Northeast	August 1966
The Role of Cultural Factors in Worker–Client Relationships: A Two Way Process [Yatsushiro]	August 1966
The Northeastern Village: A Nonparticipatory Democracy [Stephen B. Young]*	September 1966
Village Attitudes and Conditions in Relation to Rural Security in Northeast Thailand [Yatsushiro]	May 1967
Khao Teung Prachachon or Reaching the People [Liang Jayakal, former Interior Minister]	August 1967
Local Indigenous Security Unit (Homeguard): Preliminary Tables; Preliminary Tables (Villagers); Preliminary Tables (Kamman and Phuyaiban [leader of group of villages and village leader])	16 Nov. 1967; 28 Nov. 1967; 8 Dec. 1967
An Evaluation of the Home Guard by Local Officials, Members of the Guard and Villagers	3 January 1968
The Home Guard, A General Summary	7 January 1968
Field Interviews with Amphoe, Tambon, and Muban [district, subdistrict, and village] Officials and Villagers about Local Administration and Local Problems in Changwat [Province] Udorn Thani	25 January 1968

TITLE	DATE
Security and Development in Thailand's Rural Areas [Charles F. Keyes, anthropologist (University of Washington)]	October 1968
Attitude Survey of Rural Northeast Thailand	October 1968

*Although Young's paper lists Bangkok as place of origin, discusses the effect of the political assumptions of villagers on Thai government and USOM programs, and was found with other USOM/Thailand publications, its title page does not specifically indicate whether or not it is a USOM/Thailand publication.

SEADAG activities were to advise AID on "specific aid plans, programs, and policy, and the relationship of scholarship to these"; to foster "the encouragement of research on development problems in Southeast Asia with programmatic implications"; and to provide an "information clearinghouse role" between its member institutions.[43]

SEADAG also held a series of seminars (under contract with USAID) that brought together representatives from AID, U.S. and foreign government agencies, the International Bank for Reconstruction and Development, the Rand Corporation, and academics. Topics included employment, labor strategies, rural and urban development, and the problems of development under insurgency.[44]

SEADAG members, probably with USAID prompting, proposed the creation of a specific academic group to function in an advisory role to an Asian AID mission. The Academic Advisory Council for Thailand (AACT) was formed in September 1966, and the AID mission chosen was Thailand.[45] This was about one year after professors Peter Gosling and Gayl Ness of the University of Michigan had traveled to Bangkok under AID sponsorship to determine the research needs of USOM/Thailand. Their report on the visit ("Suggestions on the Elaboration of a University Role in USOM") had also suggested the creation of a "secretariat" of Thai specialists to "provide liaison" among USOM/Thailand, SEADAG, universities, foundations, and others "specializing on Southeast Asia or working on development problems."[46] By 1968 U.S. concern with the Thai insurgency had become so acute that an amendment to the original contract that had created AACT in 1966 was drafted.

USAID CONTRACT WITH UCLA

The original function of AACT was similar to that of SEADAG. The USAID contract with UCLA was an agreement to make personnel available "to support and strengthen the operations of the U.S. aid program in Thailand," especially the operations of USOM/Thailand's Research Division.[47] In pursuit of this goal,

> AID has established the Academic Advisory Council for Thailand (AACT), composed of social scientists with background specialization in Thailand to provide coordination between the academic community of Thai scholars and AID.... [the] United States' competence to foster development in Thailand is strengthened by the intellectual integration of scholars in the social sciences professionally interested in Thailand's development....[48]

The 1968 amendment modified the original contract and specifically mandated UCLA to "provide support" for AACT "to insure its maximum contribution to accomplishment of the goals of the AID program in Thailand";[49] and for AACT to provide eight "services" to AID. The first and sixth services were:

> Identify research ... that may relate to developmental and counterinsurgency activities in Thailand; evaluate, index and make such research available to AID; suggest and solicit research proposals relevant to AID activity in Thailand....[50]

> Organize, coordinate and conduct meetings, seminars or conferences, under AACT auspices, dealing with development and counterinsurgency problems, issues and activities, including research, relating to AID operations in Thailand.[51]

Other services were to prepare a list of Thai scholars and their research interests; to meet requests for assistance with regard to AID and USOM/

Thailand research needs; to evaluate reports and proposed studies; to make recommendations concerning research plan and problems of USOM/ Thailand, Research Division; to collect and maintain a library; and to "[c]arry out such other functions as shall be mutually agreed upon by AID and the Contractor."[52] The provision of mandated services was discussed at meetings held by AACT several times a year.

AACT MEETINGS

Anthropologists Charles Keyes, Michael Moerman, and Lauriston Sharp were among the academic members of AACT (see Table 5.2). Sharp and Keyes attended AACT meetings with various AID and USOM/Thailand officials in 1968 and 1969, but Moerman did not. The minutes of four AACT meetings (October 1968, and January, June, and July 1969) reveal that the participants discussed research that could aid counterinsurgency efforts, working with ARPA and AID, subverting SEADAG, and other topics.

The AACT minutes—like the minutes for the 1967 Institute for Defense Analyses Thailand Study Group—are disputed by at least one participant. Lauriston Sharp has said that the minutes are incomplete, omitting what AACT members did not want AID to see.[53] David Wyatt agrees with Sharp, calling the AACT minutes "selective."[54] The reason for this selectivity is unclear since representatives from AID were present at all of the meetings.

At the first meeting of AACT (held at the State Department) following the September 1968 amendment to the AID–UCLA contract, general organizational and membership matters were discussed, such as the services AACT would provide to AID, maintenance of a liaison with SEADAG, and exploration of possible Ford and Rockefeller funding to support research.[55]

Two factors relating to counterinsurgency work were also discussed. The first concerned ARPA:

> The participants agreed that AACT should make an effort to obtain information on ARPA programs in Thailand in order to be of possible assistance in improving the quality of research activities.[56]

The second security-related topic concerned the arrangement of conferences:

TABLE 5.2: ACADEMIC ADVISORY COUNCIL FOR THAILAND (AACT) MEMBERS AND OTHERS IN ATTENDANCE AT AACT MEETINGS [57]

NAME	AFFILIATION	MEETINGS ATTENDED
William Bradley (AACT)	Rockefeller Foundation	none
L. A. Peter Gosling (AACT)	University of Michigan, geographer	October, June
James Hoath	USOM/Thailand, director of research	July
Charles Keyes (AACT)	University of Washington, anthropologist	January, June, July
Michael Moerman (AACT)	UCLA, anthropologist	none
Frank Moore (AACT)	Stanford University	January, July
Howard Parsons	USOM/T, director	January
Gordon Pierson	AID/Washington	October
Dalip Saund	——	July
Lauriston Sharp (AACT chairman)	Cornell University, anthropologist	all
William Siffin (AACT)	Indiana University	all
Frederick Simmons	AID/Southeast Asia	all
Robert Solomon	Rand Corporation, National Security Council	June
Louis Stamberg	AID/Southeast Asia	October, January
Paul Trescott (AACT)	Miami University, later Southern Methodist University	January, June, July
Fred von der Mehden (AACT)	Rice University	all

NAME	AFFILIATION	MEETINGS ATTENDED
David A. Wilson* (AACT)	UCLA political scientist	all
David Wyatt (AACT)	University of Michigan, later Cornell, historian	January, June

*October 1968: "research coordinator"; January 1969: "coordinator/secretary"; June 1969: "executive secretary."

In discussing topics for conferences to be organized under AACT auspices, it was agreed that the subject of local authority in Thailand, including the implications for village security, should be first priority and that additional conferences should be held on innovation and diffusion in Thai society and, thirdly, on land tenure problems, including land as an incentive and land tenure as related to security.[58]

At the next AACT meeting (January 1969 at UCLA), David Wilson reported on his field trip to Thailand, discussed proposed AACT functions, and described AACT as "a packager of knowledge."[59] The January minutes do not state whom Wilson saw in Thailand in 1968, but a document of an AACT trip in November 1969 lists all persons contacted on that trip.[60] They include the American and Japanese ambassadors, U.S. Special Assistant for Counterinsurgency George Tanham, fifteen members of the USOM/Thailand office (including Director Rey Hill) and Office of Public Safety advisor Batson, the Thai minister of foreign affairs, representatives of the Thai Ministry of the Interior, Accelerated Rural Development Program, and others, three ARPA employees (including anthropologist Robert Kickert, coauthor of the *Village Security Study*, and Philip Worchel), and representatives from the Rockefeller, Ford, and Asia Foundations.

Topics of discussion at the January UCLA meeting included the relationship between AACT, AID, and USOM/Thailand and AID objectives in Thailand (among which "security" was of primary importance):

Fred Simmons reiterated AID/USOM program priorities in Thailand as

1) Strengthening civil security at the village level, principally through aid to the Thai National Police Department;

2) Accelerated rural development;

3) Coordination of RTG [Royal Thai Government] programs through the Northeast Economic Development (NEED) process and the Northeast Regional Development Committee.

Howard Parsons [director of USOM/Thailand] summed up the essential mission in Thailand as political development.[61]

Progress was made on arranging conferences, and Wilson and USOM/Thailand Director of Research James Hoath agreed on four conference topics—local authority, education, land tenure, and private investment.[62]

The first conference was titled "Local Authority and Administration in Thailand" and took place from July 24-27, 1969 at UCLA. Its objective was "to determine how USOM could most effectively use its capacities and protect its resources flowing into rural Thailand."[63] Members of the planning subcommittee were Keyes, Moerman, Siffin, and von der Mehden (chairman).[64] Many AACT members came to this conference, along with representatives from AID, USOM/Thailand, and the Thai Ministry of the Interior and Department of Local Administration.[65] A collection of conference papers edited by von der Mehden and Wilson was published under the conference title, as "Report No. 1—1970 for the United States Operations Mission/Thailand."[66]

The published conference volume included a bibliography on local government, assembled by Siffin and Keyes. Entries in the bibliography are divided by topics, including:

Local Developmental Problems and Programs;
Village Security: Perspectives, Problems, Programs; and
Studies Dealing with Aspects of Social Change.[67]

Despite the obvious distinctions between these three topics, Siffin and Keyes assert that the sources arranged under the heading Village Security are "only partially distinguishable" from those under Local Development; and that the distinction between those under Social Change and others under Village Security is "arbitrary and somewhat thin—a matter of convenience."[68] Surely all of the works available about social change or development were not about security issues. But the conceptualization of the U.S. government and AID was that issues of security, development, and social change were inseparable. This position was mirrored in the bibliographic arrangement of Siffin and Keyes.

The next meeting of AACT (June 10-11, 1969 at Cornell) included the participation of the director of research of USOM/Thailand James Hoath and a member of the Rand Corporation and the National Security Council. Three major discussions took place at this meeting: AACT members decided they were merely USAID advisors and not representatives of the larger group of Thailand scholars; AACT members decided to create a conference on Northern Thailand to bring together social science information for AID; and members talked of ensuring that AACT would control the dispersal of SEADAG research funds through the insertion of AACT chairman Lauriston Sharp onto the board of SEADAG.

The June 1969 meeting began with von der Mehden reporting on his trip to Thailand and presenting information about the Research Division of USOM, the Thai National Research Council, and ARPA research cutbacks.[69] A discussion of the three decisions followed.

First, AACT members openly described their role as follows:

In regard to the community of Thai scholars, it was agreed that AACT should abandon its pretensions to be representative of that group. It should accept its role as basically a consultative body to AID.[70]

Second, members discussed the possibility of holding a conference in conjunction with the panel on "Regional Integration in Northern Thailand" that was to be held at the annual meeting of the Association for Asian Studies in April 1970.[71] The Regional Integration panel was chaired by

Peter Kunstadter; Wilson and Gertrude Marlowe (American University) were discussants; and Moerman, Keyes, Kunstadter, and David Marlowe (Walter Reed Army Institute of Research) presented papers.[72] The purpose of the conference, AACT members suggested, would be to gather data of interest to AID, not to evaluate USOM projects:

> It was agreed that the enormous amount of social science research in North Thailand was potentially of value to the USOM and that AACT should participate in an effort to realize this value. Such an effort on the part of AACT would be to contribute to a better understanding of the character of the northern part of Thailand. It would not be concerned with the development of programs or projects for USOM in that part of the country.[73]

Finally, AACT members suggested a semi-takeover of SEADAG to improve the way it was conducting business:

> In regard to SEADAG there was considerable discontent expressed regarding the organization, development, and particularly the management of the SEADAG grant during the past year. It was agreed that AACT should seek a more active role in the granting of funds for research in Thailand through SEADAG next year. As a first step toward this it was agreed that we should seek to have Professor Lauriston Sharp appointed a member of the SEADAG Executive Committee. In addition to that it was agreed that AACT should seek a role in the screening of grants and the establishment of areas of priority research to be funded through SEADAG in Thailand.[74]

The AACT discussion about SEADAG mirrors a similar one that took place at the IDA's Thailand Study Group in July 1967. From the discussion in the Thailand Study Group minutes, it appears that before the 1968 amendment that spelled out the AACT role as an advisor to AID, several social scientists found it to be a less than satisfactory organization:

> [Herbert Phillips:] A SS [social science] Jason would be different from SEADAG and AACT in that it would have:

1) more continuity;
2) more frank exchange of views;
3) more internally generated studies.

[Michael Moerman:] Don't lump SEADAG and AACT together. AACT is a better analogy to the proposed SS Jason.

You can in a SS Jason, talk to more than one agency, other SSs and avoid the shortcomings of academic administration.

[Lauriston Sharp:] AACT could serve agencies other than AID.

[Moerman:] ARPA could co–opt AACT for its Thailand activities.[75]

When Moerman stated that AACT was an analogy to a "SS Jason," he was suggesting that it could function in an advisory capacity to various government groups about security, counterinsurgency, and other issues of interest to the Defense Department. If ARPA co–opted AACT, as Moerman suggested, the result would be a certain collusion between the Defense Department's research arm and a group of external social scientists. Although AACT, in its capacity as an advisory group to AID, was already advising the U.S. government on counterinsurgency programs and policy, such a collusion would erase any independence that its academic members still had. The suggestion that Sharp be appointed to the executive board of SEADAG in an effort to control research funding is even more disturbing in light of the IDA discussion. It must have been a disappointment to the U.S. government that SEADAG was not performing adequately, because according to AID's Curtis Farrar, it was to have "influence[d] academic open research by showing them the government's problems and data."[76]

At the final AACT meeting for which minutes are available (July at UCLA), James Hoath, Director of the Research and Evaluation Division (RED) of USOM/Thailand, was present. It was agreed that "AACT must relate as closely as possible to operations divisions of USOM in order to help identify emerging research problems."[77] In pursuit of this goal, Sharp later suggested in a letter to USOM/Thailand director Rey Hill that a system be developed through which AACT members could work at USOM/Thailand for a length of time equivalent to an academic leave.[78]

The functions of RED were also discussed, including its liaison activities with ARPA and having graduate students come to work under

RED sponsorship in Thailand. The minutes note that "RED has already used graduate students (Clark Neher [now of Northern Illinois University]) in Thailand for ongoing projects."[79] In an interview, Neher said he worked as a graduate assistant for AACT while in the department of political science at UCLA, doing mostly "bibliographic work" for Moerman and Wilson. While in Thailand, Neher asserts, he did nothing for AACT, and was "never involved in any counterinsurgency activities."[80] Whether or not Neher knew it, any research he might have done could have been used by AID as an aid to its counterinsurgency program. This is a dilemma that all social scientists face in gathering research data—how will their research data be used.

Michael Moerman devoted a large portion of his 1971 letter to the *AAA Newsletter* discussing the time he spent with AID and AACT. He wrote that he worked as a "consultant on Thai development to AID" from 1964 to May 1970 (with no consulting in 1968, one day in 1969, and two days in 1970).[81] Like Phillips and Sharp, Moerman stated that one of his reasons for consulting was to help Thai villagers by advising the U.S. government.

> My field work in Thailand (1959–61) had strengthened my conviction that US functionaries had an active ignorance of Thai culture which was amusing and appalling. Living in a small Thai village for fourteen months, I had come to identify with peasant prejudice against government officials. It seemed clear that the US and Thai governments would harm villagers less if they knew more about them.[82]

Moerman wrote that during his tenure as a consultant, his emphasis was to

> ... eliminate military support, drop the counterinsurgency rationale for development activities, cease concentrating on Northeast Thailand, consider national and urban problems, and not just rural ones, incorporate Thai—especially unofficial Thai—in program planning, shift from bilateral to multilateral aid, and incorporate research and evaluation into program planning and implementations.[83]

Finally, Moerman wrote that he eventually resigned from both groups because his ideas were not listened to and because of what he had heard at the 1967 IDA Thailand Study Group. In spite of Moerman's good intentions, his experience with AID confirmed the reality that U.S. government motives were incompatible with his own.

RESEARCH PROJECTS OF AACT MEMBERS

Members of AACT served as consultants to USAID both as a group and individually;[84] they also received funding from other government sources. According to a 1969 letter from an Acting Administrator for AID, five of AACT's twelve members were engaged in research involving Thailand, sponsored by government agencies other than AID. They were:

L. A. Peter Gosling, sponsored by the Office of Naval Research to do a study on transportation development in the Thai central plains;

Fred von der Mehden, sponsored by ARPA to study the relation of social and economic factors to organized rural violence in Southeast Asia;

Charles Keyes, sponsored by the National Science Foundation to study relationships between the Thai and the hilltribes in northwestern Thailand;

David Wilson and Michael Moerman, sponsored by the National Science Foundation to study "integration of a complex society" focused on the "integration of peasant society into Thai national life."[85]

Any one of the above projects could have been applied to the design of counterinsurgency policy in Thailand, although there is no proof that they were used as such. Certainly, the von der Mehden study was sponsored by ARPA because of its potential use to the Defense Department. The studies by Keyes/Wilson and Moerman could have contributed to an understanding of how best to bring minority groups in insurgent areas under government control. Finally, the Gosling study had the potential to be used in the establishment of transportation networks for both commerce and military mobility.

Research conducted by the Research and Evaluation Division of USOM/Thailand could serve the dual function of ascertaining how rural security programs were working, by measuring villager attitudes, while at the same time identifying "insecure" areas and villagers of questionable loyalty. The methods of the Census Aspiration Teams used in Vietnam and then Thailand were decidedly simple. Census takers would tell villagers that they were there to find out about village needs; while doing so, they would elicit how villagers felt about the government and the communists; and later they would report certain respondents as security risks or communist sympathizers. The questions asked by USOM/Thailand research teams and by Census Aspiration Teams must not have been very different, as demonstrated in the example that follows. Furthermore, it is unlikely that villagers were able to distinguish between the various government agencies that conducted surveys.

Von der Mehden assisted in an October 1966–May 1967 USOM/ Thailand survey of 1200 villagers in three insurgent–plagued provinces, including Sakorn Nakorn and Mahasarakam in the Northeastern region. [86] The purpose of the survey was to measure the impact of USOM/Thailand and Thai government projects on the "attitudes, behavior, and welfare" of villagers. [87] Findings were presented in such categories as "National Loyalty"; "Attitudes towards the CTs [communist terrorists], the Government's Suppressive Efforts, and Village Defense"; and "Village Needs and Problems." [88] These and other questions on the impact of programs are not benign. A transcript of a February 1967 meeting between villagers in Mahasarakam province and USOM/Thailand Research Division member Toshio Yatsushiro (who assisted in the von der Mehden survey) demonstrates the degree to which villagers feared and were unclear of the intentions of surveyors. [89]

> [villager:] What is your purpose in coming here, and what kinds of questions are you going to ask us?
>
> [interviewer:] We came here to study how people feel towards certain things, what people think about certain things; and we also want to study the effectiveness of certain development programs.
>
> [villager:] I mean, tonight, what do you want to ask us about tonight? You are not going to take the names of villagers and tell the police that we are communists, are you? We would die, if you did....
>
> [villager:] The reason that I ask you about communists is that I really want to know the reason why your research team is here, in

our village. We are very much afraid of communists here; we don't
know what they look like because we have never seen them. So
many people have cautioned us about them. We have heard that,
elsewhere, they send their agents in to recruit villagers, and
sometimes they come in helicopters, to take away those whom
they have recruited. If they come to take us away, in that manner,
it will surely kill us, because we are opposed to communists here.
All of us are Buddhist devotees, and are of unshakable Buddhist
faith.

[interviewer:] (explains to Dr. TY [Toshio Yatsushiro].) He says
that he doesn't even know what communists are; he has only heard
about them and what they do.

[Yatsushiro:] If you don't know about communists, why are you
afraid of them?[90]

Yatsushiro's interview questions scared the above villager because of the
many Thai and U.S.–funded research projects in Northeast Thailand that
were being used to identify villages at risk to communist subversion. The
above conversation was part of a set of forty-five reports prepared by
Yatsushiro from "intensive village studies focussed on rural security and
related conditions," which included interviews with a "communist terrorist"
and "communist sympathizers" and an account of a "brain washing meeting"
led by "a band of communist terrorists."[91]
   But even while in the employ of USAID, Yatsushiro was still willing
to use his reports to criticize the overemphasis on military countermeasures.
In a May 1966 report on village organization and leadership, he wrote:

Given the present political situation in the Northeast, threatened as
it is with communist subversion and insurgency, the thinking
concerning this problem tends too easily to overemphasize
politico–military counter–measures....[92]

Yatsushiro went on to advocate meeting the people's basic needs through
such grass-roots means as local self–determination, involving villagers in
village development, and utilizing local resources (points that Moerman said
he, too, advocated). Yatsushiro pointedly excluded military and police
strategies from his consideration; he said that the situation required "a careful

reappraisal of the entire development efforts of both the Governments of Thailand and the United States."[93]

The views of other members of the USOM/Thailand team are unknown, and the USOM/Thailand policy on the collection of data is unclear. If surveys were conducted anonymously and the data was not circulated to security agencies, then villagers were safe. However, if the survey found that village attitudes toward the government indicated that a region was not secure, then USOM and Thai government programs such as extensive police and paramilitary operations, could be increased. Thus, information about the people studied could be used against them.

It is impossible to establish a causal link between a particular USOM/ Thailand survey or paper and the activities of the Thai military or government, or to establish to what degree the Thai military took into account survey information. For example, according to one USOM Research Division study of seventeen Northeastern villages in Sakon Nakorn and Mahasarakham provinces, "the people ... would like to see the Government employ military aircraft to bomb jungle hideouts of the CTs [communist terrorists]."[94] In another survey covering 40 percent of the population of the entire Northeast, villagers were asked "What should the government do about the communists?" Sixty-seven percent of the respondents said "catch them or drive them out," and 13 percent said "kill them."[95]

Contrast the responses of villagers with the cautious words of Yatsushiro, above, on meeting the people's basic needs, or with University of Washington anthropologist Charles Keyes, who wrote in a paper for USOM/Thailand that the grievances of the peasantry (excluding certain ethnic minorities) do not constitute the basis for a mass–based revolutionary movement. To counter "terrorism" with development projects would be "absurd," Keyes wrote; he suggested, instead, offering villagers better protection and programs that would improve relations between peasants and officials.[96]

The consequences of the counterinsurgency efforts of the U.S. and Thai governments were demonstrably worse for those at the periphery of Thai government control. These included the "hilltribes" of the North and (to a lesser degree) the Northeast and many villagers, including ethnic Vietnamese and Khmer, of the Northeast. The hilltribes were pointedly excluded by Keyes when he wrote that Thai peasantry would not form the basis for an insurgency. Alfred McCoy gives the following account of counterinsurgency efforts against a group of Hmong villagers near Lom Sak in Northeast

Thailand.[97] A group of Hmong who had previously lived to the north of what the government considered a strategically important road migrated to the south of the road due to population pressure and the need for more farming land. From July to August 1967, the Thai government conducted detailed surveys of the new Hmong villages and then decided it did not want "potential" insurgents on both sides of the road. In early 1968, the Border Patrol Police forced the Hmong to move to less fertile land to the north of the road. In the process, promised relief supplies for the Hmong never materialized, and by late 1968 the Hmong were forced to steal food rather than starve. The BPP responded; the Hmong retaliated; and the Thai government accused the Hmong of being trained and armed by Vietnam and China. A full–scale rebellion developed in the region, which the Thai government was not able to put down until the Third Army deployed troops and helicopters and finally resorted to heavy bombing and napalm in early 1969.

In this account, it is clear that fear of communism caused the Thai government to grossly overreact to a local problem and to see it in terms of the international struggle with communism. As McCoy notes, the research techniques refined by ARPA, AIR, and AID, road building by ARD, training of the BPP and Thai military, and U.S. armaments came together against the Hmong. Social scientists must continually be aware of this potential use of applied research.

AACT members were aware of their relationship to USOM programs. As the von der Mehden/Wilson volume states:

> AACT is unique in that it is directly related to an operating Mission and therefore brings the academic people into direct contact with the programs and planning of foreign assistance. This unique character has its counterpart in a division for research and evaluation in the Thailand Mission that is designed to provide research support to programming activities.[98]

To bring social scientists "into direct contact with the programs" of USOM/Thailand was not always a positive factor for Thai villagers, although it certainly helped USOM in implementing counterinsurgency policy.

NOTES

[1] AID, "Amendment No. 3 to the Contract Between the United States of America and the Regents of the University of California" (1 September 1968 [mimeograph]), 4. The original contract was AID/fe–267 enacted on 6 September 1966.

[2] Ibid., 2.

[3] Tanham, *Trial in Thailand*, 72–73.

[4] AID, *Project Budget Submission Thailand FY [Fiscal Year] 1970* (n.p.: Department of State, September 1968), 22; David E. Lockwood, "The U.S. Aid Program in Asia," *Current History* 49:291 (November 1965), 258–259; Alvin Roseman, "Thailand, Laos and Cambodia: A Decade of Aid," *Current History* 49:291 (November 1965), 274.

[5] Cf.: Peter F. Bell, "Thailand's Northeast: Regional Underdevelopment, 'Insurgency,' and Official Response," *Pacific Affairs*, 42:1 (Spring 1969), 52–53:

> ... the essential fact about this counterinsurgency effort is that it is a "mending the dikes" type operation, namely a post–hoc response of a political nature to a complex phenomenon of regional disaffection, isolation, regional underdevelopment, and outside influences (spill–over effects from the Laotian and Vietnamese conflicts). More important, the counterinsurgency philosophy as currently practiced by the United States with the help of the academic community and research corporations is based on concealed assumptions regarding human behavior. This is perhaps best understood in terms of the following relation: a given political–military objective is to stabilize an area (protect it from never clearly defined "external subversion"); to this end a battery of academic investigators is called on to make elaborate researches into village loyalty patterns and socioeconomic needs with a view to manipulating the desired direction of stabilization.

[6] USOM, "U.S. Aid to Thailand—U.S. Objectives," n.d. (circa 1965), quoted in Randolph, *United States and Thailand,* 96.

[7] Lobe, Thomas, *United States National Security Policy and Aid to the Thailand Police* (Denver: University of Denver, 1977), 48. Lobe supports the conclusion that "all AID projects were selected or rejected on the basis of assisting the Thais in defeating the guerrillas" by interviews with more than eight officials, including the director and deputy director of USOM/Thailand, Special Assistant for Counterinsurgency Tanham, the chief Thai resident for the Rand Corporation, the director of the Thailand office of the Stanford Research Institute, and others. See also USOM/ Program Office, "USOM Thailand Program Goals and Projects" (26 November 1965), quoted in Randolph, *United States and Thailand,* 96; preface to United States Operations Mission Thailand, *Thai–American Economic and Technical Cooperation* ([Bangkok:] USOM/Thailand, March 1965).

[8] Testimony of Robert H. Nooter, Acting Assistant AID Administrator for East Asia, and Frederick Simmons, Director, Office of Southeast Asia Affairs, Southeast Asia Bureau (U.S. Congress. Committee on Government Operations. Foreign Operations and Government Information Subcommittee, *Hearing on Thailand and the Philippines* [John E. Moss, chairman], 16 June 1969 [mimeograph], 3).

[9] AID, *Budget Submission Thailand 1970*, passim.

[10] Ibid., 83.

[11] Lobe, *U.S. Aid to the Thailand Police,* 33–62.

There were turf battles of sorts fought by various U.S. agencies in Thailand, as Lobe makes clear. The same type of agency conflicts were probably in evidence in Laos, where a similar program of "village assistance properly backed by the military and civil authorities" was also taking place. Colonel John T. Little, commander of the U.S. Special Forces White Star Teams in Laos, wrote on civil assistance in 1961, apparently addressing his men:

> You are not in competition with other U.S. agencies; USIS and USOM; you are the spearhead and a focal point for the injection of these activities until Laos civil assistance teams are trained and in use (William P. Yarborough, (LTG, Ret.), "Civil Assistance in Laos" in *Psychological Operations,* Department of the Army, 458).

The USOM operation in Laos was also used to cover CIA aid to forces opposed to the communist Pathet Lao, much like the USOM/Thailand police training program under which CIA operatives worked with the Thai

Border Patrol Police (Judith F. Buncher, ed., *The CIA & the Security Debate: 1971–1975* [New York: Facts on File, 1976], 100).

12 U.S. Congress, *Hearing on Thailand and the Philippines,* 3.

13 Lobe, *U.S. Aid to the Thailand Police,* 3.

14 Ibid., 49, 55.

15 Randolph, *United States and Thailand,* 99.

16 Lobe, *U.S. Aid to the Thailand Police,* 23–24 and passim, for continued CIA involvement with the BPP. Randolph, *The United States and Thailand,* 97–99, cites a number of USOM documents on the Thai police, particularly the BPP, including: "A Brief History of USOM Support to the Thai National Police Department," August 1969; "The Border Patrol Police: Concept of Operations," undated (mimeograph); "Border Patrol Police: Remote Security Development Program," undated (mimeograph); and "Border Patrol Police: Remote Area Security Development Program," September 1966 (mimeograph). See also New York Times, *The Pentagon Papers,* 133–134, in which counterinsurgency legend Edward Lansdale discusses "unconventional warfare resources in Southeast Asia."

17 AID, *Budget Submission Thailand 1970,* 18.

18 Herbert Phillips and D. A. Wilson, *Certain Effects of Culture and Social Organization on Internal Security in Thailand* (Santa Monica, California: Rand Corporation, June 1964).

19 Phillips and Wilson, *Internal Security in Thailand,* iii.

20 Ibid., 37–38.

21 Lobe, *United States Aid to the Thailand Police,* 67. See, for example, [Thai] Department of Police, Department of Local Administration (DOLA), and Communist Suppression Operations Command (CSOC), *Evaluation Report: VSO (Village Security Officer] Training Project* ([Bangkok:] n.p., n.d. [post–July 1967 seems likely]).

22 Phillips, *Between the Tiger and the Crocodile,* 25 (note 9).

23 AID, *Budget Submission Thailand 1970,* 22–23; Blaufarb, *Counter-insurgency Doctrine,* 199; Lobe, *U.S. Aid to the Thailand Police,* 67–70; Tanham, *Trial in Thailand,* 136–137.

24 See the following works by Americas Watch (a division of Human Rights Watch), New York: *Civil Patrols in Guatemala,* August 1986, passim; *Closing the Space: Human Rights in Guatemala During President Cerezo's First Year,* February 1987, 41, 46, 75–79; *Messengers of Death: Human Rights in Guatemala,* March 1990, 67–71; *The Civilian Toll 1986–1987 (Ninth Supplement to the Report on Human Rights in El Salvador),* 30 August 1987, 118–121; *Human Rights in Honduras: Central America's "Sideshow,"* May 1987, 90–91: *A Certain Passivity: Failing to Curb Human Rights Abuses in Peru,* December 1987, 8; and *Tolerating Abuses: Violations of Human Rights in Peru,* October 1988, 48.

25 Phillips, *Between the Tiger and the Crocodile,* 38 (note 13).

26 Prime Minister Thanom Kittikachorn, Speech on "The Need for an Acceleration of Rural Development in Areas Threatened by Infiltrations," 9 February 1965, reproduced as Attachment C of USOM/Thailand, *Evaluation Report: Joint Thai–USOM Evaluation of the Accelerated Rural Development Project* (Bangkok: [USOM/Thailand], 30 May 1965), 2. Cf: U.S. Congress, *Hearing on Thailand and the Philippines,* 4–5:

> ... our basic objective in the area of rural development is to assist the Thai government in increasing its capacity to respond to local needs, particularly in rural areas threatened by insurgency.

27 USOM, "U.S. Aid to Thailand—U.S. Objectives (Accelerated Rural Development Program)," undated (circa 1965–66), quoted in Randolph, *United States and Thailand,* 102. The same goals are given for the Community Development program in AID, *Budget Submission Thailand 1970,* 42.

28 "A Joint Accelerated Rural Development Office and PERM Team Effort: Some Planning Challenges for ARD," I.S. No. 5 (Bangkok: Office of the Prime Minister, May 1972), 1–2, quoted in Randolph, *United States and Thailand,* 102.

29 AID, *Budget Submission Thailand 1970,* 31.

[30] USOM/Thailand, Evaluation Report: *Second Joint Thai–USOM Evaluation of the Accelerated Rural Development Project,* 2 vols. (Bangkok: [USOM/Thailand] July 1966), 3.

[31] For further information on security development projects, see AID, *Budget Submission Thailand 1970*, 29–47; Lee W. Huff, "The Thai Mobile Development Unit Program" in *Southeast Asian Tribes, Minorities, and Nations*, ed. Peter Kunstadter (Princeton: Princeton University Press, 1967), vol. 1, 425–486; Randolph, *United States and Thailand*, 102–106; Orlin J. Scoville and James J. Dalton, "Rural Development in Thailand: The ARD Program," *Journal of Developing Areas* 9 (October 1974), 53–68; USOM/Thailand, Evaluation Report: *Joint Thai–USOM Evaluation of the Accelerated Rural Development Project;* USOM/Thailand, *Evaluation Report: Second Joint Thai–USOM Evaluation of the Accelerated Rural Development Project;* USOM/Thailand, *Impact of USOM–Supported Programs in Changwad Sakon Nakorn* ([Bangkok:] Research Division, USOM/Thailand, 22 May 1967); and Tanham, *Trial in Thailand*, 73–75.

[32] U.S. Congress, *Hearing on Thailand and the Philippines*, 6.

[33] See descriptions of projects in AID, *Budget Submission Thailand 1970*, 155–174.

[34] Kanok, *Thai Counterinsurgency Policy*, 5; Randolph, *United States and Thailand*, 119–120; Tanham, *Trial in Thailand*, 51.

[35] *Bangkok (Thailand) Post*, "10,000 Share Soap Secrets," 24 August 1970; "Will the Message Wash Off?" 28 August 1970.

[36] Research Division/USOM [Toshio Yatsushiro], "The Role of Cultural Factors in Worker–Client Relationship: A Two–Way Process" (Bangkok: USOM/Thailand, August 1966), 1.

[37] USOM/Research Division [Toshio Yatsushiro, study coordinator], "Advanced Overall Summary (Revised): Village Attitudes and Conditions in Relation to Rural Security in Northeast Thailand, An Intensive Resident Study of 17 Villages in Sakon Nakorn and Mahasarakham Provinces" (Bangkok: USOM/Thailand, May 1967), 10–11.

[38] Ibid., 11.

[39] Ibid., 5.

[40] Southeast Asia Development Advisory Group, *Directory 1966/67* ([New York:] The Asia Society, circa 1966–67) (mimeograph), 5.

[41] Ibid.

[42] This is not an exhaustive list of publications, but gives the flavor of the broad range of research in which the Research Division of USOM/Thailand was engaged. I am indebted to Professor Delmos Jones of the City University of New York, Graduate Center, for providing me with copies of the documents listed.

[43] Ibid., 7.

[44] Ibid., 6. For later examples of SEADAG seminars see the following reports: SEADAG, *Ad–Hoc Seminar on Employment* (New York: Asia Society, 1972); *Ad–Hoc Seminar on Labor Strategies* (1973); *Tenth Panel Seminar on Southeast Asian Development Goals—1980* (1973); *Ad–Hoc Seminar on Communist Movements and Regimes in Indochina* (1974); and *Ad–Hoc Seminar on Development and Finance of Local Government in Thailand* (1976).

[45] SEADAG, *Directory 1966/67*, 6; Rutherford W. Poats, letter to [Senator] J.W. Fulbright, n.d. [first page missing].

[46] "Suggestions on the Elaboration of a University Role in USOM," 30 August 1965 (mimeograph), quoted in Klare, *War Without End*, 85.

[47] AID, "Amendment to the Contract," 2.

[48] Ibid., 1.

[49] Ibid., 2.

[50] Ibid., 3.

[51] Ibid., 4.

[52] Ibid.

---

53 Lauriston Sharp, telephone interview with author, 29 April 1991.

54 David Wyatt, telephone interview with author, 24 April 1991.

55 AACT, "Meeting of the AACT," 19 October 1968, 1–2.

56 Ibid., 3.

57 Biographical information on participants from: Academic Advisory Council for Thailand, "Meeting of the Academic Advisory Council for Thailand," 19 October 1968; 24–25 January, 10–11 June, and 23–24 July 1969; and Fred von der Mehden and David A. Wilson, eds., *Local Authority and Administration in Thailand* (Report No. 1) (Los Angeles: United States Operations Mission/Thailand–Academic Advisory Council for Thailand, 1970), reverse of cover.

58 AACT, "Meeting of the AACT," 19 October 1968, 3.

59 Ibid., 24–25 January 1969, 2.

60 AACT, "People Seen on AACT Trip," November 10 to December 22 1970. The date "1970" is crossed out on the document and replaced with "1969?" It is most likely that the revision is correct and that Wilson's trip took place in 1969 and not 1970.

61 AACT, "Meeting of the AACT," 24–25 January 1969, 1.

62 Ibid., 3.

63 Von der Mehden and Wilson, *Local Authority and Administration in Thailand*, iii–iv.

64 AACT, "AACT Subcommittees," attachment to "Meeting of the AACT," 24–25 January 1969.

65 Von der Mehden and Wilson, *Local Authority and Administration in Thailand*, iv–v.

66 Ibid., iii–v.

[67] W. J. Siffin and Charles F. Keyes, "Concerning Local Government in Thailand: A Brief Selective Biography of Materials," in *Local Authority and Administration in Thailand,* ed. von der Mehden and Wilson, 183–191.

[68] Ibid., 187, 189. This distinction, or lack thereof, was first noted by Wolf and Jorgensen, "Anthropology on the Warpath."

[69] AACT, "Meeting of the AACT," 10–11 June 1969, 2–3.

[70] Ibid., 8. Cf., in 1970, von der Mehden and Keyes, *Local Authority in and Administration in Thailand,* reverse of cover:

> The Academic Advisory Council for Thailand (AACT) was established to provide the Mission of the Agency of International Development in Thailand with a permanent and regular source of advice from the academic community of the United States.

[71] AACT, "Meeting of the AACT," 10–11 June 1969, 6.

[72] Association for Asian Studies, "Program of the Twenty Second Annual Meeting" (n.p.: 1970), 21.

[73] AACT, "Meeting of the AACT," 10–11 June 1969, 6–7.

[74] Ibid., 8.

[75] IDA, "Thailand Study Group," 5 July 1967, 2.

[76] Ibid., 3 July 1967, 3.

[77] AACT, "Meeting of the AACT," 23–24 July 1969, 6.

[78] Sharp, Memorandum to Rey Hill, et. al., 18 March 1970.

[79] AACT, "Meeting of the AACT," 23–24 July 1969, 4.

[80] Clark Neher, telephone interview with author, 24 April 1991.

[81] Michael Moerman, letter to the editor, *AAA Newsletter* 12:1 (January 1971), 9–11.

[82] Ibid.

[83] Ibid.

[84] Poats, letter to Fulbright.

[85] Ibid.

[86] USOM/Thailand, Research Division, *Impact of USOM–Supported Programs in Changwad [province] Sakorn Nakorn* ([Bangkok:] USOM/Thailand, 22 May 1967).

[87] Ibid., 2.

[88] Ibid., 93.

[89] USOM/Thailand, Research Division, *Village Changes and Problems: Meeting with Village Leaders and Residents of Ban Don–Du, Tambon Khwao, Amphur Muang, Mahasarakam Province, February 10, 1967* (Bangkok: USOM/Thailand, Research Division, July 1967).

[90] Ibid., 5–6.

[91] Yatsushiro, Memorandum titled "Reports Resulting from Intensive Village Studies Focussed on Rural Security and Related Conditions," n.d. [after February 1967 is most likely]. According to this memorandum, Yatsushiro and ten Thai assistants produced forty-five reports, including a summary on "Village Attitudes and Conditions in Relation to Rural Security in Northeast Thailand"; seventeen analytic "Village Summary" reports; twenty raw data "Village Meeting" reports (including the one from which the frightened villager's comments are excerpted); a three–part interview with "A CT [communist terrorist] Who Surrendered"; "A Group Interview with Nine Village Communist Sympathizers"; "A First–Hand Account of a 'Brain Washing' Village Meeting Called by a Band of Communist Terrorists"; and "Some Pertinent Village Attitudes in Northeast Thailand." A report by "D. Mitchell" titled "Background Data on Six Communist Terrorists Who Surrendered" was appended to the forty-five Yatsushiro reports.

[92] Yatsushiro [Research Division USOM/Thailand], *Village Organization and Leadership in Northeast Thailand: A Study of the Villagers' Approach to*

Their Problems and Needs (Bangkok: n.p. [Department of Community Development and USOM/Thailand], May 1966), 118.

93 Ibid., 119–120, 136.

94 USOM/Thailand Research Division [Yatsushiro], "Advanced Overall Summary (Revised): Rural Security in Northeast Thailand," 8.

95 USOM/Thailand, Research Division, "Attitude Survey of Rural Northeast Thailand" ([Bangkok:] USOM/T, [October] 1968), 88. Page seven of the study states:

> The Royal Thai Government with USOM support is actively engaged in programs to raise the living standards and to strengthen the economic base of Northeast Thailand. The programs are intended both to ends in themselves and to serve as a bulwark against communism. To evaluate the success of these programs to date and to discern the direction of future inputs into the Northeast were among the principal concerns of this study.

96 Charles F. Keyes, "Security and Development in Thailand's Rural Areas" (Bangkok: USOM/Thailand, October 1968), 3, 11–12.

97 Alfred W. McCoy, "Subcontracting Counterinsurgency," *Bulletin of Concerned Asian Scholars* (Special Issue: Vietnam Center at S.I.U. [Southern Illinois University], December 1970), 56–70. The following account is from this source.

98 von der Mehden and Wilson, *Local Authority in Thailand*, reverse of cover.

CHAPTER SIX

AAA INVESTIGATION

Is one's primary loyalty to the truth, to one's own integrity, to the Thai people, to one's profession and colleagues, to one's nation, to one's political beliefs? I do feel that the establishment of such priorities is essentially one's own moral business, not something to be established by some external moral authority (an Ethics Committee?) to be imposed on anybody.

—Herbert Phillips, letter to Eric Wolf, April 1970

It is clear that anthropologists now have to face the possibility that a publication of routine socio-cultural data about identified village communities ... might be used for the annihilation by bombing or other forms of warfare of whole communities....

—Report of the Ad Hoc Committee to Evaluate the Controversy Concerning Anthropological Activities in Thailand [the Mead Committee], September 1971

The Student Mobilization Committee to End the War in Vietnam sent copies of the primary documents of the Thailand Controversy to Eric Wolf and Joseph Jorgensen, members of the Ethics Committee of the American Anthropological Association, before publishing them in the *Student Mobilizer*. Wolf and Jorgensen immediately issued a public statement condemning the actions of colleagues whose professional expertise was being harnessed to the U.S. counterinsurgency effort in Southeast Asia. Their public condemnation caused an internecine controversy in the anthropological community. Some members of the AAA, a professional body that had only recently created an Ethics Committee, and those who saw themselves as having been "smeared" by the documents felt that, before such a public statement was made, there should have been a more careful investigation of the documents, the circumstances in which they were obtained, and the individuals mentioned in them. As a bureaucratic institution, the AAA wanted to proceed with caution, ever conscious of the possibility that passing judgement on the ethical conduct of its members could lead to the fragmentation of the association.

The sequence of events within the professional anthropological community that followed the expose of the Thailand Controversy documents began with members of the Student Mobilization Committee (SMC) reading statements from Eric Wolf, Joseph Jorgensen, Gerald Berreman, and Marshall Sahlins at press conferences in Washington D.C. and San Francisco on April 2. These were followed by angry denials of ethical wrongdoing by those who felt "accused" by the *Student Mobilizer* presentation of documents. Michael Moerman, Herbert Phillips, and Lauriston Sharp, in turn, called for an investigation of the ethics and tactics of Wolf and Jorgensen. The events culminated with the report of a committee chaired by anthropologist Margaret Mead that exonerated "the accused" and rebuked Wolf and Jorgensen, only to have the Council of Fellows of the AAA vote to reject the Mead Committee Report.

RELEASE OF THAILAND CONTROVERSY DOCUMENTS

Since the 1965 Project Camelot fiasco, the AAA had been moving steadily toward the establishment of professional ethical guidelines for anthropologists. The early 1967 Beals Report, commissioned by the AAA Executive Board, had led to the approval by the Association Fellows of the *Statement on Problems of Anthropological Research and Ethics* (Appendix B) later that year. Although the *Statement* carried no provision for enforcement, it urged anthropologists to avoid "clandestine intelligence activities" and "constraint, deception, and secrecy."

The AAA membership was divided over what some saw as the new "political" turn that the Association was taking. Some members decried any ethical guidelines as an infringement on the personal freedom to make one's own choices outside of political boundaries. Others saw the absolute need for a codified standard of conduct in light of the revelations of Project Camelot and U.S. activity in Southeast Asia.

Interest in ethics continued within the AAA, and an Ad Hoc Ethics Committee formed in late 1968 held its first meeting in January 1969. It consisted of David Schneider (University of Chicago) and David Aberle (University of British Columbia) as cochairmen, and members Richard N.

Adams (University of Texas), Joseph Jorgensen (University of Michigan), William Shack (University of Illinois, Chicago Circle), and Eric Wolf (University of Michigan).[1] The Ad Hoc Committee proposed the creation of detailed ethical standards as part of its function, but this, along with most of its other suggestions, was rejected by the Executive Board.

The first standing Ethics Committee of the AAA was elected in the fall of 1969. Its members were Norman Chance (University of Connecticut), Robert Ehrich (Brooklyn College, CUNY), Wayne Suttles (Portland State University), Terence Turner (University of Chicago), Oswald Werner (Northwestern University), and Gerald Berreman (University of California-Berkeley). In addition, three members were carried over from the Ad Hoc Committee—Joseph Jorgensen, William Shack, and Eric Wolf (who was named the chair). David Aberle, then a member of the Executive Board of the AAA, was appointed liaison member to the Committee.[2] In 1969 the AAA Executive Board charged the the newly formed Ethics Committee to

> consider the earlier report of the Interim (or Ad Hoc) Ethics Committee, the body of AAA resolutions concerning ethical matters ... and recommend to the [Executive] Board what its functions should be.[3]

There would later be a debate over what exactly was the proper function of the Ethics Committee and how it should best complete its mandate. According to former AAA president George Foster, an explanation of the ballot for the 1969 election of AAA officers, including Ethics Committee members, included the following assurance about the Ethics Committee: "[I]ts activities will be under direct review and control of the Executive Board...."[4] In any event, Ethics Committee members saw their task as best completed through the collection of anonymous case studies of ethical dilemmas among its members. With this in mind, a notice was published in the *AAA Newsletter* in March 1970, which stated:

> The Ethics Committee of the American Anthropological Association has begun to build up a file of anonymous cases diagnostic of ethical conflicts....
>
> We ask the Fellows and Members of the Association to acquaint us with the details of cases in which they have been involved, or which they have collected on their own. From such case material

we hope to extract or to document general principles of the formulation of an ethical code for anthropologists.[5]

Meanwhile, in June 1969 UCLA anthropologist Michael Moerman had hired a graduate student to work in his office as a typist under an NSF grant for ten months, ending in mid-March 1970.[6] According to a letter by Moerman, he had been the student's M.A. committee chairman and had hired her only because a colleague recommended her and she pled poverty. Moerman says he had been about to fire her when she quit, but not before stealing parts of his personal files from an unlocked cabinet in his office. Although Herbert Phillips and Lauriston Sharp echoed Moerman's charge of stealing, it seems that Moerman's assistant copied and replaced the documents from files to which she most likely had access.[7] One version of the next step is that the assistant showed the copied documents to her husband, a graduate student in political science, and he suggested they be given to the Student Mobilization Committee to End the War in Vietnam (SMC).[8] According to Moerman, when he learned the name of the male graduate student who had passed the documents on to the SMC and found it matched that of his former graduate assistant, he was able to establish who had copied the documents.

As its name makes clear, the SMC was devoted to ending the Vietnam War. The SMC editors must have seen the documents as one more example of academics aiding the U.S. military in Southeast Asia and sought to expose it through their newspaper the *Student Mobilizer*. The Thailand Controversy documents were seen to be incriminating for academics in general, not solely for anthropologists.

The SMC planned to release the documents at press conferences in early April in both Washington, D.C., and in San Francisco, where the Association for Asian Studies was holding its annual conference. Before doing so, the SMC provided copies of the documents to a number of academics in the hope of eliciting statements from them. At least four anthropologists complied, issuing statements condemning the work described in the documents. The anthropologists were Gerald Berreman, Joseph Jorgensen, and Eric Wolf (all members of the AAA Ethics Committee), and Marshall Sahlins. Jorgensen, Sahlins, and Wolf were members of the Department of Anthropology at the University of Michigan, and Berreman was a member of the Department of Anthropology at University of California-Berkeley. Although the Ethics Committee had published a request in the March 1970 *AAA Newsletter* for information on "ethical conflicts" to be used to help in the "formulation of an ethical code for anthropologists," this was almost certainly not the reason for the SMC having approached these particular academics.[9] Berreman, Jorgensen, and Wolf all cited their work in the anti–war movement as a likely reason for their having been being contacted.[10] Berreman noted that he had previously written on the compromising effect of receiving certain kinds of funding and had been slated to give a talk on funding and research at the 1970 San Francisco AAS meeting. Marshall Sahlins, who had created the concept of the teach–in and was involved with a group of students and faculty opposed to the war, was the first person to be contacted at Michigan.[11]

The entire texts of the statements by Berreman, Jorgensen, Sahlins, and Wolf are reproduced below, because their content and the way in which the signatories identified themselves framed the counter debate on the ethics of the members of the Ethics Committee. Wolf and Jorgensen cosigned the following statement, which was distributed at the SMC press conference in Washington, D.C.:

30 March 1970

The undersigned members of the Ethics Committee of the American Anthropological Association have had occasion to see xeroxed copies of the following documents:

1. Minutes of the Jason Summer Study, Institute for Defense Analysis [Analyses], Falmouth Intermediate School, Falmouth, Mass., June 20th-July 6th, 1967;

2. A proposal to the Advanced Research Projects Agency, Pittsburgh, Pa. [actually the location of AIR], entitled "Counter-Insurgency in Thailand: The Impact of Economic, Social and Political Action Programs," American Institutes for Research, Dec. 1967;

3. Trip Report for a visit to Amphoe Nong Han, Changwad Udon, May 28th-June 6th, 1969;

4. Agenda for an Advisory Panel Meeting, American Institutes for Research, June 30th-July 4th, 1969;

5. Amendment to a Contract between the United States of America, represented by the Agency for International Development, and the Regents of the University of California, to facilitate advice and assistance on the part of the academic community for the Academic Advisory Council for Thailand, Sept. 1st, 1968;

6. Minutes of the Academic Advisory Council for Thailand, Oct. 19th, 1968-July 24th, 1969.

Since these documents contradict in spirit and in letter the resolutions of the American Anthropological Association concerning clandestine and secret research, we feel that they raise the most serious issues for the scientific integrity of our profession. We shall therefore call the attention of the American Anthropological Association to these most serious matters.

> Eric. R. Wolf, Professor of Anthropology
> Chairman, Ethics Comm., AAA
> Joseph Jorgensen, Associate Prof. of Anthropology[12]

Wolf also cosigned the following statement with Sahlins, which was distributed by the SMC in Washington, D.C:

We have seen the dossiers on S.S. Jason, AACT, ARPA, etc., held by the Student Mobilization Committee. The documents tell of massive U.S. intervention in Thailand, political and military intervention prepared with the active help of American social scientists and serviced under contract by at least one major American university. The spirit of the documents is organized contempt for the Thai people, their government, and their institutions. If verified, the participation of American scholars is a perversion of their science, as the participation of the university would be corruption of its purpose. Over the short run, anthropologists, sociologists, and political scientists who lend themselves to the counterinsurgency projects of the Defense Department render their fields physically impossible as well as intellectually meaningless. The dangers over the long run are to the existence of this country, and not only from foreign defeat, but from the application to the U.S. of the methods of totalitarian manipulation now being perfected by our scientists abroad—a prospect that one of the Thailand research proposals finds "exciting."

> Prof. Marshall Sahlins, Prof. Eric Wolf, Dept. of
> Anthropology, University of Michigan.[13]

Finally, Gerald Berreman issued the following "Statement by Professor Gerald D. Berreman, Professor of Anthropology and Member Center for South and Southeast Asian Studies, University of California, Berkeley," which was distributed by the SMC in San Francisco on April 3:

> I have carefully read the Student Mobilization Committee's report on American social scientist's role in counterinsurgency research and advising in Thailand under sponsorship of such governmental agencies as AID and with the blessing support of their academic institutions.
>
> The evidence clearly demonstrates the direct complicity of scholars in the antischolarly task of implementing counter insurgency programs in Thailand. This comprises untenable corruption of social science and scholarship which promises to discredit not only those who have participated, but to cast suspicion on all of those who study and work in Asia and, in fact, anywhere else. It also betrays social scientists and area specialists in their role as scholars within American society, for it identifies them as hirelings to agencies whose purposes are, as this document confirms, to intervene politically in the internal affairs of sovereign nations. This is an intolerable affront to the academic community and the public which supports it. It is an insult to the people we area specialists know, study, work with and trust in Asia and elsewhere....[14]

Berreman, Jorgensen, Sahlins, and Wolf felt the Thailand Controversy documents were important enough to warrant immediate comment. Wolf and Jorgensen held that the activities detailed in the documents violated the letter and spirit of the *Statement on Problems of Anthropological Research and Ethics* (Appendix B).[15] In his statement written with Jorgensen, Wolf identified himself as the chairman of the AAA Ethics Committee. Berreman did not identify himself as an Ethics Committee member in his statement because, at first, it did not occur to him that being a member of a professional ethics committee of anthropologists was important in light of the Thailand Controversy documents.[16] Michael Moerman, Herbert Phillips, Lauriston Sharp, and others later objected to the conflict of interest implied in members of the Ethics Committee publicly prejudging the activities of others before a thorough investigation.

When Michael Moerman arrived in San Francisco on April 2 for the beginning of the AAS conference, he was told by Herbert Phillips that the SMC had held a press conference in Washington, D.C. at which copies of the Thailand Controversy documents were released. At first Phillips and David Wilson (UCLA Department of Political Science and AACT), suspected that Moerman had passed the documents to the SMC and, as Moerman later wrote, had "caused great damage to them and to the scholarly community and its ability to influence government policy."[17] SMC activists circulated during the AAS conference and offered to send copies of the documents to interested scholars. A heated discussion developed at the panel on Regional Integration in Thailand, chaired by Peter Kunstadter.[18]

On April 3, Wolf sent private letters to Michael Moerman, Herbert Phillips, Steven Piker, and Lauriston Sharp. The identical letters read:

Dear Prof. [name]

The enclosed note will show you that Joe Jorgensen and I have had occasion to see a number of documents bearing on the involvement of anthropologists in secret research, and we feel that we must raise the issue once again at the next meeting of the AAA Ethics Committee to deal with cases on as anonymous a basis as possible, in an effort to develop an approach to cases without penalizing any individuals; and we shall honor this commitment as much as practicable. However, I should like to invite you to make any statement to the Committee that you wish, especially in view of the past resolutions of our Association on the subject of clandestine research and restricted, non–public publication of research results.

Eric R. Wolf, Chairman, Ethics Comm., AAA.[19]

Moerman, Phillips, and Sharp reacted with outrage to the Wolf letter, saying Wolf had already publicly judged them guilty in his statement to the SMC and was now proposing to be able to deal impartially with the information in the Thailand Controversy documents as the chairman of the AAA Ethics Committee. The question of ethics became twofold: Did the conduct of the anthropologists mentioned in the Thailand Controversy documents violate codified or uncodified ethical standards for academics? And did the conduct of Wolf and Jorgensen violate the ethical standards required of their positions on the Ethics Committee? While both questions are important, it would difficult to argue that they are equally significant. One ethical dilemma involved activities that may have been used to physically harm the people studied; the other had the potential for ruining people's reputations.

The public statements of Wolf, Jorgensen, and Berreman were undeniably judgmental of the activities of their colleagues, calling them gross violations of ethical standards. But Wolf's letter written as chairman of the Ethics Committee to the four anthropologists who figure prominently in the Thailand Controversy documents stated that the Ethics Committee was withholding any judgement. Moerman, Phillips, and Sharp felt they had reasonable cause to feel adjudged "guilty" without the benefit of due process. The result of the conflict was a heated exchange of letters between Wolf and Moerman, Phillips, and Sharp. The latter three expressed varying degrees of indignation, personal hurt, and anger. Piker's response to Wolf, however, expressed none of these sentiments and, thus, serves as an interesting contrast to the others.

ANTHROPOLOGISTS' RESPONSES & CAMPUS REACTIONS

Steven Piker

In his response to Wolf, Piker expressed a willingness to cooperate with the Ethics Committee in providing information. He wrote that the American involvement in Thailand was detrimental to the Thais. At the same time, he stressed the responsibility of citizens to respond to requests for information from government officials, with the important caveat that he would undertake no research that would endanger those studied:

Thank you for your letter of 3 April. I am deeply concerned, as no doubt many others are, about the implications of government–related research generally, and "clandestine research" particularly, for the future of Anthropology. I am happy, therefore, to make known to your committee—and to anyone else who might inquire—the specifics of all research and professional work generally in which I have been involved since my association with Anthropology began as a graduate student more than ten years ago. I hope the following remarks will suffice; but, in the event that you or your associates desires further specifics on any matter, I urge you to be in touch with me....

[re: Institute for Defense Analyses, Project Jason] I was explicitly given to understand that the purpose of the meeting [of the Thailand Study Group] was to evaluate the effects of these [development] programs, and American involvement generally....

My own participation ... involved in fact the presentation of my own opinions—which at the risk of over–summarization, could then and can now be stated as follows: American involvement in Thailand (especially military, but also AID), is highly detrimental to the best interests of the Thai nation and the Thai people, and is working both to their short and long run disadvantage.....

I consider myself a concerned citizen ... and if people in a position to make important decisions solicit my opinions in areas in which I have some degree of competence, I am generally inclined to make my opinions known (and to support them as strongly as I can), because it seems to me that by so doing I both discharge some of my responsibilities as a citizen and, in some small sense, perhaps achieve a measure of effectiveness in areas that are of concern to me. I would not consider undertaking any consulting work, however, that entailed violating the kind of confidences Anthropologists enjoy from their respondents in carrying out field work; nor, consulting aside, would I carry out or participate in actual research the results of which could not be made fully public according to long established professional standards. I will, however, make my opinions concerning the feasibility and desirability of government programs (as well as their morality) known to government agencies if my opinions are solicited....

Piker wrote that he had been approached by members of SEADAG and of AACT to join those organizations, but declined because he was

strongly opposed to American policy and involvement in SE Asia, and I do not want in any way to be a part of it; and, second, even if my views were otherwise, my own research in SE Asia is such that the activities and projects of these organizations would be of no interest to me.

He listed all research support and then continued:

Other than personal confidences, I have nothing that cannot and (I hope) will not be made public to all interested parties, anthropologists and others.

Finally, although it is not directly pertinent to the question of clandestine research, I feel I should make my position on the SE Asian situation known to you since that is the crisis area at present and my own work has been exclusively in this area. I am now and have been for some years unequivocally opposed to American involvement in Vietnam and SE Asia, and to American policy in that part of the world generally.

He mentioned his activities in opposition to the war and concluded:

I suppose in rehearsing all this I am attempting to make it as clear to you as it is to me that I could under no circumstances allow myself to become involved in any work—research or otherwise— that is in support of any aspect of American policy in that part of the world. Our professional standards concerning openness of research in any event are my guide, and I subscribe to them—as I gather do you and your associates—without reservation. In this instance, however, my feelings in such matters are reinforced by my long–standing conviction that American policy in SE Asia has amounted to a practical catastrophe and a moral outrage. My involvement with this policy (if indeed such a pretentious term as "involvement" is appropriate) has been restricted exclusively to attempting to change it, whether I have addressed the general public or (as in one instance) a government agency. This has involved no clandestine research....[20]

Piker was the only one, in his responses to Wolf, to stress his opposition to U.S. policy in Southeast Asia, although Phillips and Sharp insisted in later interviews that they had been opposed to many, if not all, U.S. programs in Southeast Asia.[21] Wolf praised Piker for "the calm and well–thought–out manner" in which he discussed the issues and said that he, Wolf, was

> ... personally very happy to learn of your own efforts to change our disastrous policy in Southeast Asia and of your awareness of the ethical implications of the anthropologists role in such a complex setting.[22]

The public political opinions and positions of each anthropologist are reflected in his response to Wolf. Piker, who opposed the Vietnam War and the U.S. role in Southeast Asia, supported the right of an ethics committee to investigate issues. Moerman, Phillips, and Sharp, who first expressed ambivalence and then opposition to U.S. policy in Southeast Asia, did not support the right of an ethics committee to investigate the individual choices of anthropologists—particularly not an ethics committee chaired by Wolf.

Michael Moerman
Moerman, after asserting that he had been a student of Wolf and Sahlins and had been influenced by them both, wrote in response to Wolf's action:

> [Y]ou are behaving inhumanely and, which bothers me less, unprofessionally toward me. The inhumanity, abstractly expressed, is to judge ... another human being solely through some prejudicially selected sampling of his "objective" behavior with no concern for the choices, orientations, goals, contexts, and moral textures which motivated, informed, and created his actions. To do that is always wrong. To do it to someone you know as a person, to someone whom you could have phoned and to do it on the basis of a document put together with narrowly political interests from papers stolen by someone whom I trusted is appalling.

I have read the AAA's Statement of Ethics and know that I have not only done nothing inconsistent with them, but have worked to support them. I also know that any personal political purposes I have had (and perhaps fulfilled, until this blew up) are closer to yours than you imagine. But these considerations matter far less to me than the damage you have done to the whole fabric of trust upon which the academy is based, and less than my pained knowledge that you have lost the moral and professional authority which would require or permit me to try to justify myself to you.[23]

Moerman's tone of personal injury at the hands of a colleague whom he felt had behaved inhumanely towards him moved the discussion away from that of the ethics of anthropology in the highly charged arena of U.S. involvement in Southeast Asia. He wrote of the violation of the fabric of trust that stripped Wolf of any authority—professional or moral—to hear Moerman's side of the issue. While Moerman's criticisms of Wolf's personal and professional role in the controversy are valid, they sidestep the specific ethical issues that should have been the central focus of the discussion.

Moerman further stressed the personal political purposes that he had been able to pursue until the blowup, making clear his belief that the best place from which to influence policy was from the inside. Phillips was also a proponent for working for change from the inside. Obviously, Wolf, Jorgensen, Berreman, and Sahlins favored the position of working from the outside.

In his response to Moerman, Wolf wrote that he and Jorgensen had seen the SMC documents on March 30; and that while Wolf had sent the SMC a message stating that he would call to the attention of the AAA the issues raised by them, no names of individual anthropologists had been used in his public statement. In a similar vein, he wrote that he and Sahlins had sent a telegram to the SMC in their capacity as *individual* anthropologists, but again no names had been mentioned. Finally, he reiterated the function of the Ethics Committee, which he said was

> ... not a judicial agency. It neither intends to sit in judgement over individuals, nor to pass on their merit. It *is* concerned with the ethical implications of actions taken by anthropologists. As far as practicable we deal with these actions anonymously. It does not

bring charges, nor does it ask justification of anyone [emphasis in original].[24]

Wolf's response is problematic in that he claims to be making one judgement as an individual—that others have breached ethical standards—while stating that as a member of an Ethics Committee he would be able to "deal with cases on as anonymous a basis as possible, in an effort to develop an approach to cases without penalizing any individuals" (Wolf's letter to Moerman, Piker, Phillips, and Sharp). Furthermore, while Wolf did not name names in his public statements, the statements were distributed by the SMC along with copies of the "Counterinsurgency Research on Campus Exposed" issue of the *Student Mobilizer* that decidedly *did* name names. The result was that anyone at the Association for Asian Studies conference in 1970 or any individuals involved in the anti–war movement would be able to access the names in the newspaper and match them with the statements of Wolf and others. Thus, the statements of Wolf, Jorgensen, Berreman, and Sahlins were hardly innocuous for the individuals implicated in the documents, particularly Moerman, Phillips, and Sharp. These two issues—the public and private positions of Wolf and Jorgensen and others and their almost naming names—were used by Moerman, Phillips, and Sharp in an effort to discredit the Ethics Committee chaired by Wolf.

Herbert Phillips

Herbert Phillips issued a statement to his Berkeley colleagues, on April 4, 1970, regarding the Thailand Controversy documents, before responding publicly to the accusations.[25] He described the information in the *Student Mobilizer* as being comprised of a mixture of truth and falsehoods that linked scholars to counterinsurgency solely on the basis of their having spoken to U.S. government officials (whom, Phillips wrote, deserved to be condemned). He wrote that the University of California should not have been a party to the contract with USAID that had mandated cooperation on counterinsurgency research. He further asserted that the counterinsurgency activities of the U.S. government in Thailand were damaging to Thai citizens.

While acknowledging that U.S. counterinsurgency activity in Thailand was socially destructive to the Thais, Phillips felt these issues should be discussed in a civil manner, not disseminated indiscriminately so as to harm those academics who had spent their lives studying Thai society. He proposed, for example, that his experience at IDA's Thailand Study Group could be written up as a criticism of the corrupt morality of U.S. government officials.

In an interview, Phillips said that of all the anthropologists implicated by the Thailand Controversy documents, "I was the most heavily involved with the U.S. government." He stressed that to affect policy, "access to ˙ndividuals" is far more important than controlling funding. Further, to speak out publicly against what ARPA was doing "would not have had any value whatsoever"; there was "far more effectiveness" for change by working from within. In spite of this, Phillips asserted, "I terminated my association with ARPA because they were not listening to me, and they were having a far greater deleterious effect with what they were doing..." Phillips said he told them they "were doing this wrong and doing that wrong, and not doing anything useful." It was his perception that the government often wanted consultants to legitimize what the government was already doing.[26]

In spite of his disenchantment with ARPA, in 1969 or 1970 Phillips undertook a study as a member of a Kissinger–appointed panel called National Security Studies Memorandum 51 (NSSM 51). According to Phillips, NSSM 51 was a

> thorough assessment of U.S. involvement with Thailand since 1952. [It was to] serve as the basis of U.S. policy toward Thailand.... [My] assessment was negative—stop, stop, stop. The general thrust was upsetting the lives of individuals unnecessarily.

He says that there was no suspicion about the goals or intents of NSSM 51 by its members, partly because many (although not Phillips) were friends of Kissinger. NSSM 51 went down the drain with the U.S. invasion of Cambodia. Phillips concedes that by this time he was "totally disgusted with the U.S. government. There is no indication that things have changed with time gone by." But more than this, he felt what he describes as "a profound sense of adult sadness" at the turn of events.

Phillips also had a profound sense of "disenchantment" with his colleagues in anthropology. He says their actions had arisen from a fair first reading of the Thailand Controversy documents, that is, as they appeared. However, he criticizes the legitimacy and accuracy of the documents, calling them misleading. Phillips responded to Wolf's letter on April 5, stressing the need for due process and personal contacts with those involved:

[H]ow could a person of your sensitivity consider the materials presented by SMC to be "evidence"? Likewise, how could you so pervert reality by saying that the scholars slandered by SMC have "contempt for the Thai people, their government, and their institutions"? [referring to the Wolf–Sahlins statement reproduced earlier in this chapter] How could you say this without looking into the writings of these people, without inquiring into their side of the story, without permitting them to defend themselves? You seem *in this instance* so dominated by your political interests (or perhaps by a momentary inexplicable passion) that you are ready to abandon the most elementary rules of evidence, due process, and professional trust....

You are in the very delicate position of being chairman of the AAA's Ethics Committee, a role which, I assume, requires special regard for the rules of evidence, due process, the rights of defense and professional courtesy. I would suggest that in issuing your public statements you have prejudged this matter and have forfeited any adjudicative and investigatory role whatsoever in determining the merit of either the material in the SMC dossiers of any "defense" that the accused parties might choose to present to any forum. Simply stated, I am suggesting that you resign from the Ethics Committee. I would further suggest that in announcing *publicly* that you are bringing to the attention of the AAA a series of implicating documents, the nature of which are in no way specified and the individuals implicated in no way cited, and having done this without first informing the implicated parties, you and Professor Jorgensen have behaved in an administratively irresponsible manner, and he too should resign from the Ethics Committee....

I am sure you understand that these issues are not easy for any of us. You always have been to me one of the most stimulating thinkers in modern social anthropology. I only hope that this convulsion is momentary, and that we can return to the task of being anthropologists—trusting each other, appreciating the people we study and work with, and advancing knowledge [emphasis in original].[27]

One day later, on April 6, Phillips followed up with another letter:

[W]hat really stimulates my fury is your letter of April 3rd in which you say, "It is the announced purpose of the Ethics Committee to deal with cases on as anonymous a basis as possible." How can you have the effrontery to make this assertion when your statement of March 30th was freely circulating among the members of the Association for Asian Studies *at the same time* as the 70–page SMC document and the SMC newspaper was referring to these same documents, providing detailed information (as well as rich fantasy) on the names of the alleged principals? I am not sure whether you are being deceptive, have no control over your fellow Committee members, or are simply compounding the utter madness of this entire affair.

I am no longer sure, Eric, which part of this tangled web is enveloping whom? Whose integrity is on trial: Your own? The Ethics Committee's? The AAA's? Gerry's? [Berreman] Mike Moerman's? Lauri Sharp's? My own?... Is this kind of thing, if taken further in a public forum, going to tear the AAA apart? And what is the AAA if not you, Marshall [Sahlins], Mike, Lauri, Gerry, myself, and every other individual connected with this business? And of what merit is the AAA if its members lack integrity (or, I might add, possess a bit too much hubris)?

There are many "instrumental" problems in this whole affair. But perhaps the most fundamental is that we have all been marching around *presuming* things about each other, principally because of lack of knowledge. May I suggest that you step down from Olympus, telephone the persons involved, and talk with them as a human being not as a moral paragon.

If the thrust of this letter is one of personal outrage or personal hurt (I am not sure which) please remember that it is I, not you, who has given fifteen years of my life trying to understand the Thai people. It is I who know the Thai peasants as vibrant individuals, not as abstract categories of an ethical calculus. It is I, not you, who has tried to induce any U.S. government official who would listen to leave the Thai alone and to let them "tamcaj tua eng" (follow their own hearts). There is nothing intrinsically noble about this, but it is sufficiently valuable not to have been violated by your presumption [emphasis in original].[28]

Phillips took up many of the same issues that Moerman did, with an admitted tone of "personal outrage or personal hurt," while shifting the discussion away from the ethical conduct of anthropologists in the context of U.S. goals in Southeast Asia.

If, as Phillips writes, there were no "political, legal, or military justifications" for U.S. counterinsurgency operations in Southeast Asia, we must assume that Phillips's role at IDA's Thailand Study Group and in ARPA were attempts at privately convincing U.S. officials of this. Similarly, his published work with David Wilson on *Certain Effects of Culture and Social Organization on International Security in Thailand*, written for the Rand Corporation, may have been circulated for the same reasons. Finally, if Phillips's experience at IDA's Thailand Study Group could have been written up as an indictment of the incompetence and corruption of U.S. government officials, as he suggests, why did he not do so at the time? Presumably, his answer would be that a public forum was not the place to do so.

One month later, in April 1970, Phillips did decide to publicly air his criticism of U.S. policy in a letter (later published in Thai)[29] to the Thai elder statesman Khukrit Pramoj, editor of *Siam Rath* [Thai Nation] newspaper. He wrote:

I love your country second only to my own. My son is a Thai citizen and when I die I hope that my ashes will be returned to Thailand. I also feel that what we call "Thai culture" is one of the most humanly satisfying and distinctive creations of mankind, and that as a teacher and author I have been privileged in trying to communicate some of these qualities to persons who have been unable to know Thailand first hand.[30]

Phillips went on to criticize the U.S. presence in Thailand:

I have seen the towns of Nakornrajasima, Ubon, Udorn, Nakornphanom, and the village of Sathaheep suddenly transformed from peaceful and happy communities into noisy centers of warfare; it is from these centers that American airmen have gone to kill people who have never done any harm to your countryman nor to mine. I have seen Thai citizens in their own towns being treated in the same way that black people have been treated by white hooligans in some of the towns in the State of Mississippi. I have talked with American Military Advisors who are angry at Thai officers and soldiers for refusing to kill Thai citizens whom Americans call "communist terrorists" but whom Thai officers correctly recognize as frustrated and misguided countrymen who need jobs and the help of their own government. I have seen as much as one million baht of my countrymen's taxes being wasted on "counterinsurgency research in Thailand" that nobody reads, nobody wants, and that benefits nobody except a few (and for the most part, incompetent) American research technicians....

For a time I thought I could serve as an advisor to my government and by reaching people in high places I could diminish some of this pain.... Despite my enumeration above, I know that there are many socially desirable things that the United States has done in Thailand.... I also know that along with our many shortsighted and incompetent American officials, there are other men of wisdom and good will. My problem was to be selective in the kind of advice that I gave and to present it in a way that would not permit it to be perverted. I have had great hopes, but grave doubts, about any value that my contribution might have had.

The President's recent decision to expand American bombing and destruction in Laos and Cambodia—to kill innocent people who, excepting their language and citizenship, are almost indistinguishable from the people of Thailand—has convinced me that incompetence or cruelty continue to dominate the conduct of American affairs in Southeast Asia, and that nations or people who continue to associate themselves with such conduct do so at the greatest peril to themselves.... the people living in Thailand's Northeast today may be the very people who will die next year from American bombs. Make no mistake about this: U.S. soldiers would no more hesitate to bomb and kill Thai citizens than they have hesitated to bomb and kill Vietnamese, Laotians, Khmers, or American college students in Kent, Ohio.[31]

Wolf, in his April 12, 1970, response to Phillips, repeated the claims made in his response to Moerman's letter—that his telegram to the SMC had been written as an "individual" anthropologist and that he had not mentioned specific names:

> I want to reiterate at the outset that I have no intention of assigning guilt to individuals; I *am* concerned with clarifying a situation which indeed does have implications for the integrity of the social sciences, including anthropology.... I wrote to [the anthropologists mentioned in the SMC documents] in the hope that they would be able to acquaint us with the aspect of the situation of which we might be ignorant. This was not done to point a finger at anyone....
>
> I addressed a telegram to Student Mobilization at their Washington Office in our capacity as individual anthropologists concerned with the purposes to which social science is put by agencies of our government and with the problem of co–optation of social scientists in the counterinsurgency effort. We were not interested in assigning guilt or absolving individuals from it.... If I can make you realize that we are participants in a common cause and not in any struggle to impugn the integrity of any individual, this letter will have accomplished its primary purpose [emphasis in original].[32]

Phillips's April 16, 1970, reply criticized Wolf's assertions, but then suggested a possible rapprochement between Wolf and the wronged parties. While it addressed the weakness of Wolf's public–private position, it avoided responding to the documents of the Thailand Controversy, even in their prejudged *Student Mobilizer*–published form. Phillips wrote:

> I have been implicated only in the most peripheral way and I have no acute need to feel umbrage, to condemn, or to protest. All of this is to say that, if it is at all possible, I would prefer to resolve the problem on the personal level.
>
> However, I am not at all certain that our problems can now be dealt with in this manner.... you gave [the SMC] your imprimatur, as well as the imprimatur of the AAA, and in the complete absence of

further evidence, due process, and an interest in professional trust, you indicated that you shared their judgements about your colleagues. You could have said nothing. You could have pondered the matter. You could have written, phoned, or telegraphed me. But you chose to do none of these things.... You knew that the SMC materials mentioned individual personalities, and I assume you knew that the *sole* function of SMC is to present a political point of view to the public. To have sent that statement to them three or four days earlier than you sent it to me ... is clear demonstration that you were more concerned with endorsing their political judgements than with serving the interests of the Ethics Committee, the AAA, and your anthropological colleagues.... Almost all my inclinations ... impel me to trust your good intentions and your good judgment. However, I must in all frankness indicate that events of the past few weeks require that such trust now be demonstrated by you rather than be assumed by me. I also want you to know that I am as much bewildered as I am disturbed by these events: I really do not understand what prompted your actions or how ideological commitments could so dominate considerations of truth, integrity, and intellectual complexity. I mention the last because I do not understand your unwillingness to recognize the possibility of there being some very complex professional and moral issues involved here. Is it not possible that your Thai colleagues [that is, American academics who study Thailand] could have been prompted by the desire to reduce rather than to serve the destructiveness of U.S. Government programs in Thailand?... Is it not possible that they might be more concerned with the social effectiveness and the social consequences of their activities than with simply expressing (for the sake of expression or for other selfish psychological reasons) a sense of righteousness? Is it not possible that there are many routes for reducing the destructiveness of U.S. activities in Thailand...? ... Is it not possible that they might have actually weighed what the consequences of their "speaking out" as contrasted with "speaking with government officials" as contrasted with "doing nothing" might be to (1) what the U.S. Government will continue to do or will terminate doing in Thailand; (2) to their own credibility as

Thai specialists; (3) to their own professional and moral integrity?...

A retreat to ideological formulae may be psychologically comfortable, but it is of little value in resolving the concrete choices that must be made.... Is one's primary loyalty to the truth, to one's own integrity, to the Thai people, to one's profession and colleagues, to one's nation, to one's political beliefs? I do feel that the establishment of such priorities is essentially one's own moral business, not something to be established by some external moral authority (an Ethics Committee?) to be imposed on anybody....

I would hope that you, Gerry [Berreman], Marshall [Sahlins], and [Joseph] Jorgensen would publish in the AAA *Newsletter* a dignified retraction of your earlier statements, and seriously consider resigning from the Ethics Committee. I would then be happy to sit down with you—at San Diego or elsewhere—and hash out in concrete detail many of these problems, with a view to presenting a unified statement on them to a reconstituted Ethics Committee of the AAA Executive Board. However, in the present circumstances, where I am uncertain about your motives and distrustful of your judgment, I cannot honor any further request that you might make to me as Chairman of the Ethics Committee.[33]

Phillips made clear that he believed Wolf, on the basis of his previous statements, had forfeited his right to chairmanship of the Ethics Committee; and he accused Wolf of being guided by his political beliefs. But again, Phillips avoided the ethical issue of anthropologists working to further U.S. counterinsurgency goals in Southeast Asia.

Lauriston Sharp

Lauriston Sharp replied to Wolf only after issuing public statements of his own and writing letters to his colleagues at Cornell University. In an April 8, 1970, letter to "Officers of Cornell University," he said that the charges against AACT "are based on purloined documents, including private correspondence, all of which would have been made available for the asking."[34] (Whether or not Moerman would have opened his files to the Ethics Committee, in fact, is open to question.)

On April 1 Sharp responded to the accusations against the Academic Advisory Council for Thailand that had been circulated by the SMC at the end of March. AACT, he wrote,

> [is] a group of independent American scholars ... who advise and consult with staff of the Agency for International Development who are concerned with Thailand. AACT has never conducted research on banditry, terrorism, or insurgency, which for some years in the late 1960s were of grave concern to the Thai government and which seriously interfered with Thai development programs in the country's northeast. Thai government efforts to control these illegal activities, generally called counterinsurgency measures, were naturally of concern also to AID official, but at no time did they ask AACT to study or report on these problems....
>
> Had SMC done their research with some scholarly thoroughness and honesty ... they would have learned that AACT is dealing with problems of agricultural production, education, regionalism in North Thailand, population increase, urbanization and the urban–rural gap, and means for supporting more research by Thai in Thailand.[35]

Until the SMC circulated the Thailand Controversy documents, Sharp may not have been aware of the September 1968 revised contract between the U.S. government and the Regents of the University of California (discussed in Chapter Five), which specifically mandated that AACT provide services to AID that included identifying and evaluating research related to counterinsurgency and organizing seminars about "counterinsurgency problems."[36] And, in the heat of the moment, Sharp may have doubted the validity of such an amendment as recounted by the SMC. He did repudiate the amendment, however, in a later interview,[37] as did Phillips in an April 13 letter to the [Berkeley] *Daily Californian*, cosigned with Gerald Berreman and fifteen others.[38]

In the earlier April 1 statement, Sharp commented on the AACT conference on local authority held in July 1969 at UCLA:

> The meetings dealt with administration and authority at the village and commune level and the problems of effective linkage with district officials appointed by the government. Civil security at this

> level in isolated villages all over Thailand is often inadequate, and this was discussed. It has been a long standing problem that has troubled Thai officials.
>
> SMC in its ignorance of Thai conditions and eagerness to depict AACT as sinister concluded gratuitously that "security" in this context is really "counterinsurgency." The SMC statement or misstatement is thick with false imputations of this kind, attempts to show guilt by association ... and out and out falsifications....
>
> Members of AACT may not agree with every detailed program goal of AID and its predecessors in Thailand, but they obviously agree with its general objectives, judge its work to be benevolent and on the whole beneficent and wanted by most Thai.

In an April 1991 interview with the author, Sharp asserted that there is "nothing illegal about an established government wanting order."[39] And, indeed, there is not. However, Sharp's treatment of the terms "order," "security," and "counterinsurgency" as though they were not conflated in the Thailand Controversy documents and by U.S. and Thai government officials is misleading. Furthermore, the "general objectives" of AID *were* directed at counterinsurgency.

Some academic members of AACT did acknowledge the security and counterinsurgency interests of AID. David A. Wilson, professor of political science at UCLA and a member of AACT, issued a statement of his own on April 3, 1970, in which he said:

> AACT's interest in insurrection is very marginal except in the broad sense that a more productive and just society in Thailand may make the aspirations of the few foreign supported insurgents less likely to be realized.[40]

When asked about his awareness of AID policy in Thailand, Wilson said he was "perfectly aware of what AID program" was doing in Thailand, and that AACT members "didn't discuss policy—we discussed programs and types of social science research that might help with what they [AID] were doing."[41] He particularly wanted to clarify that AACT was not engaged in "hurting people." Regarding the AID obsession with the counterinsurgency label in its programs, Wilson said, "Nobody thought much of it because everybody knew counterinsurgency was in the air."

David Wyatt, AACT member and professor of history at Cornell University, described the atmosphere at the AACT meetings as follows: "The common feeling was everyone was pissed off at the way the [U.S.] government was going about things in Thailand."[42] Even though "some people" at AID were willing to listen to AACT, Wyatt described his anger at the "narrow focus" of U.S. policy that justified U.S. presence in Southeast Asia for its own sake.

On April 10, 1970, in a letter to the "academic community," Sharp wrote that AACT was created because

> the development efforts associated with U.S. aid were creating situations, conditions and social changes that provide unique opportunities for better understanding of social processes. Scholars could be given a better opportunity to observe and study these complex problems. At the same time the people involved in these efforts would be able to better understand, plan and evaluate their own work.[43]

The specific "complex problems" in which AACT was interested and the "people" who would benefit from this interest were clearly identified at meetings of AACT. Members present at the September 1968 meeting, including Sharp, agreed to learn about ARPA programs in order to improve the quality of its research.[44] By June 1969 AACT members had agreed that the group "should abandon its pretensions to be representative" of the community of Thai scholars and "accept its role as basically a consultative body to AID."[45]

Although Wilson described AACT meetings as "open minded, without inhibitions,"[46] criticism of counterinsurgency goals is conspicuously absent from the meeting minutes. The explanation of both Sharp and David Wyatt for this is that things spoken about by AACT members at meetings that the members did not want AID to see were left out of the minutes.[47] The purpose for so editing the minutes is unclear since AID staff also attended the meetings.

Finally, writing on the Institute for Defense Analyses, Sharp said in his April 3 statement and a subsequent April 9 letter to "anthropology colleagues" that

SMC's account of the Institute of Defense Analyses and its Project Jason is as befuddled as its account of SEADAG.... Project Jason, normally concerned with weaponry and other problems, decided that in 1967 it should consider the possibility of adding a social science section to its other capabilities. To this end, and under the leadership of its Nobel laureate member, Murray Gell–Mann, it would see what was known of a country important in U.S. policy, and how that knowledge might be organized systematically as "social science."... Information on Thailand was provided by a series of visiting experts. Many of these were concerned by the alleged insurgency in Northeastern Thailand, the magnitude of which was just then being emphasized by the Thai Government. Quite naturally, a good deal of the study group's discussion turned on this problem. In conclusion, the group was impressed with how little firm or useful information they could obtain on what was really happening in Thailand, and how little science there was in "social science."... It is certain, however, that this ephemeral group went out of existence in 1967 without carrying out "research" or "operations," "counterinsurgent" or otherwise....[48]

... I have now confirmed through others my recollections of the informal and, in a technical sense, perfectly "open" or non–secret meetings of an ephemeral group of people interested in Thailand held in 1967 under Institute of Defense Analyses, Project Jason, auspices.... Participants in or visitors to the meetings needed no clearance of any kind; they met in absolutely unrestricted, unguarded and thus "open" rooms of what I took to be a city school. Their discussions on a wide variety of topics, involving as far as I know no secret information, could hardly be called "research," and they had, as a group, no possibility of carrying out "counterinsurgency," "clandestine," or any other operations.[49]

While the Thailand Study Group meetings were not classified, neither were they advertised publicly among academics, nor did any journalists cover the meetings. It seems that the discussions were sensitive enough to be limited, although participants could have publicized what they heard at the meetings had they wanted to. And although no counterinsurgency or clandestine research was carried out at the meetings, the Study Group *was* called together to discuss how social scientists might aid the U.S. counterinsurgency effort in Thailand.

Based on his statements at the time and a recent interview,[50] it seems that Sharp had a more favorable outlook on some U.S. goals in Southeast Asia than did Phillips. Sharp had conducted "applied social science research" for AID under a contract with Cornell University in 1963.[51] The purpose of this project, whose results were published as a *Report on Tribal Peoples in Chiengrai,* had been to help Thai government and AID officials in planning policy decisions. It included a study of the integration of minority groups into the national society. Recommendations that would have benefited minority groups included the use of "tribal" languages and encouraging the Thai government to better understand local customs and laws. There was nothing sinister about this research, except the use to which it could have been put by the U.S. or Thai governments, a consideration whose probability appeared remote until the U.S. became involved in a ground war in Southeast Asia. By the late 1960s, AID was specifically linking all of its programs in Thailand to combating the insurgency.

Sharp said he entered the discipline of anthropology after serving with the U.S. State Department, during which time he was "appalled by the ignorance" of program planners. He saw a need for planners who knew something about the people they were to help. During his association with USAID, Sharp said he spent a lot of time "trying to get AID to insist on research before making grants."

Sharp mentioned "feeling unhappy about the wording of AID projects," but attributed the linkage of projects to "counterinsurgency" to "Washington politicians trying to get funds from Congress. The actual people in AID were not as communist obsessed." He spoke of the absurd logic through which persons fear communism and at the same time predict its failures. He said he was sympathetic to several insurgents whom he knew personally, but that the best position for a scholar was not to assist "the establishment or the insurgents."

Sharp said he felt that AID people sometimes had appreciated his positions; but overall he had been discontented with AID's program in Thailand, including its "avuncular attitude" toward the Thais. In 1970 Sharp wrote that one of the reasons he had joined AACT was to help the Thai people live a more "productive, humane, and just life."[52] But, in 1991, he said retrospectively, "AACT was not very effective in the long run." There was a "lack of enthusiastic support" that worsened until AACT disbanded.

In direct reply to Wolf on April 17, Sharp acknowledged receipt of the Wolf–Jorgensen letter with the list of six documents and their "bearing on the involvement of anthropologists in secret research":

> I point out at once that in their original state the last two documents on your list, which have to do with the Academic Advisory Council for Thailand (AACT), of which I am chairman, have absolutely no such bearing, and would not be likely to have. None of AACT's work or records or publications has been or is secret or in any way restricted....

> I have now carefully gone through these and other documents relating to AACT from my own file. I can state categorically that they contain no evidence whatsoever that any member of the Council, including the anthropologists [Charles] Keyes, Moerman, and me, has been involved in secret or clandestine research or with "restricted, non–public publication of research results."

Sharp concluded with a criticism of the Berreman and Wolf-Jorgensen statements, calling them "false and libelous" and "malicious and libelous." He called for the resignation of Wolf, Jorgensen, and Berreman from the AAA Ethics Committee:

> In the midst of these defamatory and libelous public pronouncements against unidentifiable people, you suggest that the facts may not yet be verified! But this minor obstacle, which could have been overcome very easily with a telephone call or two, in no way inhibits your dishonest and vicious attack, which has been widely broadcast, and has already done irreparable damage to my professional reputation among colleagues and students, both Americans and Thai.[53]

Sharp covers two bases in the above statements. He criticizes the nature of the "purloined" documents and urges the resignation of Wolf, Jorgensen, and Berreman from the Ethics Committee; but he also makes an attempt to answer specific criticisms of AACT, unlike Moerman or Phillips, who address their connections only insofar as to say they were made for the purposes of altering damaging U.S. programs. Moerman and Phillips, believing the charges to be completely baseless, may have felt that no response was necessary. Sharp, equally feeling the charges to be baseless, nevertheless felt compelled to address them.

Wolf and Jorgensen's response to Sharp reiterated their defense of public and private positions on the Thailand Controversy, not naming names, and the Ethics Committee not being a judicial body.[54] Berreman also wrote Sharp, defying him to prove the accusation of libel.[55]

Campus Reactions

Back on the campuses of UCLA, Berkeley, and Cornell, student and faculty reaction was mixed. At UCLA Moerman had a difficult time with both students and colleagues.[56] David Wilson recalls harassment by radical students and that the AACT office was broken into by "a small mob of students."[57] Phillips notes the campus accusations against Moerman, as well as those against Charles Keyes and Peter Kunstadter at University of Washington, but said he suffered none of these at Berkeley, with the exception of what he describes as the attention of some emotionally disturbed individuals.[58]

One of the most emotionally charged campus reactions occurred at Cornell. Although Sharp had been near retirement at the time the documents were released, he said the Thailand Controversy did affect his working relationship with students. Sharp and David K. Wyatt, a historian of Thailand and member of AACT, attended a public forum at Cornell where they were questioned by students and faculty on their work for AACT. Sharp said that "in terms of the accusations" leveled by students and the SMC, it was "a justifiable meeting" and that there was a "good deal of misunderstanding" by the accusers.[59] David Wyatt said that what had bothered him about the meeting was "the assumption that anyone who had anything to do with the U.S. government was evil."[60]

David Marr, a historian of Vietnam now teaching at the Australian National University, who was teaching at Cornell on a visiting appointment at the time of the Thailand Controversy, had travelled to the San Francisco AAS meeting with David Wyatt. While in San Francisco, he learned that his name had been identified with the *Student Mobilizer* Thailand Controversy issue as someone opposed to those accused of wrongdoing. Marr recalls speaking at the Cornell meeting:

I first explained that I knew nothing of the events prior to hearing and reading [of them] at the AAS meeting. However, after reading the evidence available, and listening to subsequent explanations, it seemed to me that the critics of Sharp, David Wilson, etc., had some justification.[61]

Marr believes that "this whole episode helped to eliminate my chances for a tenure–track position at Cornell."[62]

Another person present at the meeting cited (not for attribution) the "hatchet job" Marr did and said it was not surprising that the other faculty members reacted unfavorably to him. David Wyatt disputes the assumption that the controversy over AACT cost Marr a tenure position at Cornell, citing:

(1) Marr was here [at Cornell] on a two–year visiting appointment.
(2) There was, so far as I know, no possibility at that time of there being a position to which he could have been appointed: we already had two tenured professors of Southeast Asian history, and there was no possibility of there being a third—in a History Department which at the time numbered only 26 for all fields of history.[63]

The Cornell meeting was apparently tape recorded and its contents circulated. Yale graduate students in Southeast Asia listened to the recording, and it is likely that others did as well.[64]

The Thailand Controversy had an effect throughout the academy, on both professors and students, as well as among members of professional organizations like the AAA. The nature of professional ethics became an issue of major importance on campuses throughout the country. Reputations were threatened and relationships with students and colleagues were imperiled.

By the time letters had been exchanged between the "accused" and the "accusers"—late April 1970—the primary issues within the professional community of anthropologists had been articulated. Those in the camp of Wolf and Jorgensen accused Moerman, Phillips, and Sharp of unethical conduct that specifically violated the AAA statements on ethics. Those in the camp of Moerman, Phillips, and Sharp, in turn, accused the Wolf–Jorgensen camp of violating, through their accusations and judgements, the most basic norms of due process.

One camp believed that the Thailand Controversy documents showed Wolf and Jorgensen to be correct in drawing the connections between U.S. social scientists and counterinsurgency policy, in spite of the inappropriateness of their public statements. The other camp did not agree with this conclusion and called for ad–hoc investigations, independent of the Wolf–chaired Ethics Committee, of both the actions of Wolf and Jorgensen and of the anthropologists named in the Thailand Controversy.

CALL FOR INVESTIGATION OF MEMBERS OF AAA ETHICS COMMITTEE

By April 1970 the President of the American Anthropological Association, George Foster, Jr., had been inundated with letters calling for an ad–hoc investigation of the actions of Wolf and Jorgensen. The charges against Wolf and Jorgensen were that they and others had used the tactics of "McCarthyism"; they had failed to abide by the rudiments of due process; they had issued "slanderous, libelous, and defamatory charges"; they had damaged the profession of anthropology; and they had used stolen documents as the basis for falsely accusing colleagues of ethical transgressions. The accusers asserted that the Thailand Controversy documents *did not* show what Wolf and Jorgensen had said they did; and that because of their actions, Wolf, Jorgensen, and Berreman should resign from the Ethics Committee.[65]

Some time in April, Foster, in turn, requested from Ralph Beals an opinion on the charges of unethical conduct levied by Wolf and the others.[66] Beals was respected as the author of "Background Information on Problems of Anthropological Research and Ethics," which had led to the "Statement on Problems of Anthropological Research and Ethics" approved by the Fellows of the AAA 1967 (See Appendix B). He was also the author of the *Politics of Social Research*, which discusses the research that led to his earlier "Background" report.

In his May 1, 1970, response to Foster's request, Beals wrote that the "Statement on Ethics" said nothing relevant to the subject of serving as consultants to government agencies, except that it rejected clandestine activities, secrecy, and having research results made classified:

> The assumption that by attendance at conferences or serving on a consultant basis means the persons involved thereby endorsed everything said or the policies of government agencies is wholly unwarranted. A good many anthropologists who have attended conferences or served as consultants to government agencies have done so in the hope of preventing unwise decisions and policies.

Whether government policies may best be influenced by
maintaining contact with its agencies or through external criticism
is an individual decision....[67]

Beals criticized the actions of Wolf, Jorgensen, and Berreman as being
unethical and stated that their claims to having spoken as individuals, not as
members of the Ethics Committee, were "indefensible." He called for the
resignation from the Ethics Committee of Wolf, Jorgensen, and Berreman.
Before a decision was made on these complaints, the Wolf–chaired Ethics
Committee issued two statements in support of Wolf and Jorgensen.

STATEMENT OF THE WOLF–CHAIRED ETHICS COMMITTEE

On May 2, 1970, the Ethics Committee, composed of Gerald Berreman,
Norman Chance, Robert Ehrich, Joseph Jorgensen, William Shack, Wayne
Suttles, Terence Turner, Oswald Werner, and Eric Wolf issued two
unanimous[68] statements to the President and the Executive Board of the
AAA. In the first statement, the Committee said it "strongly supports the
propriety" of Wolf and Jorgensen having addressed the March 30 statement
of the SMC, as well as their letters to the four anthropologists associated
with the Thailand Controversy. It also supported Wolf, Berreman, and non–
member Sahlins in their claim to be acting as "individuals" in commenting
on the controversy.[69]

The second May 2 statement reads:

Our examination of the documents available to us pertaining to
consultation, research and related activities in Thailand convinces
us that anthropologists are being used in large programs of
counterinsurgency whose effects should be of grave concern to the
Association. Those programs comprise efforts at the manipulation
of people on a giant scale and intertwine straightforward
anthropological research in Southeast Asia and in other parts of the
world.

Although involvement by anthropologists seems to range between
acceptance of the goals of counterinsurgency activities and rejection
of them, the orientations of individual anthropologists are not our
concern. On the other hand, the effects of their participation

concern us deeply. They generate conflicts between the ethical standards of the Association as expressed in the "Statement on Problems of Anthropological Research and Ethics," of 1967, and the personal ethics of individual anthropologists. They polarize members of the Association, threatening a deep and lasting division within it. They downgrade the credibility of social science and social scientists. Such participation also entails direct and fateful intervention in the lives of the people of Southeast Asia.[70]

When the Ethics Committee statements reached Phillips, he immediately wrote a letter to its members on May 19, 1970, in which he both chastised them for their lack of knowledge about Thailand and condemned ARPA activities:

[Y]ou care almost nothing about the professional issues posed for anthropologists working in a counterinsurgency "situation" or about the affects of "counterinsurgency research" upon the people of Thailand, about which you know hardly anything, and have asked even less. Rather, like your chairman and the SMC, you seem primarily concerned with public scandal and the political use of such scandal.... That you are animated more by the desire to condemn than to inquire is attested to by the simple fact that *none* of you has ever asked any of our group of Thai anthropologists *anything* about counterinsurgency research in Thailand. And had you asked, as Mr. Wittenberg [sic: Rittenberg], the student at the University of Chicago, asked me in 1967—you certainly would have been told.... Any social scientist who has been in Thailand for a week knows about the role that ARPA—with its annual budget of 5–12 million dollars—plays in subverting the purpose and direction of social science research in that country. After Professor Berreman became a member of the Ethics Committee and indicated in informal conversation that counterinsurgency involvement might be of interest to your Committee, I volunteered on two separate occasions to discuss with him ARPA activities, principally because I knew of two professional anthropologists who were employees of ARPA and I felt their activities crystallized a kind of problem which would be of interest to your Committee. Berreman said he was interested but never actually responded to my offer [emphasis in original].[71]

Who the "two professional anthropologists" were and whether or not Phillips was one of them remains unclear. In his unpublished manuscript *Between The Tiger and the Crocodile,* Phillips makes reference to three anthropologists working on counterinsurgency projects; another anthropologist who worked for USOM/Thailand and later for ARPA (probably Toshio Yatsushiro); and Colonel Donald Marshall, an anthropologist and U.S. Army colonel who had prepared a study on Thailand for the Army in the mid–1960s.[72] Phillips also knew of Austrian anthropologist Robert Kickert, who had studied for a time at Berkeley and worked for ARPA in Thailand.

SUTTLES–CHAIRED ETHICS COMMITTEE REPORT

Sometime in May, the Executive Board of the AAA prepared a statement of instruction to the Ethics Committee in preparation for the issuance of its annual report. In its instructions (published in the June *AAA Newsletter*), the Board reaffirmed the AAA "Statement on Ethics" (Appendix E) and wrote, in part:

1) Actions by anthropologists in Thailand or elsewhere which contravene the above statement of ethics are a breach of the ethical standards of the association.

2) Evidence so far available, on either side of this issue, is incomplete and not adequately verified; hence, no evaluation of the Thai issue is possible at this time.

3) Current discussion confirms the necessity and desirability of a viable Committee on Ethics of the American Anthropological Association.

4) The Chairman (Wolf) and a member (Jorgensen) of the Ethics Committee, in communicating on this matter outside the Ethics Committee, went beyond the mandate of the Executive Board to that Committee and were speaking as individuals and not on behalf of the Committee or the Association.

The Board instructs the Ethics Committee to limit itself to its specific charge, narrowly interpreted, namely to present to the Board recommendations on its future role and functions, and to fulfill this charge without further collection of case materials or by any quasi–investigative activities.[73]

The Executive Board statement was preceded by a prefatory section that briefly traced the history of the controversy. It said the Executive Board had given "careful consideration of the documents and of all letters and other statements of the principals in the case" and included this sentence:

Five anthropologists whose names appear in the documents and who fear their professional reputations have been adversely affected have raised the question of the propriety of the actions of two Ethics Committee members in this matter.[74]

In a letter to the *AAA Newsletter*, board members David Aberle and David Schneider criticized this introductory material (apparently written by George Foster without the approval of the entire Board)[75] because it

had the effect of laying entire stress on the Ethics Committee procedures and gave virtually no attention to the substantive issues raised by that Committee....

It is not correct to say the Board reviewed the documents it received in any full and far–reaching fashion. It is correct to say that it came to no conclusion as a result of such review as it did give to them, but it did not go into them with enough care to say whether they did provide significant evidence on some *issues* [emphasis in original].[76]

After reading the Executive Board statement, Wolf and Jorgensen resigned from the Ethics Committee on May 25, noting that the charge

appears designed to appease all contending parties rather than to grapple with the substantive issues posed by the documents assembled by the Student Mobilization Committee. In its Statement the Board wishes the Ethics Committee to limit itself to its specific charge, narrowly interpreted, but it is not equally specific about its own intention to cope with the issues raised by an applied anthropology which has for its focal concern the internal security of the present Thailand government. In drawing attention to the actions of particular members of the Ethics Committee, the Board evidently hoped to avert a threat to the internal harmony of our Association. In not applying themselves with equal diligence to an analysis of the issue which prompted these individual actions, the Board averts its eyes from the real source of a danger which threatens not only the integrity of the Association, but the fate and welfare of the peoples among whom we work. In view of the failure of the Board to interpret its mandate to the Ethics Committee to include a concern of vital relevance to the profession, we ourselves fail to perceive how the Committee can "present to the Board recommendations on its future role and functions." We therefore tender our resignations as Chairman and Member of the Committee on Ethics....[77]

In September 1970 the remaining members of the Ethics Committee, Wayne Suttles (acting chairman), Gerald Berreman, Norman Chance, William Shack, and Terence Turner (without Ehrich and Werner),[78] responded to the charge of the Executive Board. They wrote they were in full agreement with points (1) and (3) of the above Executive Board statement. However, with regard to point (2)—that "no evaluation of the Thai issue is possible at this time"—the Ethics Committee wrote that this is "true only with respect to the question of the ethical status of the actions of the individuals named in the documents."[79] But, the Ethics Committee continued:

We believe, after careful examination of the documents made available by SMC that they constitute adequate grounds for the conclusion that a general pattern of government–sponsored research activity exists in Thailand that involves clandestine research. It is clear, moreover, whatever the character of the involvement of the individuals named in the documents may have been, that the government has followed a general policy of attempting to involve anthropologists in this pattern of research activity. This is the major issue raised by the documents, one which transcends in importance and exists quite apart from the question of the nature of the activities of particular individuals.

With regard to point (4) of the Executive Board statement, which addressed the public statements of Wolf and Jorgensen, the Suttles–chaired Ethics Committee wrote:

> The situation was fraught with extraordinary pressures and danger to the good name of the Association as a whole: national publication, accompanied by sensational publicity, of the documents was imminent. Under the circumstances, there was no time to convene a meeting of the Ethics Committee or for that matter the Executive Board. Wolf and Jorgensen were faced with the choice of (a) replying with a "no comment" on the grounds of alleged lack of information or doubts as to the authenticity of the documents (b) refusing to comment on the grounds that it would be necessary to wait to go through the proper channels; (c) commenting as they did; or (d) commenting further than they did. We feel that (a) would have been inappropriate because of the convincing character of the documents themselves and that (d) would likewise have been inappropriate on grounds of discretion. Alternative (b) in the context of the rapidly breaking news story, would have amounted to a refusal to react in time to affect the story, and would have doubtlessly been exploited by SMC as evidence that anthropologists, like doctors, Senators and musk oxen, close ranks to protect their own regardless of circumstances. We therefore feel that a limited response of the kind Wolf and Jorgensen actually made, acknowledging receipt of the documents and referring to the 1967 declaration, was the most appropriate reaction to a very difficult situation.

While the Suttles–chaired Ethics Committee supported the public–private distinction between the actions of Wolf and Jorgensen, it said that the language of their letter to the four anthropologists was "not entirely appropriate." Nevertheless, the committee felt that the entire Ethics Committee, which supported Wolf and Jorgensen, should have been censured, not only Wolf and Jorgensen.

Finally, writing on the Thailand Controversy documents themselves, the Ethics Committee stated:

> The documents consist almost entirely of official correspondence, memos, and minutes of exploratory discussion meetings oriented

toward the inception, promotion, and programming of social science research that could be of use to various American governmental agencies and programs in Thailand, including those connected with counterinsurgency and political control in rural areas. They indicate clearly enough that several government agencies were considering or proposing programs of research which, if implemented, would necessarily have had to be at least partly clandestine, *if "clandestine" is defined to include deliberate distortion or withholding of research aims from the subject population....* These programs were to have been concerned, among other things, with ascertaining optimal policies and methods of securing the political loyalty, or at least passivity, of the rural population....The documents strongly suggest that some anthropologists were involved in at least some of these programs. The documents, in short, clearly contradict the *spirit* of the Association's resolution against clandestine research [emphasis added].

By defining "clandestine" according to the *Random House Dictionary of the English Language* ("characterized by, done for, or executed with secrecy or concealment, esp. for purposes of subversion or deception; private or surreptitious"),[80] the Suttles–chaired Ethics Committee clearly implicated the actions of those anthropologists named in the Thailand Controversy documents.

Phillips responded to the published report of the Suttles–chaired Ethics Committee with a long letter published in the *AAA Newsletter* of January 1971.[81] He took issue with the Ethics Committee and said he would not participate in any examination that it instituted without a simultaneous examination of the conduct of the Wolf–chaired Ethics Committee. In the same issue of the *AAA Newsletter*, Michael Moerman also published a letter in which he detailed his connections with the government agencies and private organizations mentioned in the Thailand documents.[82]

THAILAND CONTROVERSY IN AUSTRALIA

In November 1970, the same month in which the Ethics Committee report was published in the *AAA Newsletter*, Wolf and Jorgensen published "Anthropology on the Warpath in Thailand" in the *New York Review of Books*.[83] The *Review* article discussed the history of the .Thailand Controversy (without using the use of names of the anthropologists implicated) and included brief excerpts from the documents. Wolf and Jorgensen wrote:

> As the Thailand papers show, the [U.S.] government is less interested in the economic, social, or political causes of discontent than in techniques of neutralizing individual or collective protest.[84]

They called on anthropology to "disengage itself from its connection with colonial aims."

In the article, Wolf and Jorgensen also added two new items to the Thailand Controversy. The first was a discussion of the functions of the Tribal Research Center in Chiang Mai, Thailand, and the contribution of Australian anthropologists to its research. The second was the mention of a "lone dissenter" who had refused to participate in any activities that might endanger people studied in Northern Thailand. Both of these additions turned out to be problematic for Wolf and Jorgensen, as their opponents accused them of getting their facts wrong in recounting the stories of both the Tribal Research Center and the lone dissenter.

Regarding the Tribal Research Center, in their *Review* article Wolf and Jorgensen discussed a "Consultants' Meeting" that took place in Chiang Mai in January 1970, under what they said was Tribal Research Center auspices. According to Wolf and Jorgensen, officials at the Consultants' Meeting made it clear that a Tribal Data Center was to be established to centralize information (with a computer) on the "tribal people" of Northern Thailand for use by interested parties. Further, Wolf and Jorgensen wrote that thirty-two social scientists, twenty-two affiliated with American universities, were invited to attend the Meeting. The actual Tribal Research Center/Tribal Data Center story is more complex, does not mention a computer, and involves two meetings. But Wolf and Jorgensen are correct in the essentials of their story, especially in their contention that ARPA was involved in attempting to recruit social scientists to its cause.

The Tribal Research Center was founded in 1965 following the suggestion of Hans Mannsdorf of Austria, who had been working in Thailand under UNESCO and Asia Foundation sponsorship. Mannsdorf recommended that a Tribal Research Center collect data on "hill tribes" and evaluate Thai Department of Public Welfare programs aimed at the hill tribes.[85] W. R. Geddes, an anthropologist at the University of Sydney, Australia, was the first advisor to the Tribal Research Center. Geddes proposed and initiated six basic tribal studies, which were carried out by foreign anthropologists assisted by Thai students, in spite of what Geddes said was "opposition" from ARPA officials, "who were more interested in sponsoring research under American control."[86] Geddes's salary and the cost of jeeps provided to the Tribal Research Center were paid by the Australian government "from its allocation of Australian funds to the SEATO [Southeast Asia Treaty Organization] aid programme."[87] Geddes has written that he was responsible to and submitted reports to the Thai Director of Public Welfare. He also submitted reports to the Secretary General of SEATO and the Australian ambassador, but said he was not obliged to do so.[88]

Geddes was succeeded as advisor to the Tribal Research Center by his former student Peter Hinton, who served as advisor from 1965–1969. According to Hinton, during this time, research was to focus on improving agriculture, health, education, and administration. Funds were provided by the Thai Budget Bureau (about $25,000 per year) and from foreign sources, predominantly the Australian Aid Projects Branch of the Department of Foreign Affairs (about $15,000 per year).[89] Hinton later said SEATO "only provided the channels through which unilateral aid from Australia, New Zealand, Britain, and America passed."[90] According to the SEATO Secretary–General at the time, however, SEATO's interest in the Tribal research Center was more specific. General Vargas of SEATO wrote in the SEATO Report for 1967–1968:

> The Hill Tribes Research Center, in Chiang Mai in Northern Thailand, continues to make significant progress in its primary task of producing worthy studies on the tribal peoples in Thailand. Such studies are becoming increasingly important as the Communists have concentrated much effort to subvert the hill tribes people of the country. To counteract Communist subversion, it is important to have a wide knowledge of these people.

And in the SEATO Report for 1968–1969, Vargas wrote:

> The Center, with the assistance of well–qualified advisers from
> SEATO member nations has produced during the year worthy and
> timely studies on the hill tribes in Thailand, which reveal their
> vulnerability to Communist subversion.[91]

Thus, despite Hinton's assertion that "the TRC was not concerned with
counterinsurgency research, and no efforts were spared to maintain its
autonomy from US agencies which were,"[92] it seems that SEATO was
prepared to use the information in another manner. By 1970, a SEATO
medical official was able to remark that,"All of the foreign staff at the Tribal
Research Centre have been appointed and supported through SEATO."[93]

While Hinton was at the helm of the Tribal Research Center, ARPA
approached him several times seeking closer "'coordination,'" but this
proposal was rejected by his Thai colleagues at the Center.[94] According to
Hinton, after being rebuffed, ARPA went to the Dean of Social Sciences at
Chiang Mai University and created the Lanna Thai Research Center as a
joint ARPA–Faculty of Social Sciences operation. In 1969 ARPA financed
the creation of the Tribal Data Center, which was to use the facilities of the
Tribal Research Center.[95] According to Hinton, he was doing research in a
village for much of 1969 and left Thailand in October, "strongly opposed to
the drawing together of the TRC and the ARPA–financed TDC but no
longer in a position to do anything about it."[96] The process by which
ARPA managed circumvent and then subvert a legitimate research center
should give pause.

The Tribal Data Center (TDC) was at first quite different from the
Tribal Research Center (TRC). According to TDC documents, the idea for a
Tribal Data Center "to centralize all available information concerning tribal
peoples and their environment" was originally proposed by W. R. Geddes.[97]
Geddes remembered it slightly differently, but was not opposed to such
collection of information nor its use by defense departments. In a May 1971
letter to Margaret Mead, Geddes wrote:

> I cannot recall ever having made such a specific proposal. But I did
> write in the 1967 United Nations report [on reducing opium
> production] that successful socioeconomic planning to improve or
> maintain the welfare of the hill tribes required accurate statistical
> information on them....

> I did not envisage a separate Tribal Data Centre.... I cannot find any sound argument, however, against the decision to give the work to a special Tribal Data Centre. It makes the information more accessible to persons in the north where the tribal populations are....

> I do have an inborn suspicion of any kind of data bank....

> Like all publicly available information the information from the Tribal Data Centre may be used by the Defense Department of the Thailand Government. The anthropologist cannot prevent this situation. It is a logical consequence of the principle that the information be open to all. The Defense Department may use the information for counterinsurgency. The anthropologist also has no abstract ethical right to prevent this. Governments may oppose insurgency because government and insurgency are logically contradictory. [footnote: By insurgency I do not mean criticism of government, but violent attempts to do away with it.][98]

In December of 1969, the Dean of the Chiang Mai University Faculty of Social Sciences invited eighty people to a January 14, 1970, conference on the uses of ARPA's Tribal Data Center (TDC). The TDC self–consciously scheduled its meeting just a few days before the "Seminar on Shifting Cultivation and Economic Development in Northern Thailand," January 18-24, 1970, so that some of the participants at the Shifting Cultivation seminar, including Hinton and Geddes, could attend the TDC conference.[99] Hinton and Geddes did go to the Seminar, but declined to attend the TDC Meeting. Wolf and Jorgensen may have confused the invitations to the Seminar and the Meeting. Some academics were invited to both, including Peter Kunstadter (University of Washington) and A.Y. Dessaint (University of Hawaii).

Dean of Social Sciences Nibhond Sasidhorn's invitation letter at no time stated that the TDC was an ARPA project. It did, however, describe TDC's goal and urged invitees to contribute to it:

> [The Tribal Data Centre] is intended to develop systems of collecting coding, processing, integrating, storing, updating, checking, retrieving and publishing data concerning tribal people of Northern Thailand and contiguous areas.

We understand that in the course of your work you may be in a position either to supply us with raw data concerning tribal communities, to utilize processed data, or to give us technical advice as to systems of data collection and processing.[100]

"Raw data" may seem like a benign collection of information, but the "Proposal for Village Data Card" circulated at the meeting called for data collection far exceeding that necessary for ethnographers.[101] In addition to questions on the village name and number of houses, categories include map coordinates of the village, name of village headman and influential persons, number of Border Patrol Police living in village, name, race and occupation of occasional residents, and weapons in the village. This bears a passing resemblance to the questionnaire used in ARPA's Rural Security Systems Survey, which surveyed villages in Northeast Thailand (see Appendix D).

According to TDC documents, persons attending the meeting included seven from ARPA/MRDC (including anthropologist Robert W. Kickert) and representatives from SEATO, the Thai Ministry of the Interior, the Border Patrol Police, the Tribal Research Center (although Geddes and Hinton declined to attend), the Thai National Security Council, the Communist Suppression Operations Command, USOM/Thailand (including Research and Evaluation Division's James Hoath), the Peace Corps, representatives from six Christian missions, and persons from different departments at Chiang Mai University, the University of Paris, and the University of Munich.[102]

At the actual "Meeting of Consultants and Interested Persons," ARPA's James L. Woods made it clear that ARPA was financially supporting the TDC as a "cooperative project between the Faculty [of Social Sciences] and the Tribal Research Centre."[103] He also said that the TDC would serve the needs of all the groups represented at the meeting, thus linking non–military users, such as academics, with those users who wanted to help with military planning, such as ARPA. A chart of "Administrative and Funding Channels," appended to the Record of the Meeting, indicates that funds were transferred from ARPA to its joint Thai–U.S. Military Research and Development Center (MRDC), to the U.S. Army's 9th Logistical Command, to the Applied Scientific Research Corporation of Thailand, to the Lanna Thai Social Science Research Centre, and finally, to the Tribal Data Centre.[104] While everyone could benefit from such a project, the information was going to be used as an aid to ARPA projects.

Participants at the meeting spoke about the data they might have to contribute to the TDC, their usage requirements, and channels of communication to the TDC. In addition to the non–counterinsurgency related commentary from Ministry of Agriculture, Malaria Eradication Center, the Faculty of Medicine, and others, the following comments by participants make it clear that the data gathered by the TDC would be used as a tool in counterinsurgency programs.[105]

James Woods said ARPA was interested in "migratory patterns and the reaction of the populace to Royal Thai Government programs." Colonel Phoon Phon Asanachinta, professor of Geography at Chiang Mai University and a member of the ARPA–financed Trail Study Project, said maps of trails and environmental features of land around trails would be made available to the TDC. A BPP officer said his organization would be able to provide information on "tribespeople" and would be interested in "data concerning aspects of border security." Representatives from the Christian missions indicated their willingness to provide information to the TDC, including correcting topographical maps.

The Communist Suppression Operations Command official said his agency was concerned with "'winning the war' against communist infiltration" and would provide information "relevant to tribespeople," while being interested in a broad spectrum of "tribal data." At this point, Gary Oughton, the agricultural adviser to the Tribal Research Centre,

> highlighted the usefulness of aerial photography in speedily updating geographical and environmental information. He expressed the hope that the various agencies concerned with either aerial survey or photointerpretation could be coordinated in regard to the needs of tribal data collection.

Wanat Bhruksasri, the Director of the Tribal Research Center and later co–editor of the book *Highlanders of Thailand*,[106] commented on the inauguration of fourteen "Contact Teams" that would be attached to each rural district in Chiang Mai and Mae Hong Son provinces. The Contact Teams would

> ... establish friendly relations with each tribal community in their assigned districts. Later they will be able to conduct socio– economic surveys among each tribal community in their districts on behalf of the TDC.

Following the comments of B. P. Whitlock, Program Advisor to the Hill Tribe Radio Station, the TRC's Mr. Oughton spoke from previous experience of the value of broadcasting to Thai and tribal villagers information on impending surveys. After hearing such broadcasts, "nearly all villagers ... had been very cooperative in answering detailed questions." This method for informing villagers could just as easily be used to deceive them, as the CIA Census Aspiration Teams project that mimicked USOM and other surveys to gather information on subversives (discussed in Chapter Five).

The Thai NSC representative stated that although the NSC did not have any raw data of use to the TDC,

> it would probably be important to establish a section for classified information obtained from such sources as CSOC, the Border Patrol Police, the Third Army Command, the MRDC, and Governor's Assistants.

Oughton commented that

> in planning the establishment of the TDC, thought *had* been given to establishing a classified section. However, it was considered that it would be essential to start the Center operating smoothly with the accumulated unclassified data already available before proceeding to a classified section. It should not be difficult, in any event, to arrange to consign all such material to the classified section of the [ARPA] Thailand Information Centre in Bangkok [emphasis in original].

In a letter to Eric Wolf and the *New York Review of Books* in December 1970, after Wolf's article had appeared in the *Review*, Oughton claimed his position on classified research was somewhat different:

> ARPA has been adamant that the Tribal Data Project maintain an open facility, and that it not handle "classified" material ... Had this not been the case, I am assured that the Director of the Tribal Research Centre would not have accepted U.S. financial assistance. I would certainly have been reluctant to render my services in an advisory capacity.[107]

Oughton's comment at the TDC Meeting was a corrective to his letter to Wolf. It appears that ARPA preferred that the TDC *begin* as a wholly open facility; it could later establish a classified section. Oughton did not seem disturbed at the suggestion of the Thai NSC representative that a classified section be established; but for the time being, he suggested steering classified documents to ARPA in Bangkok.

Returning to the original Wolf and Jorgensen assertions in their *Review* article, the Consultants' Meeting was convened by the Tribal *Data* Center, not the Tribal *Research* Center. But, as the above history has demonstrated, by late 1969 ARPA, through the Tribal Data Center, had effectively coopted the Tribal Research Center. TRC director Wanat Bhruksasri went so far as to say, "The logical place at which the [Tribal Research] Center should store such information [its data] is, of course, the TDC."[108] The Dean of Social Sciences as Chiang Mai had assured that the Tribal Data Center would be headquartered at the Tribal Research Center.[109] Finally, as "the only foreign advisor attached to the Tribal *Research* Center," Oughton's views on cooperation with ARPA were substantially different than those of his predecessors Hinton and Geddes:

> It must be accepted as a fact of life that the very information required in order for a government to establish a just and peaceful administration over its domain is also sought after by those who wish to disrupt, or to hinder the establishment of, such an administration through subversive activities. The same information is required also by those who need to engage in short–term measures to counter insurgency. I do not see this as a justification for refusing to involve in the gathering of information in an honest and open way.[110]

The fact that there was not a computer at the TRC or the TDC and other minor errors should not dilute the thrust of Wolf and Jorgensen's article. In a July 1971 letter to the editor of the *New York Review of Books*, the two pointed out that they were trying to draw attention to the "extraordinary alliance between counterinsurgents and academics." They urged that "the political and military contexts in which academic findings are increasingly used [and] the cooptation of academics into the 'intelligence community'" must not be "lost sight of in the course of arguments concerning who did what, when, and where."[111]

A footnote to the Thailand Controversy in Australia is that a small Australian journal reprinted an article written by Alfred McCoy in 1970 on the overreaction by the Thai military to population pressure, causing a group of Hmong people to move (discussed at the end of Chapter Five).[112] The journal apparently asserted that W. R. Geddes had been instrumental in the death of Hmong at the hand of the Thai military. Geddes sued the journal and won a libel article that bankrupted it.[113]

CASE OF THE "LONE DISSENTER"

The second issue brought to the surface by Wolf and Jorgensen was the case of the "lone dissenter" from this nexus of military–academic cooperation. This tangent becomes important because some academics who opposed Wolf and Jorgensen saw the case of the lone dissenter as an example of their poor scholarship. In their *Review* article, Wolf and Jorgensen championed an individual who "refused to make available his field research data" and "called on anthropologists to help create radical political alternatives for the people among whom they work."[114] They also recounted their version of this person's reasons for pursuing research in northern Thailand and how he became aware of the use to which research could be put by the Thai government and Border Patrol Police.

In an April 8, 1971, letter to the *Review*, Wolf and Jorgensen identified their lone dissenter as CUNY anthropologist Delmos Jones.[115] Unfortunately, Jones did not find the individual described in Wolf and Jorgensen's 1970 *Review* article to match himself: "Since this unnamed individual has now been named, and I find to my great surprise that it is me, I feel that some statement is required on my part."[116] Jones went on to draw a careful distinction between himself and what he called the "half truths and distortions" of Wolf and Jorgensen's description of him and his positions, which were originally articulated in an article Jones had written in August 1970, but which was not published in *Current Anthropology* until June 1971.[117]

Although Jones was uncomfortable with Wolf and Jorgensen's interpretation of his comments, it bears a closer resemblance to his original comments than Jones prefers to admit. Jones's article is a carefully reasoned and powerfully argued discussion of the philosophical issues involved in making ethical decisions in anthropology, or anywhere. In it he asks:

Was it an accident that the strategic and political concerns about the hill areas and the questionable loyalty of the hill people to Thailand coincided with the growing anthropological concern about the lack of knowledge of the area? Was it also an accident that, about the same time, a considerable amount of money became available for basic research on this "little–known area"?[118]

He suggests a possible answer:

It is extremely unlikely that there would be any official awareness of social and economic conditions among the hill people—much less any attempt to improve those conditions—if they did not occupy the important strategic position that they do.[119]

Jones goes on to attack the "illusion of neutrality" under which anthropologists labor while doing research, and notes that "... by presenting descriptive materials we have provided a tool which the more powerful can use against the powerless."[120] Jones concludes:

Most anthropologists would no doubt express concern over what is happening and what is going to happen to the people among whom they have worked. Few, however, would consider that one of the ways to protect their people in politically dangerous situations is to refrain from publishing books and articles describing their way of life. This is the conclusion that I have reached....

If we decide not to publish, we may jeopardize promotions, raises, and even job security. But we cannot have it both ways. We must not only "think twice" when asked to provide services, which directly and indirectly, support the war effort.... if we do not support the war, we must refuse to provide these services. A true radical cannot do otherwise.[121]

In his corrective to Wolf and Jorgensen,[122] Jones pointed out that his *Current Anthropology* piece stressed general, and not individual, issues of ethics. He corrected personal details (for example, that he had, in fact, published on the tribal group he had studied and that he was not at a particular TRC conference as assumed by Wolf and Jorgensen). Wolf and Jorgensen responded to the Jones letter by acknowledging their factual errors. However, they also presented excerpts from Jones's letter and wrote, "these are brave words and we believe that Dr. Jones will not want to go back on them now."[123]

MEAD COMMITTEE

The AAA Executive Board had been under pressure by participants involved on both sides of the Thailand Controversy to conduct an investigation of all aspects of the controversy. In November 1970 the Executive Board voted to establish

> an ad hoc committee of inquiry to deal with the controversy over research and other activities of United States anthropologists in Thailand and their implications for anthropology as a profession and for anthropological research throughout the world.[124]

The result was the creation of the "Ad Hoc Committee to Evaluate the Controversy Concerning Anthropological Activities in Thailand." Because it was chaired by Margaret Mead, the Committee was known informally as the Mead Committee.

The selection process for the composition of the Mead Committee was rather informal. According to former AAA Executive Board chairman George Foster, the president, president–elect, and the six other Board members met and discussed candidates.[125] (The other Board members were David Aberle, Cyril Belshaw, James Gibbs, Eugene Hammel, Dell Hymes, David Schneider, and Charles Wagley.) In a recent interview, Foster said there was quite a spread of political opinions among Board members, which assured that the Mead Committee would be composed of "fair and objective people."[126] Cyril Belshaw noted, however, that the fact that no Thai anthropologists had been asked to comment on the matter put the AAA in a particularly "ethnocentric" position; he was leery of being lumped (as a Canadian) with any American institutional positions that might come out of the AAA.[127]

Foster has said that Margaret Mead was the "obvious choice" for chairperson, because, "We all knew Mead and knew she was genuinely respected by her colleagues for her demonstrated concern with ethical and moral problems."[128] Added to this is Foster's description of Mead as a "mother–goddess" in terms of her relationship to the tribe of American anthropologists. Wolf recalls that, among American anthropologists, Mead had the "status of a senior medicine woman"; Steven Piker characterizes her stature to have been "virtually pantheanic–transcendental."[129]

In addition to Mead, the other three Committee members chosen by the Board were David Olmsted (University of California-Davis), William Davenport (University of California-Santa Cruz), and Ruth Freed (New York University). Freed acted as executive secretary.[130] The charge to the Mead Committee included the following points:

> 1. Through consideration of the existing documentation and solicitation of additional written statements from concerned persons, inquire into and make findings of fact concerning the activities of members of the AAA in, and in relationship to, Thailand since the issuance of the "Statement on Problems of Anthropological Research and Ethics" ...

> 2. Determine what, if any, aspects of these activities violated the principles of that 1967 statement or subsequent resolutions pertaining to ethics and professional conduct passed by the Association.

> 3. Inquire as to the actions of the Ethics Committee and its members and former members, and similarly of the Board, in relation to the Thailand controversy....

> Were there research activities or other activities, carried on in Thailand or concerning Thailand, including consultation or the preparation of reports and memoranda, for governments or contract, grant, or employing agencies that violated (i) existing canons of ethics as embodied in the 1967 statement and/or (ii) canons of ethics since established by the Resolutions of the Council, and/or (iii) canons of ethics embodied in the Code of Professional Conduct [reproduced as Appendix E] now before the Council for ratification or rejection, and/or (iv) raised ethical issues not considered in any of these documents yet, in the opinion of the Ad–Hoc Committee, of grave concern to the profession?...

> [The Committee will also consider] the validity and propriety of statements made (i) by members of the Ethics Committee who so designated themselves [Wolf and Jorgensen]; (ii) by a member of

the Ethics Committee who did not so designate himself [Berreman]; (iii) by the Ethics Committee as such.[131]

A published account of the research procedure of the Mead Committee was written, after the fact, by member William Davenport.[132] He wrote that all material in the possession of the AAA Ethics Committee was turned over to the Mead Committee, which also had requested written statements from the people involved in the Thailand Controversy. According to Davenport's published account, no formal interviews were conducted. However, in a later interview, he did say that George Foster had talked to him during this time and Mead had conducted some interviews when she had passed through Australia during the summer of 1971.[133] Committee member David Olmsted has also said that interviews were conducted, including his meeting with those in geographic proximity to him, such as Foster (at Foster's request).[134] That there was no formal interview process set up—but that they occurred nonetheless at the instigation of Committee members or others—resulted in what may have been an unbalanced information gathering system.

Davenport wrote that approximately 700 pages of material was collected by the Committee, including some public documents but not counting the documents provided to the Ethics Committee by the Student Mobilization Committee.[135] Olmsted remembers "mountains of material" being collected by the Mead Committee.[136] According to an August 25, 1971, bibliography of the material collected by the Mead Committee, the material included extensive correspondence with sixty individuals, issues of the *AAA Newsletter*, the Thailand Controversy documents that had been copied from Moerman's files, and correspondence between the Ethics Committee and anthropologists.[137] The Mead Committee Report itself cited 212 requests for information, 67 responses, and about 6000 pages of material.[138]

According to Davenport, the Mead Committee met first in the spring of 1971 to set up its procedures and again in September 1971 to write its report.[139] In between, members were in communication with each other directly and through the executive secretary, Ruth Freed. Mead was out of the country from June 19 through September 4, 1971, travelling and attending conferences in Europe and New Guinea.[140] How she was able to read the assembled documents is unclear.

After the Report was written in September 1971, the members of the Mead Committee wanted it to be distributed initially only to the members of the Executive Board. After this, they wanted it distributed at the AAA Council of Fellows meeting, which took place at the AAA annual meeting in New York in November. At the Council of Fellows meeting, the Mead Committee would be available to answer questions from the floor, but under no circumstances did the Mead Committee want its report distributed to the general membership of the AAA before the annual meeting.[141]

Normal procedure, however, was for the Executive Board to decide how a report was to be released, and reports were usually released in advance of the meetings at which they were discussed.[142] Executive Board member David Aberle remembers each Board member receiving a copy of the report with a statement saying it was not to be circulated prior to the annual meeting. He called Edward Lehman, then Executive Director of the AAA, to voice his concern. He was told that, were he to be thinking of releasing the report in advance, there were distinct mistakes on each copy to allow for the tracing of leaks. Aberle asked if anything could be done to distribute the report prior to the meeting. Lehman answered that the Board could not meet prior to that time, but that its members could be polled if anyone chose to do so.[143] Aberle then initiated a telephone vote of Board members that overrode the Mead Committee's wishes, and the report was distributed to the AAA membership by mail in early November. Thus, the members of the AAA had time to review the report in preparation for the discussion that was sure to follow at the annual meeting.

The Mead Committee Report (reproduced as Appendix G) opens with criticism of the "Indochina war," calling it "unconstitutional, unwise, and unnecessary."[144] The report continues:

> News of atrocities perpetrated by the United States and its allies produces deep psychic disturbance among many people, because the incidents stem in part from racist attitudes which stain our social fabric and at the same time contravene our most revered ideals and cherished views of ourselves.[145]

The Report's preamble follows an earlier suggestion by Mead Committee member Olmsted regarding the language of the report:

> ... if we are to have any chance of persuading newleftish types that we are correct in reprimanding Wolf and Jorgensen, we must include enough of a section on the Indochinese war—revealing attitudes as "pure" as their own—so that they cannot write off our

censure as just another defense mechanism of the establishment. They may do so anyway, but if there is a chance of persuading them, it will come, in my judgement, by way of the realization that "correct" attitudes toward the war do not justify McCarthyite tactics.[146]

The Report noted that the U.S. had merged its social and military objectives in Thailand, but that anthropologists were not aware of this merging. Of those who became aware, the report said, some "abandoned all their government connections" while others "continue to believe that they can still moderate polices and continue to try to bring the programs in which they are involved into closer fit with Thai social and cultural aspirations."[147] The report continued that, in spite of the interests of the U.S. military, all research was carried out "in conjunction and cooperation with the Royal Thai Government."[148]

The report then briefly traced the history of the names under which research funds were given:

[R]esearch funds were not forthcoming from public sources unless the project could be made to appear directly pertinent to some "practical" end of high value to those holding the public purse strings.... much social science, including anthropological research was supported because it was described as related to health, in particular "mental health.".... It happened that, during the Kennedy administration, the nation's military policy was changed from one of nuclear–confrontation–or–nothing to one including an alternative labeled "limited wars" or "counterinsurgency operations." The latter term—counterinsurgency—soon became the label under which funds were given, just as "communication" and "mental health" had been previously. The responses of individuals to the committee and other relevant documents list such activities as: construction of roads, schools and organization of medical care, water supplies, cooperatives, and marketing facilities, as well as village security and mapping of trails, under the heading of counterinsurgency; these are much the same activities that were called "community development" at an earlier time.... [S]uch activity is well within the traditional canons of acceptable behavior for the applied anthropologist, and is counterinsurgent only for present funding purposes; a decade ago it might have been "mental health."[149]

In spite of the fact that these activities were, in the view of the Committee, "well within the canon of acceptable behavior" for anthropologists, its members felt the need to state that "a new ethical dilemma" was evolving:

> It is clear that anthropologists now have to face the possibility that a publication of routine socio–cultural data about identified village communities ... might be used for the annihilation by bombing or other forms of warfare of whole communities.... [150]

The Report roundly condemned Wolf and Jorgensen for their public statements that were issued at the time of the SMC release of documents:

> The ad hoc committee does, however, find reprehensible certain actions taken by various members of the Ethics Committee, viz, their unauthorized identification of themselves as members of said committee in connection with their public denunciations, thus involving the Association; their use of unethically procured documents without public denunciation of the sources of such materials; accusations of colleagues ... without opportunity for due process; or even proper notification of those concerned.... [T]he result was an unjustified, inaccurate, and unfair attack, which has endangered research access for all anthropologists in Thailand and probably elsewhere as well. [151]

Finally, the Report exonerated all non-military members of the AAA from the charges that they had acted unethically:

> No civilian member of the American Anthropological Association has contravened the principles laid down in the 1967 Statement on *Problems of Anthropological Research and Ethics* (Beals Report) in his or her work in Thailand. [152]

The release of the Mead Committee Report to AAA members in early November allowed those who were opposed to its findings to prepare rebuttals for the 70th annual meeting of the AAA, which was to take place on November 18-21 in the Statler Hilton Hotel in New York City. The Report was presented to the Council of Fellows on November 19 at a session that George Foster describes as a "bloodbath." [153] When the acrimonious debate ended in the early morning hours, the Mead Report had been rejected, section by section, by the Fellows of the AAA.

As members of the AAA arrived for the annual meeting beginning on Thursday, November 18, two rebuttals to the Mead report were circulated. One had been written by Wolf and Jorgensen and the other by May N. Diaz and Lucile F. Newman (University of California–Berkeley and University of California–San Francisco, respectively).[154] The Wolf and Jorgensen rebuttal included the following (phrases in quotations are references from the Mead Committee Report; original line numbers have been omitted):

It is incorrect to state that the projects carried out by anthropologists in Thailand are "well within the traditional canons of acceptable behavior for the applied anthropologist." On the contrary, it is the very hallmark of applied anthropology to be aware, to the fullest extent possible, of the larger context within which research is to be applied.... [P]rojects like "village security and mapping of trails" were not at all "much the same activities that were called "community development" at an earlier time...."

Participation in research funded under the label "mental health" is not like participation in research funded under the label "counterinsurgency." Funds extended by NIH, for example, did not require a specific goal and a specific product.... Research under the aegis of counterinsurgency is intended by the granting agency to accomplish specific purposes; the granting agency can only be rewarded for its funds by the delivery of information on groups of people specifiable in time and place.

The consequences of taking money from a given source of funds do not end with the cashing of the check. The anthropologist is not only responsible to himself, but also to his informants and to his profession. This requires that he give some thought to the possible uses to which the material he collects can be put by the granting agency....

Research for the purpose of curing people under the label of "mental health" is, after all, not the same as research for the purpose of "containing" and killing people under the label of "counterinsurgency."

The committee fails to draw fundamental distinctions between a government, the people subject to it, and populations over whom a government wishes to extend its sway. "Thai social and cultural aspirations" are *not* isomorphic with the interests of the Royal Thai government nor with the interests of the hill people who differ from the Thai linguistically and culturally. The inexcusable failure of a committee of *anthropologists* to grasp such distinctions raises serious doubts regarding its ability to understand any or all parts of the controversy. It is the height of naivete to believe that no ethical problems exist as long as "US Government programs with which anthropologists have been associated were carried out in conjunction and cooperation with the Royal Thai Government," or as long as the Royal Thai Government could veto all intended research by US anthropologists.

If the ad hoc committee is satisfied that the activities of anthropologists in Thailand in no way exceeded the usual concerns of applied anthropology, why then need it fear the misuse of data, to the extent of "annihilation by bombing or other forms of warfare of whole communities" ?

The committee errs in stating that it has discovered a "new ethical principle, never envisaged before and never clearly stated in any document submitted to the ad hoc committee." It was precisely recognition of this dilemma which informed the actions of members of the Ethics Committee in the first place....

It is diagnostic of the committee's understanding of the case that it holds us also responsible for endangering "research access for all anthropologists in Thailand and probably elsewhere as well." It is not the symbiosis of anthropology and counterinsurgency which threatens our discipline, but public discussion thereof.[155]

Committee member Davenport noted that while Mead was adamant about the "new ethical principle" of anthropologists having to contend with their data being used by others, "There is nothing new about that. We all know that most intelligence [agencies] use this [data] from ordinary sources."[156]

The Diaz–Newman rebuttal articulated an interesting point regarding the receipt of government funds:

> If the report is correct in assuring us that the research undertaken in Thailand under the label of "counter–insurgency" did in fact restrict itself to projects of "applied anthropology" or "community development," we can only conclude that money was taken under false pretenses.... Either individuals engaging in that research did not do counterinsurgency research but claimed that they did to the funding agencies, or they did such research and claimed not to have done so to the [American Anthropological] Association.[157]

The sequence of events during which the Mead Committee Report was debated and rejected is as follows:[158] On Thursday afternoon, November 18, the Executive Board received the Report, without accepting or rejecting it; this decision was up to the Council of Fellows. At the time, AAA members were classified as Corresponding Members, Voting Members, and Fellows, and only Fellows could vote on the Mead Committee Report. The next day, Friday, November 19, at about nine p.m., the Report was placed on the agenda under old business for "committee reports." About 700 people were gathered in the grand ballroom of the Hilton. Mead proposed that the report be received but not put to a vote. "Neither acceptance nor rejection is appropriate," Mead insisted. From the floor came hisses, which Mead called "silly ... childish behavior"; she said, "The only time I was publicly hissed before was when I advocated that China be admitted to the United Nations." The response was more hissing.[159]

The presiding officer, new AAA president Anthony F. C. Wallace, asked if there were any questions from the floor. With most of the principals of the Thailand Controversy present, the well–organized opposition began leveling critiques at the Mead Committee Report. Eric Wolf and Gerald Berreman read portions of documents to demonstrate that the activities of anthropologists had aided the counterinsurgency objectives of the U.S. and Thai governments. Berreman read excerpts from the American Institutes for Research proposal (*Counterinsurgency in Thailand: The Impact of Economic, Social, and Political Action Programs*) discussed in Chapter Four.

Wolf read a description of a frightening document published in June 1965 by the Military Research and Development Center titled "Low Altitude Visual Search for Individual Human Targets: Further Field Testing in Southeast Asia." Wolf did not identify the author of the report (D. J.

Blakeslee), although he did say that the author was a member of the AAA. What Wolf did not know was that the author was *not*, in fact, a member of the AAA, but bore the same name as a AAA member. The "project description text" that Wolf read to the hushed ballroom was as follows:

> This report is a detailed study of quantitative information on the ability of airborne observers to sight and identify single humans on the ground. The target background for most of the testing was rice paddy with scattered bushes and trees at the end of the dry season in Southeast Asia. An analytical relationship between identification and slant range, velocity, search strip width, and visual performance factors was used with the test data. The conclusion is that limiting velocities for effective search for more difficult targets are so low that they lead to high aircraft vulnerability; and increasing the velocity can mean very narrow search strip widths and, therefore, many search passes for complete coverage of large areas, again compromising vulnerability.[160]

The document from which this excerpt was taken had been provided to Gerald Berreman by the U.S.–Thai Military Research and Development Center (MRDC) in response to a written request.[161] When Berreman and Wolf compared the names of the authors of various MRDC publications with the list of members in the AAA Directory, they found what seemed to be three matches—D. J. Blakeslee, Lee W. Huff, and Robert Kickert.[162] Huff was, in fact, a Voting Member and Kickert a Fellow. However, the Donald J. Blakeslee listed as a Voting Member in the Directory was a graduate student in anthropology at the University of Wisconsin–Milwaukee specializing in North American archaeology, while the Donald J. Blakeslee who authored "Visual Search for Human Targets" was a Rand Corporation employee, not an anthropologist. This information became known to a small group of people after Herbert Phillips later wrote to Donald Blakeslee the AAA member asking for clarification on his role.[163]

The MRDC document requested by Berreman also listed the *Village Security Pilot Study, Northeast Thailand*, coauthored by D. J. Blakeslee, L. W. Huff, and R. W. Kickert. It is an unfortunate example of overwhelming circumstantial evidence that these three names were given as those of individual authors of various MRDC publications and coauthors of the *Village Security Pilot Study* and that the same three names appeared on the AAA membership list. But it cannot be denied that further checking would likely have established that Donald Blakeslee the AAA member was not Donald Blakeslee the MRDC author. The importance attributed to the name confusion seems to correlate with one's position on the Thailand Controversy.

Lee W. Huff, who was a part of the ARPA Research and Development unit in Thailand in the early 1960s and a director of behavioral sciences for ARPA in the mid-1960s, has a doctorate in political economy and development, not in anthropology. In an interview, Huff said he was a member of the AAA and other professional associations in the 1960s and early 1970s because he needed to keep abreast of activities in the social science fields. He is no longer a member of the AAA and had left ARPA and Asia by the time the Thailand Controversy erupted.[164]

Robert Kickert is a more problematic case. According to Herbert Phillips, Kickert, who was not an American citizen, had studied at Berkeley, but did his Ph.D. in anthropology at the University of Vienna. Kickert worked for ARPA, apparently as an anthropologist, from the early 1960s until he resigned shortly before the invasion of Cambodia.[165]

The cases of Huff and Kickert are illustrative of the problem that the AAA would have in instituting a binding ethical code. Membership in the Association is open to anyone, whether or not the person is an anthropologist (as in the case of Huff) and whether or not the person is an American citizen (as in the case of Kickert). How would ethical regulations apply to non–anthropologists or to non–American anthropologists? Huff said that, although Kickert was part of a team working on the *Village Security Pilot Study*, the study had many parts, including a concern with fields of fire; but "anthropologists weren't running around measuring fields of fire."[166] Kickert, or any other anthropologist, could make a similar argument, however specious it might seem.

Returning to the grand ballroom—there was a hushed silence when Wolf and Berreman finished reading their excerpts. The Mead Committee Report, divided into three sections, was voted upon by the Fellows in attendance, section-by-section. A motion to reject the first part (from the beginning to page four, line six) was passed by a vote of 308 to 74. The second part (page four lines 7 to 122) was rejected by a vote of 243 to 57. And as midnight passed, a motion to reject the final section and "to consider the issue of anthropologists in Thailand unresolved" was passed by 214 to 14. The session ended with unanimous approval of a motion thanking the Mead Committee "for its considerable efforts in behalf of our

Association."[167] Even Mead and Committee members Davenport and Olmsted voted with the majority to reject the final section of the report and pass the motion that stated the issue was "unresolved."

Phillips and Olmsted are adamant in their belief that it was Wolf's reading of the *Visual Search for Human Targets* excerpt that was decisive in the Fellows voting to reject the Mead Committee Report.[168] Davenport believes, "It was the clincher, but it was not the winning point. What it did was that it effectively cut off any further debate."[169] Wolf, Jorgensen, and Berreman identify it as an important moment, but none cited it as the single item that decided the voting.[170] The excerpt notwithstanding, Wolf and Jorgensen's criticisms of the Report were valid and precise and must have influenced those who attended and voted on the Report.

The Report as written was intended to heal the wounds that threatened to divide the AAA; as such, it glossed over the issues in order not to damage the profession of anthropology. For example, the Mead Committee did not seem to have made any effort to contact the Defense Department, the Institute for Defense Analyses, or the Advanced Research Projects Agency for information on their use of social scientists, particularly anthropologists. By contacting only anthropologists and not conducting much research of its own, the Committee reduced its account of the historical use of social science knowledge to aid counterinsurgency to a brief preface.

Furthermore, the Committee likely knew more than it was able to tell. William Davenport remembers conversations with individuals who spoke on the condition that the information they gave not be used.[171] According to Davenport, one of these was an anthropologist not associated with the Thailand Controversy, who told of being in a village in Thailand that was bombed. He came to the realization that his information on trails and the like was being used by the military. Davenport says he was not convinced that the story was true, although he had heard another version second or third hand.

In his own manuscript on the controversy, Herbert Phillips, while maintaining that the anthropologists accused of wrongdoing on the basis of the Thailand Controversy documents were innocent, cited "forty-one social science counterinsurgency research projects, involving a minimum of 300 American researchers, *including three professionally trained anthropologists*" [emphasis added].[172] This manuscript was sent to the Mead Committee along with a letter calling attention to the three (unnamed) anthropologists and telling of two more involved in similar research. Stories like these should have prompted more assiduous digging by the Mead Committee.

In any event, on Sunday, November 21, two days after the Mead Report was rejected, the new Executive Board of the AAA unanimously passed the following motion:

1. Specific problems posed by the events referred to as the "Thailand Controversy" stand essentially unresolved.

2. Certain issues laid bare by the discussion of the controversy are matters of deep concern to all anthropologists; most specifically that the anthropologist must recognize an obligation to protect data on socially constituted human populations, where exposure of the data may expose the population to destruction.

Therefore, the Board does not believe further committee investigation of past events involving anthropologists' acts in Thailand would be productive at this time....[173]

The rejection of the Mead report was significant outside of the spectrum of the Thailand Controversy. It represented an organized body of younger anthropologists rejecting the values of its elders. Mead had the status as *the* senior anthropologist in the United States. News reports noted what few anthropologists voiced publicly: Anthropologists "came within a hair of giving their most celebrated living colleague—Margaret Mead ... a public slap in the face," and "the association's younger members see the 69–year-old Dr. Mead as a kind of anthropological Uncle Tom."[174] In spite of Mead's status (some might say because of her status), the Mead Committee's Report was rejected.

NOTES

[1] *AAA Newsletter* 10:9 (November 1969), 9–10; AAA, *Annual Report 1969 and Directory* (The Bulletins of the American Anthropological Association) (Washington, DC: AAA, 1969), 21.

[2] Gerald D. Berreman, "Ethics Versus 'Realism' in Anthropology" in *Ethics and the Profession of Anthropology: Dialogue for a New Era*, ed. Carolyn Fluehr–Lobban (Philadelphia: University of Pennsylvania Press, 1991), 43.

[3] *AAA Newsletter* 10:9 (November 1969), 9–10.

[4] George Foster, letter to the editor ("Anthropology on the Warpath: An Exchange"), *New York Review of Books*, 8 April 1971, 43.

[5] *AAA Newsletter* 11:3 (March 1970), 9–10.

[6] Michael Moerman, letter to Foster, 24 April 1970. Subsequent information in paragraph is from this source.

[7] Herbert Phillips, letter to Berreman, et. al., 4 April 1970; Lauriston Sharp, letter to Eric Wolf, 17 April 1970. Contrast this with Berreman, "Ethics Versus 'Realism,'" 42; and Eric Wolf and Joseph Jorgensen, "Anthropology on the Warpath in Thailand," *New York Review of Books* (19 November 1970). Although in his letter Phillips wrote that the theft would likely result in criminal charges being filed against the thief, this does not seem to have happened, probably because of questions of the graduate assistant's legitimate access to Moerman's files and the lack of laws at the time regarding the personal copying of documents. I was unable to go over these events with Moerman himself because he declined to be interviewed.

[8] Berreman, telephone interview with author, 14 May 1991.

[9] *AAA Newsletter* 11:3 (March 1970), 9–10. See the final pages of Chapter Two of this volume for the full text of the request.

[10] Berreman, interview, 14 May 1991; Jorgensen, telephone interview with author, 10 May 1991; Wolf, personal interview with author, 4 May 1991.

[11] Jorgensen, interview, 10 May 1991; Berreman, interview, 14 May 1991.

[12] Wolf and Joseph Jorgensen, Statement, 30 March 1970.

[13] Marshall Sahlins and Eric Wolf, Statement, [30 March–2 April 1970].

[14] Berreman, Statement, 3 April 1970.

[15] Jorgensen, interview, 10 May 1991; Wolf, interview, 6 April 1991. See also Wolf and Jorgensen, "Anthropology on the Warpath."

[16] Berreman, interview, 14 May 1991.

[17] Moerman, letter to Foster, 24 April 1970.

[18] Ibid.

[19] Wolf, letters to Moerman, Phillips, Piker, Sharp, 3 April 1970.

[20] Steven Piker, letter to Wolf, 6 April 1970.

[21] Phillips, telephone interview with author, 1 May 1991; Sharp, telephone interview with author, 29 April 1991.

[22] Wolf, letter to Piker, 12 April 1970.

[23] Moerman, letter to Wolf, 8 April 1970.

[24] Wolf, letter to Moerman, 14 April 1970.

[25] Phillips, letter to Berreman, Joseph Fischer, and Frederic Wakeman, 4 April 1970. I am enjoined by Phillips from quoting this letter directly.

[26] Phillips, interviews, 1 and 21 May 1991. The following information and thoughts by Phillips are from these interviews.

27 Phillips, letter to Wolf, 5 April 1970.

28 Ibid., 6 April 1970.

29 Phillips, along with seventeen others, rejected the AID contract revisions discussed in Chapter Five as "entirely inappropriate and contrary to the essential educational and research functions of the University" in a letter to the [Berkeley] *Daily Californian* on 13 April 1970. [John Gumperz, et. al., letter to the editor, *Daily Californian*, 13 April 1970.] This was a year and a half after the AID–UCLA contract amendment became operational and eleven days *after* the SMC issue appeared, although there is some indication that many of the members of AACT were unaware of the contract revision until the SMC issue "Counterinsurgency Research on Campus Exposed" was published.

30 Phillips, letter to Khukrit Pramoj, 6 May 1970.

31 Ibid.

32 Wolf, letter to Phillips, 12 April 1970.

33 Phillips, letter to Wolf, 16 April 1970.

34 Sharp, letter to Officers of Cornell University, 8 April 1970.

35 Sharp, Statement of Lauriston Sharp, 1 April 1970.

36 AID, "Amendment No. 3 to the Contract Between the United States of America and the Regents of the University of California," 3–4.

37 Sharp, interview, 29 April 1991.

38 John J. Gumperz, et. al, letter, *The Daily Californian*, 13 April 1970.

39 Sharp, interview, 29 April 1991.

40 David Wilson, "Statement by David A. Wilson," 3 April 1970.

41 Wilson, telephone interview with author, 2 May 1991. Subsequent quotations by Wilson from this source.

42 David K.Wyatt, telephone interview with author, 24 April 1991.

43 Sharp, letter to the Academic Community, 10 April 1970.

44 AACT, "Meeting of the AACT," 19 October 1968, 3.

45 Ibid., 10–11 June 1969, 8. Cf., in 1970, Fred R. von der Mehden and David A. Wilson, *Local Authority and Administration in Thailand*, reverse of cover:

> The Academic Advisory Council for Thailand (AACT) was established to provide the Mission of the Agency of international Development in Thailand with a permanent and regular source of advice from the academic community of the United States.

46 Wilson, interview, 2 May 1991.

47 Sharp, interview, 29 April 1991; Wyatt, interview, 24 April 1991.

48 Sharp, Statement of Lauriston Sharp, 3 April 1970.

49 Sharp, letter to Anthropology Colleagues, 9 April 1970.

50 Sharp, interview, 29 April 1991. The reflections by Sharp in the next few paragraphs are from this interview.

51 Lucien M. Hanks, Jane R. Hanks, Lauriston Sharp, Ruth B. Sharp, *A Report on Tribal Peoples in Chiengrai Province North of the Mae Kok River (Bennington–Cornell Anthropological Survey of Hill Tribes in Thailand)* (Ithaca, NY: Cornell University, Department of Anthropology, Comparative Studies of Cultural Change, 1964). All information in the text paragraph from this source. The goals of the 1963 project fit clearly into AID–security concerns, but the recommendations are quite benign and, in several cases, progressive:

> In 1963, the Department of Anthropology at Cornell University contracted with the Agency for International Development to conduct applied social science research. A principal goal of this research is to aid foreign government officials and the Agency for International Development project administrators, technicians, policy and program planners to arrive at sound policy decisions

through a better understanding of the total socio–economic context of the problems to be solved. The research also aims toward improving the long range planning of U.S. assistance programs. One of the specific problem areas the Cornell research group has undertaken to analyze is that of the integration of tribal, ethnic, and other subordinated subcultural groups into national societies (xiii-xiv).

Recommendations included the introduction and furthering of wet–rice agriculture, tools for industrial development, marketing of native crafts, sorting out problems in administration; use of tribal languages, better understanding by the government of tribal customs and laws, and teaching literacy in native languages to indigenous ethnic groups.

52 Sharp, letter to the Academic Community, 10 April 1970.

53 All quotations from Sharp, letter to Wolf, 17 April 1970.

54 Wolf and Jorgensen, letter to Sharp, 26 April 1970.

55 Berreman, letter to Sharp, 22 April 1970.

56 Moerman, letter to Foster, 24 April 1970.

57 Wilson, interview, 2 May 1991.

58 Phillips, interview, 1 May 1991.

59 Sharp, interview, 29 April 1991.

60 Wyatt, interview, 24 April 1991.

61 David Marr, letter to author, 16 April 1991.

62 Ibid.

63 Wyatt, letter to author, 25 April 1991.

64 Marr, letter to author, 16 April 1991; Alfred W. McCoy, letter to author, 13 February 1991.

[65] "McCarthyism" in Moerman, letter to Foster, 24 April 1970; "slanderous ..." in Charles Keyes and Peter Kunstadter, letter to Foster, 29 April 1970. See also Melford Spiro, letter to Foster, 24 April 1970; Spiro, letter to Wolf, 27 April 1970; Moerman, letter to Foster, 30 April 1970; Berreman, letter to Foster, 30 April 1970; Sharp, letter to Foster, 8 May 1970; Phillips, letter to Foster, 9 May 1970.

[66] Ralph Beals, letter to Foster, 1 May 1970.

[67] Ibid. Subsequent quotations from this source.

[68] Ethics Committee member Ehrich subsequently disassociated himself from the two statements (Robert Ehrich, letter to the editor, *AAA Newsletter* 11:9 [November 1970], 2). See also the comments of Ethics Committee member Oswald Werner, *AAA Newsletter* 11:9, 2 and 7; and Robert Ehrich, letter to the Executive Board of the AAA, 10 May 1970.

[69] AAA, Committee on Ethics, letter to the President, et. al. of the AAA, 2 May 1970 [letter that begins "Considering ..."].

[70] Ibid., 2 May 1970 [letter that begins "Our examination ..."].

[71] Phillips, letter to Members of the Committee on Ethics of the AAA, 19 May 1970, 3.

[72] Phillips, *Between the Tiger and the Crocodile*, 11; Phillips, letter to Mead, 24 April 1971.

[73] *AAA Newsletter* 11:6 (June 1970), 1, 10.

[74] Ibid., 10.

[75] Wolf and Jorgensen, letter to the editor ("Anthropology on the Warpath: an Exchange"), 45. See also, David Aberle, letter to the editor, *AAA Newsletter* 11:7 (September 1970), 19.

[76] Aberle and Schneider, letter to the editor, *AAA Newsletter* 11:9 (November 1970), 7–8.

[77] Wolf and Jorgensen, letter to the President, et. al. of the AAA, 25 May 1970; published as letter to the editor, *AAA Newsletter* 11:7 (September 1970), 2–3, 19. Aberle also resigned his position as liaison member of between the Executive Board and the Ethics Committee at the time of Wolf and Jorgensen's resignation (Aberle, letter to the editor, *AAA Newsletter* 11:7 (September 1970), 19).

[78] See Ehrich, letter to the editor, *AAA Newsletter* 11:9 (November 1970), 2.

[79] AAA, Committee on Ethics, *Annual Report of the Committee on Ethics*, September 1970. All excerpts are from pages 7–11 of the typewritten report. The report was also published in the *AAA Newsletter* 11:9 (November 1970), 9–16.

[80] AAA, Committee on Ethics, *Annual Report*, Appendix C, September 1970.

[81] Phillips, letter to the editor, *AAA Newsletter* 12:1 (January 1971), 2, 7–9.

[82] Moerman, letter to the editor, *AAA Newsletter* 12:1 (January 1971), 9–11.

[83] Wolf and Jorgensen, "Anthropology on the Warpath."

[84] Ibid.

[85] W. R. Geddes, letter to Mead, 27 May 1971; Peter Hinton, letter to the editor ("Anthropology on the Warpath: An Exchange"), *New York Review of Books*, 8 April 1971, 44.

[86] Geddes, letter to Mead, 27 May 1971.

[87] Ibid.

[88] Ibid.

[89] Peter Hinton, letter to the editor, *AAA Newsletter* 12:3 (March 1971), 12. An abbreviated version of this letter also appeared as a letter to the editor

in the *New York Review of Books*, ("Anthropology on the Warpath: An Exchange"), 44.

90 Tribal Research Centre [TDC], "Six Years Later: An Interview with Peter Hinton," n.p., 20 May 1976 (mimeo.), 2.

91 SEATO Reports quoted in Wolf and Jorgensen, ("Anthropology on the Warpath: An Exchange"), 45. Wolf and Jorgensen credit Chandra Jayawardena, an anthropologist at Macquarie University in Australia, for bringing to their attention the SEATO reports. They incorporated, with his permission, Jayawardena's unpublished letter to the editor of the *Review* (21 January 1971) into their response.

92 Hinton, letter to the editor, *AAA Newsletter* (March 1971), 12.

93 TDC, "Record of the Meeting of Consultants and Interested Persons," 14 January 1970, 2.

94 Hinton, letter to the editor, *AAA Newsletter* (March 1971), 12.

95 G. [Gary] A. Oughton, letter to Wolf, 15 December 1970. Oughton's letter was also sent as a letter to the editor to the *New York Review of Books;* I do not believe it was published.

96 Hinton, letter to the editor, *AAA Newsletter* (March 1971), 12.

97 Tribal Data Centre Project, "Meeting of Consultants and Interested Persons," 14 January 1970, 1.

98 Geddes, letter to Mead, 27 May 1971.

99 Hinton, letter to the editor, *AAA Newsletter* (March 1971), 12; Oughton, letter to Wolf, *Review* (15 December 1970); "Seminar on Shifting Cultivation and Economic Development in Northern Thailand, Draft Programme—January 18 to 24, 2513 [1970]," n.d. [December 1969].

100 Nibhond Sasidhorn, letter of invitation to Tribal Data Centre Project Meeting of Consultants and Interested Persons, 23 December 1969.

101 [TDC], "Proposal for Village Data Card," n.d. [January 1970].

102 TDC, "List of Consultants and Interested Persons, Attending the Consultants' Meeting," n.d. [December 1969 or January 1970].

103 TDC, "Meeting of Consultants and Interested Persons," 14 January 1970, 1.

104 TDC, "Record of the Meeting of Consultants and Interested Persons, Chart II: Administrative and Funding Channels," n.d. [January 1970].

105 TDC, "Record of the Meeting," 2–10, summarizes the comments of participants. The following quotations are from this source.

106 John McKinnon and Wanat Bhruksasri (eds.), *Highlanders of Thailand*, Kuala Lumpur: Oxford University Press, 1983.

107 Oughton, letter to Wolf, *Review*, 15 December 1970.

108 TDC, "Meeting of Consultants," 5.

109 Sasidhorn, letter of invitation, 23 December 1969.

110 Oughton, letter to Wolf, *Review*, 15 December 1970.

111 Wolf and Jorgensen, "Anthropology on the Warpath: An Exchange," 38.

112 McCoy, "Subcontracting Counterinsurgency." No one seems to remember the name of the journal that reprinted the article.

113 See TDC, "Six Years Later: An Interview with Peter Hinton," 2; Alfred W. McCoy, letter to author, 13 February 1991; and Geddes, "Research and the Tribal Research Centre," in *Highlanders of Thailand*, 3-12.

114 Wolf and Jorgensen, "Anthropology on the Warpath."

115 Wolf and Jorgensen, "Anthropology on the Warpath: An Exchange," 45.

116 Delmos Jones, letter to the editor ("Anthropology on the Warpath: An Exchange"), *Review*, 22 July 1971, 37.

117 Jones, "Social Responsibility and the Belief in Basic Research: An Example from Thailand," *Current Anthropology* 12:3 (June 1971), 347–50.

118 Ibid., 347.

119 Ibid., 348.

120 Ibid., 348–349.

121 Ibid., 349–350.

122 Jones, "Anthropology on the Warpath: An Exchange," 37.

123 Wolf and Jorgensen, "Anthropology on the Warpath: An Exchange," 38.

124 *AAA Newsletter* 12:1 (January 1971), 1.

125 Foster, telephone interview, 30 May 1991.

126 Ibid.

127 Cyril Belshaw, letter to the editor, *AAA Newsletter* 11:8 (October 1970), 2, 12. Also Aberle, interview, 8 May 1991.

128 Foster, interview, 30 May 1991.

129 Wolf, interview, 4 April 1991; Piker, interview, 5 April 1991.

130 *AAA Newsletter* 12:4 (April 1971), 1.

131 *AAA Newsletter* 12:3 (March 1971), 1, 6–7.

132 William Davenport, "The Thailand Controversy in Retrospect," in *Social Contexts of American Ethnology, 1840–1984*, ed. June Helm, (1984 Proceedings of the American Ethnological Society) (Washington, DC:

American Anthropological Association, 1985), 65–72. The following account is from this source.

133 Davenport, interview, 18 June 1991.

134 Olmsted, interview with author, 29 April 1991; See also, Olmsted, letter to Mead, Davenport and Freed, n.d. [1971]; Freed, letter to Mead, 14 June 1971.

135 Davenport, "The Thailand Controversy," 67.

136 Olmsted, interview, 29 April 1991.

137 "AAA–CTC Bibliography" [AAA–Committee on Thailand Controversy ("CTC" is shorthand for "Ad Hoc Committee to Evaluate the Controversy Concerning Anthropological Activities in Thailand," the official name of the Committee.)], 25 August 1971.

138 Davenport, et. al., "Report in Relation to Thailand," 2.

139 Davenport, "The Thailand Controversy," 68.

140 "Itinerary for Dr. Margaret Mead: June 19, 1971–September 4, 1971," Mead Papers. Aberle, Berreman, and Wolf all remember Mead being out of the country during this period. While Olmsted does not recall whether or not she was in country, he said it was no secret that in general Mead "organized the situation so other people did a lot of the work for her." [Telephone interviews with Aberle, 8 May 1991; Berreman, 14 May 1991; Wolf, 21 May 1991; and Olmsted, 21 May 1991.]

141 Mead, letter to Edward Lehman, 24 September 1971; Ruth Freed, letter to Mead, 12 October 1971.

142 Freed, letter to Mead, 12 October 1971. In this letter Freed, herself, is surprised that the report was not to be published in the *AAA Newsletter* for November and passes on to Mead the comments of AAA Executive Director Lehman as to the usual public distribution of reports.

143 Aberle, interview, 8 May 1991.

144 Davenport, et. al., "Report of the Ad Hoc Committee to Evaluate the Controversy Concerning Anthropological Activities in Thailand," 27 September 1971, 1.

145 Ibid., 2.

146 Olmsted, letter to Mead, Davenport, and Freed, n.d. [1971].

147 Davenport, et. al., "Report in Relation to Thailand," 2.

148 Ibid.

149 Ibid., 3.

150 Ibid., 4.

151 Ibid.

152 Ibid

153 Foster, interview, 30 May 1991.

154 Reproduced as Wolf and Jorgensen, letter to the editor, *AAA Newsletter* 13:1 (January 1972), 3; and May N. Diaz and Lucile Newman, letter to the editor, *AAA Newsletter* 13:1 (January 1972), 3–4.

155 Wolf and Jorgensen, letter to the editor, *AAA Newsletter* 13:1 (January 1972), 3.

156 Davenport, interview, 18 June 1991.

157 Diaz and Newman, letter to the editor, *AAA Newsletter* 13:1 (January 1972), 3.

158 My description of the meeting and meeting procedure is taken from the following sources, with specific quotations individually cited: Personal interview with Wolf, 4 April 1991; telephone interviews with Berreman, 14 May 1991; Davenport, 18 June 1991; Foster, 30 May 1991; Jorgensen 10 May 1991; Olmsted, 29 April 1991; and Wolf, 21 May 1991; *Behavior Today,* "Outlook: Anthro Convention: Ethical Hassle," 29 November 1971;

Berreman, "Ethics versus 'Realism' in Anthropology"; Davenport, "Thailand Controversy"; Freed, letter to Mead, 16 November 1991; Stephen Isaacs, "Asia Anthropology: Science or Spying?" *Washington Post*, 23 November 1971; Israel Shenker, "Anthropologists Clash Over Their Colleagues Ethics in Thailand," *New York Times*, 21 November 1971; Charles Wagley, letter to Mead, 20 October 1971.

159 Shenker, "Anthropologists Clash."

160 [MRDC, untitled fragmentary document listing unclassified MRDC projects], 32. "Low Altitude Visual Search for Individual Human Targets: Further Field Testing in Southeast Asia," by D. J. Blakeslee [*not* the anthropologist], is listed as "AD–468 413" with the additional identifying numbers of "(965–19)(Div.18/2,18/7,6/5)".

161 Berreman, interview, 14 May 1991.

162 AAA, *Annual Report 1970 and Directory* (4:1), Washington, D.C,. April 1971, 85, 131, 138.

163 Donald J. Blakeslee [the anthropologist], letter to Phillips, 27 January 1972; Lee W. Huff, telephone interview with author, 21 May 1991.

164 Huff, telephone interview, 21 May 1991.

165 Phillips, interview, 21 May 1991; Phillips, letter to James F. Gibbs, 29 December 1971.

166 Huff, interview, 21 May 1991.

167 *AAA Newsletter* 13:1 (January 1972), "Council Rejects Thai Controversy Committee's Report," 1 and 9.

168 Olmsted, interview, 29 April 1991; Phillips, interview, 1 May 1991.

169 Davenport, interview, 18 June 1991.

170 Wolf, interview, 4 April 1991. Telephone interviews with Berreman, 14 May 1991; Jorgensen, 10 May 1991; and Wolf, 21 May 1991.

171 Davenport, interview, 18 June 1991.

172 Phillips, *Between the Tiger and the Crocodile*, 11.

173 *AAA Newsletter* 13:2 (February 1972), 6.

174 *Behavior Today*, "Anthro Convention" and Isaacs, "Asia Anthropology."

CHAPTER SEVEN

THE AFTERMATH

Specifically, no secret research, no secret reports or debriefings of any kind should be agreed to or given [by anthropologists].

—Principles of Professional Responsibility of the AAA, 1971

Anthropologists are under no professional obligation to provide reports or debriefings of any kind to government officials or employees, unless they have individually and explicitly agreed to do so in the terms of employment.

—Principles of Professional Responsibility of the AAA, 1990 revised version

The aftermath of the Thailand Controversy was uneven for the anthropologists involved and for the profession of anthropology. Many of the anthropologists whom I interviewed felt the effect on the profession had been minimal or at least temporary; and later generations of anthropologists know very little about it. Yet, the issues raised remain seminal to social scientists doing research in any discipline and to the use to which other parties may put such research.

Perhaps the most interesting of the immediate after-effects of the controversy developed shortly after the rejection of the Mead Committee Report. Before the November 1971 Council of Fellows meeting, the Mead Committee had discussed the appropriate way to deal with the assembled material; destroying all or part of the material was one consideration.[1] After the September meeting of the Mead Committee, Mead wrote to Freed that the *bibliography* of assembled material should

not [be] given to the [Executive] Board. If the Board had it, there would immediately be questions about the people who hadn't answered, etc. You will destroy the address cards.[2]

By the time the final version of the Report was issued, the Mead Committee had committed itself in the preface of its Report to presenting its accumulated material (or at least part of it) to the AAA:

> The documentation for the ad hoc committee's work will be deposited in the archives of the American Anthropological Association.[3]

Following the rejection of their report at the November meeting, however, the Mead Committee's members all agreed to *destroy* the material they had collected, rather than to have it archived for the use of future scholars. According to William Davenport:

> The Ad Hoc Committee's response to the rejection was to destroy all the documentation that it had collected. This was not done in a fit of pique. The action was taken in order to prevent the materials from being used, in the manner that the SMC had treated the original six documents, to revive the issue.[4]

Davenport mailed his copies of the documents to Margaret Mead, probably by way of Ruth Freed, for them to be disposed of.[5] But David Olmsted, in a more ritualistic manner, tossed his copies into a wood-burning stove in his study.[6]

When Edward Lehman, the executive secretary of the AAA, wrote to Mead in March of 1972, requesting that she forward the assembled material to the AAA as it had been agreed upon,[7] Mead responded with the following three-sentence letter:

> After the continuing display of irresponsibility, the committee decided to destroy the files. This was done. You have the complete financial record and the report.[8]

Mead's response could hardly *not* be called a "fit of pique." What the Committee would have done had its report not been rejected by the Fellows remains a mystery. Both Davenport and Olmsted said that they thought the material could have been used in a way to harm innocent people. Olmsted said, "Some material was damaging to innocent people and might [have] cause[d] another Wolf-like [episode]."[9] Davenport said, "There was clear out-of-context stuff in the most innocuous documents."[10] The committee displayed an admirable concern for fellow anthropologists—although Mead's comments about "irresponsibility" can be read to mean both fear of misuse and indignation at the Report being rejected. Even if there was no damning information in any of the material collected by the Mead Committee, by destroying it, the end result is an unanswerable curiosity, which can never be satisfied through legitimate scholarly access to the documents.

For individual anthropologists, the results of the Thailand Controversy were mixed. At the University of California-Berkeley, working on the same floor were Gerald Berreman, George Foster, Herbert Phillips, and Eugene Hammel of the Executive Board. The friendship that had existed between Berreman and Phillips suffered; and although they have had something of a rapprochement, the two do not speak about the Thailand Controversy with each other.[11] Lauriston Sharp had been Berreman's advisor at Cornell, and, according to Berreman, many people thought it was "reprehensible" for him to have made statements that implicated Sharp in the controversy.[12]

Berreman later published a volume titled *The Politics of Truth: Essays in Critical Anthropology*, in which he discussed the controversy and anthropological ethics.[13] In a recent interview, he recounted the effect the controversy had on his running for president of the AAA in 1970, after the controversy had broken.[14] The AAA Nominating Committee had chosen three candidates for the post of president: Albert C. Spaulding (University of California-Santa Barbara), James N. Spuhler (University of New Mexico), and Anthony F. C. Wallace (University of Pennsylvania). Although the Nominating Committee generally chooses only three candidates, the signatures of five Fellows and Voting members of the AAA is all that is needed to nominate other candidates. Berreman was so nominated. Spaulding and Spuhler withdrew from the race after Berreman's candidacy became known, leaving Berreman to face Wallace, who won.

According to Berreman, years later Spaulding told him that he had been asked by George Foster to withdraw from the race (and to ask Spuhler to do the same) to prevent a takeover by "the radicals." When asked about Berreman's version of the election, Foster conceded that,

> We [the Executive Board] were concerned that the normal vote would be split among the other three candidates and Berreman, and felt Berreman would not represent the Association in as balanced a way as a candidate nominated according to accepted procedures.

Foster acknowledged that Board members David Aberle and David Schneider did not feel this way. However, Foster strongly and clearly asserted that, "No candidate was asked to withdraw from the race. I asked no one to withdraw from the race."[15]

I could not confirm Berreman's account with Spaulding, as he is deceased. However, James Spuhler's memory of his withdrawal from the election corresponds with Foster's account.[16] Spuhler, who describes himself as "a lifelong liberal," remembers the event as follows:

Al Spaulding called me and we talked about it and we realized that there was a very good chance if the vote were split four ways, the write-in candidate would win.... It was clearly a political nomination. The Marxist clique was going to write this guy in and he might win.... We independently believed that [his] being a Marxist candidate at that time would have been wrong [for the Association].

Spuhler said, "It was foolish not to withdraw," and "I am absolutely convinced we did the right thing." Spuhler also said unequivocally that Spaulding did not say anything about Foster asking him to withdraw from the race: "I am absolutely convinced that Spaulding didn't mention anything about George Foster, and Foster is a very honest person."

Herbert Phillips continues to be bitter about the "kind of behavior" that the Thailand Controversy brought out in some people.[17] When it was over, he quit the AAA and has never rejoined. A year later, he joined Berkeley's Committee for the Protection of Human Subjects, which was established originally as an effort to protect research subjects in medical experiments, but has since been broadened to include other fields. While Phillips has continued his research focus on Thailand, he has shifted from studies of peasants to that of Thai literature.

Phillips continues to argue that, in spite of the seeming inability of government agencies to listen to consultants, the best way to ameliorate deleterious U.S. influences is through work within the government and not by criticizing it from outside. Phillips began a book on the subject of the Thailand Controversy, which was never published, in which he argues his position. The following excerpts are taken from that unpublished manuscript:

The Thai specialists accused by their anthropological colleagues of "implementing counterinsurgency programs in Thailand" and other indicting activities certainly did none of these things. But more important, neither did they do what they aspired to do: ameliorate significantly the disruption and pain of counterinsurgency programs and other U.S. efforts in Thailand.

... to expect that as an advisor to the government he can significantly modify the governmental decisions that created that reality requires that he have extraordinary hubris, talent or luck. If he has sufficiently strong feelings about the horrendous nature of the U.S. role in Thailand, and how it is a perversion of American's national purposes, he can go to the opposite extreme, and attack the role frontally ...

I know of no scholar-consultant who was foolish enough to believe that the government would accept his advice because it was self evidently true, or because it was persuasively and elegantly presented, or because he is a sincere, well-informed expert.... You do it because you hope you can make the world a little better, not because you expect that you will.[18]

Lauriston Sharp retired soon after the controversy. Although it affected his working relationships with students, retired professors at Cornell cannot sit on graduate committees.[19] Michael Moerman, still teaching at UCLA, is one of the few principals who declined to be interviewed by the author. Many other people interviewed, however, cited the emotional toll the controversy took on him. Steven Piker continues to teach at Swarthmore College, where there was no discernable reaction to the Thailand Controversy.[20] Eric Wolf is Distinguished Professor of Anthropology at the City University of New York. He has published extensively and recently received a MacArthur Fellowship. Delmos Jones, the "lone dissenter," discontinued studying the Lahu ethnic group in Northern Thailand and focussed his research in the U.S., but said the change cannot be wholly linked to the Thailand Controversy. He returned to Thailand on a small grant in 1979 and continues to teach at the CUNY graduate center.[21]

Joseph Jorgensen now teaches at the University of California-Irvine in the Program in Comparative Culture. In a recent letter, he recounted attending a meeting in Chicago in the spring of 1973 at which Margaret

Mead was present. About a dozen anthropologists, including Sol Tax, Marshall Sahlins, and Jorgensen, were seated in a circle as Mead was going around the table greeting them. As Jorgensen describes it:

> Mead stopped in front of me while I was sitting in a chair and spit on me. She couldn't spit like Ted Williams, but she made her point.[22]

It is hard to judge the long-range effect of the Thailand Controversy on the profession of anthropology without a more thorough survey. Most younger anthropologists have only a vague understanding that something happened involving anthropologists who specialized in Thailand during the Vietnam War. Anthropologists associated with the controversy differ in their opinions as to its effects. Berreman believes, "It made people think about the sources [of funding]. Many people became concerned about the issue,"[23] while Davenport has commented that the effects are "None whatsoever. It might just as well not have happened."[24] Foster concurs with both Davenport and Berreman:

> After the 1971 bloodletting, the whole thing disappeared as an issue. I don't believe that three-quarters of the anthropologists practicing today know about it.... There are more anthropologists working for the government—ten times more—than before. Most anthropologists would be careful about the nature of the research that they do. They have seen how it can be used—once burned, twice cautious ... anthropologists who remember the 1970 events probably are more cautious in considering possible pitfalls in war-related defense-related assignments than would previously have been the case.[25]

Wolf believes that "everybody tried to forget it."[26]

Apparently, it was forgotten enough to allow for a complete rewriting of the 1971 AAA Principles of Professional Responsibility (PPR) (Appendix E), which removed all provisions forbidding secret and clandestine research.[27] A Draft Code of Ethics prepared in 1982 had suggested several fundamental changes, including downplaying anthropologists' "paramount responsibility to those they study" (preface to #1 in original PPR), elimination of accountability and the possibility of sanction (final sentence of epilogue in original PPR), and the elimination of the responsibility of anthropologists to speak out "to contribute to an 'adequate definition of reality'" (#2.D in original PPR).[28] The version of the Principles of Professional Responsibility amended through October 1990 (Appendix G) omits six standards that prohibit secret work.

Regarding the relationship between the anthropologist and the people studied, the original PPR read:

> In accordance with the Association's general position on clandestine and secret research, no reports should be provided to sponsors that are not also available to the general public and, where practicable, to the population studied [1971:1.G].

This is replaced with:

> Whether they are engaged in academic or nonacademic research, anthropologists must be candid about their professional identities. If the results of their activities are not to be made public, this should be made clear to all concerned from the outset [1990:I.6].

Other deleted segments are: Responsibility to the public:

> Anthropologists should not communicate findings secretly to some and withhold them from others [1971:2.A].

Responsibility to the discipline:

> Anthropologists should undertake no secret research or any research whose results cannot be freely derived and publicly reported [1971:3.A].

> Anthropologists should avoid even the appearance of engaging in clandestine research, by fully and freely disclosing the aims and sponsorship of all research [1971:3.B].

Responsibility to sponsors:

> They should enter into no secret agreements with sponsors regarding research, results, or reports [1971:3.B].

Responsibilities to one's own government and host governments:

Specifically, no secret research, no secret reports or debriefings of any kind should be agreed to or given. If these matters are clearly understood in advance, serious complications and misunderstandings can generally be avoided [1971:6].

The latter is replaced in 1990 with:

Anthropologists are under no professional obligation to provide reports or debriefings of any kind to government officials or employees, unless they have individually and explicitly agreed to do so in the terms of employment [1990:VI].

No one can say what the changes in the Principles of Professional Responsibility will mean for the conduct of individual anthropologists. Today, just as in the 1960s, there are social scientists who feel bound by no ethical code other than their own. There are people who will engage in secret or clandestine research or who will conduct research with no intention of publishing it. Ultimately, it is only the personal ethical scruples of individual anthropologists that will decide what they will do. However, perhaps the scrutiny of colleagues can help to prevent them from being misled by funding sources or governments and can identify potential ethical transgressions. The responsibilities of anthropologists to the people they study remain unchanged, as do the desires of anthropologists to work for change (from both the inside and outside). But the ability and willingness to legislate and enforce ethical conduct by a professional organization like the American Anthropological Association remains unclear.

The desire of governments for social science information has increased since the Thailand Controversy. In many instances, the goals of governments and social scientists may complement each other, in which case the social scientists are not confronted with an ethical dilemma. However, when the goals of the two groups come into conflict with each other, the social scientist must be diligent in asking questions: Why is the data needed? To what use will it be put? Can it in any way be used to harm people? These are not new questions and they are not complex, but the fact that social science discourse so rarely centers on them can only lead to future ethical dilemmas.

NOTES

[1] Ruth Freed, letter to Margaret Mead, 27 August 1971:

> The committee at the September meeting should decide how it
> wants to dispose of the mass of papers now in its hands ... in some
> cases destroy them.

[2] Mead, letter to Freed, 20 September 1971.

[3] William Davenport, et. al., "Report in Relation to Thailand," 2.

[4] Davenport, "The Thailand Controversy in Retrospect," 68.

[5] Davenport, telephone interview with author, 18 June 1991.

[6] David Olmsted, telephone interview with author, 21 May 1991.

[7] Edward Lehman, letter to Mead, 28 March 1972.

[8] Mead, letter to Lehman, 10 April 1972.

[9] Olmsted, interviews, 21, 29 May 1991.

[10] Davenport, interview, 18 June 1991.

[11] Herbert Phillips, telephone interview with author, 1 May 1991.

[12] Gerald Berreman, telephone interview with author, 14 May 1991.

[13] Berreman, *The Politics of Truth: Essays in Critical Anthropology* (New
Delhi: South Asian Publishers, 1981).

[14] Berreman, interview, 14 May 1991; Berreman, "Ethics versus
'Realism,'" 67 (note 2).

[15] George Foster, telephone interview with author, 30 May 1991.

16 James Spuhler, telephone interview with author, 3 July 1991. The following quotations are taken from this interview.

17 Phillips, interview, 1 May 1991.

18 Phillips, *Between the Tiger and the Crocodile*, 4, 16, 29.

19 Lauriston Sharp, telephone interview with author, 29 April 1991.

20 Steven Piker, telephone interview with author, 5 April 1991.

21 Delmos Jones, personal interview with author, 2 May 1991.

22 Joseph Jorgensen, letter to the author, 15 April 1991; telephone interview, 10 May 1991.

23 Berreman, interview, 14 May 1991.

24 Davenport, interview, 18 June 1991.

25 Foster, interview, 30 May 1991.

26 Eric Wolf, personal interview, 4 April 1991.

27 Prior to this, the Principles of Professional Responsibility had had only three amendments affixed to it since 1971. They were to prohibit plagiarism (3.D in 1974), to tell informants that their anonymity may be revealed unintentionally (1.C(1) and (2) in 1975), and to proscribe exclusionary policies against colleagues (3.E in 1975). In addition, masculine pronouns were removed throughout the document around 1976. These changes are noted in Berreman, "Ethics versus 'Realism,'" 50.

28 Berreman, "Ethics versus 'Realism.'"

APPENDIX A

REGISTER OF PRINCIPALS

David F. Aberle

Role: Member of the AAA Executive Board; liaison between the Executive Board and the AAA Ethics Committee.

Title: Professor of anthropology emeritus.
Institution: University of British Columbia.

Dissertation: The Reconciliation of Divergent Views of Hopi Culture Through the Analysis of Life–History Material (Columbia University, 1950).

Ralph L. Beals

Role: Author of "Background Information on Problems of Anthropological Research and Ethics" (the Beals Report of the AAA).

Title: Professor of anthropology (deceased).
Institution: University of California–Berkeley.

Dissertation: (University of California-Berkeley, 1930).

Gerald D. Berreman

Role: Member of AAA Ethics Committees.

Title: Professor of anthropology.
Institution: University of California–Berkeley.

Dissertation: Kin, Caste, and Community in a Himalayan Hill Village (Cornell, 1959).

William H. Davenport

Role: Member of the Mead Committee.

Title: Professor of anthropology, Curator of University Museum.
Institution: University of Pennsylvania.

Dissertation: A Comparison of Two Jamaican Fishing Communities (Yale, 1956).

George M. Foster

Role: President of the AAA.

Title: Professor of anthropology emeritus.
Institution: University of California–Berkeley.

Dissertation: A Primitive Mexican Economy (University of California–Berkeley, 1942).

Ruth S. Freed

Role: Executive secretary of the Mead Committee.

Title: Research Associate.
Institution: American Museum of Natural History.

Dissertation: Culture, Change, Acculturation, and Types of Community (University of California–Berkeley, 1958).

Delmos Jones

Role: Championed by Wolf and Jorgensen as "lone dissenter" from counterinsurgency research among Thai specialists.

Title: Professor of anthropology.
Institution: CUNY Graduate Center.

Dissertation: Cultural Variation Among Six Lahu Villages, Northern Thailand (Cornell, 1967).

Joseph Jorgensen

Role: Member of (Wolf–chaired) AAA Ethics Committee.

Title: Professor of anthropology, Program in Comparative Culture.
Institution: University of California–Irvine.

Dissertation: The Ethnohistory and Acculturation of the Northern Ute (Indiana, 1965).

Margaret Mead

Role: Chairperson of the Mead Committee.

Title: Adjunct professor of anthropology (deceased).
Institution: Columbia University.

Dissertation: An Inquiry into the Question of Cultural Stability in Polynesia (Columbia, 1928).

Michael Moerman

Role: Attended Institute for Defense Analyses Thailand Study Group (1967); American Institutes for Research panel member; Academic Advisory Council for Thailand member.

Title: Professor of anthropology.
Institution: University of California–Los Angeles.

Dissertation: Farming in Ban Phaed Technological Decisions and Their Consequences for the External Relations of a Thai–Lue Village (Yale, 1964).

David L. Olmsted

Role: Member of the Mead Committee.

Title: Professor.
Institution: University of California–Davis.

Dissertation: The Phonology of Polish (Cornell, 1950 [Language and Literature]).

Steven Piker

Role: Attended Institute for Defense Analyses Thailand Study Group (1967).

Title: Professor of anthropology.
Institution: Swarthmore College.

Dissertation: An Examination of Character and Socialization in a Thai Peasant Community (University of Washington, 1964); advisors: Melville Jacobs (chair), Melford Spiro, Kenneth Read, Simon Ottenberg.

Herbert P. Phillips

Role: Attended Institute for Defense Analyses Thailand Study Group (1967); Advanced Research Projects Agency consultant (1967–1968).

Title: Professor of anthropology.
Institution: University of California–Berkeley.

Dissertation: Thai Peasant Personality: A Case Study of Bang Chan Villagers (Cornell, 1963).

Marshall Sahlins

Role: Critic of ARPA, AIR, AACT activities.

Title: Charles F. Grey Distinguished Service Professor of Anthropology.
Institution: University of Chicago.

Dissertation: Social Stratification in Polynesia: A Study of Adaptive Variation in Culture (Columbia, 1954).

Lauriston Sharp

Role: Member of Academic Advisory Council for Thailand; Attended Institute for Defense Analyses Thailand Study Group (1967).

Title: Professor of anthropology emeritus.
Institution: Cornell University.

Dissertation: The Social Anthropology of a Totemic System of North Queensland (Harvard, 1937).

Wayne P. Suttles

Role: Chair of AAA Ethics Committee following Wolf resignation.

Title: Professor of anthropology.
Institution: Portland State University.

Dissertation: The Economic Life of the Coast Salish of Haro and Rosario Straits (University of Washington, 1951).

Eric R. Wolf

Role: Chair AAA Ethics Committee.

Title: Distinguished Professor of Anthropology.
Institution: CUNY Graduate Center.

Dissertation: Culture Change and Culture Stability in a Puerto Rican Coffee Community (Columbia, 1951).

APPENDIX B

American Anthropological Association
Statement on Problems of Anthropological Research and Ethics[1]

(approved by the Fellows of the American Anthropological Association, April 1967)

The human condition, past and present, is the concern of anthropologists throughout the world. The study of mankind in varying social, cultural, and ecological situations is essential to our understanding of human nature, of culture and of society.

Our present knowledge of the range of human behavior is admittedly incomplete. Expansion and refinement of this knowledge depend heavily on international understanding and cooperation in scientific and scholarly inquiry. To maintain the independence and integrity of anthropology as a science, it is necessary that scholars have full opportunity to study peoples and their culture, to publish, disseminate, and openly discuss the results of their research, and to continue their responsibility of protecting the personal privacy of those being studied and assisted in their research.

Constraint, deception, and secrecy have no place in science. Actions which compromise the intellectual integrity and autonomy of research scholars and institutions not only weaken those international understandings essential to our discipline, but in so doing they also threaten any contribution anthropology might make to our own society and to the general interests of human welfare.

The situations which jeopardize research differ from year to year, from country to country, and from discipline to discipline. We are concerned here with problems that affect all the fields of anthropology and which, in varying ways, are shared by the social and behavioral sciences.

I. Freedom of Research

1. The Fellows of the American Anthropological Association reaffirm their resolution of 1948 on freedom of publication and protection of the interests of the persons and groups studied:

---

[1] Reprinted by permission of the American Anthropological Association.

Be it resolved: (1) that the American Anthropological Association strongly urge all sponsoring institutions to guarantee their research scientists complete freedom to interpret and publish their findings without censorship or interference; provided that (2) the interests of the persons and communities or other groups studied are protected; and that (3) in the event that the sponsoring institution does not wish to publish the results nor be identified with the publication, it permit publication of the results, without use of its name as sponsoring agency, through other channels.

—American Anthropologist 51:370 (1949)

To extend and strengthen this resolution, the Fellows of the American Anthropological Association endorse the following:

2. Except in the event of a declaration of war by the Congress, academic institutions should not undertake activities or accept contracts in anthropology that are not related to their normal functions of teaching, research, and public service. They should not lend themselves to clandestine activities. We deplore unnecessary restrictive classifications of research reports prepared under contract to the Government, and excessive security regulations imposed on participating academic personnel.

3. The best interests of scientific research are not served by the imposition of external restrictions. The review procedures instituted for foreign area research contracts by the Foreign Affairs Research Council of the Department of State (following a Presidential directive of July, 1965) offer a dangerous potential for censorship of research. Additional demands by some United States agencies for clearance, and for excessively itineraries and field plans from responsible scholars whose research has been approved by their professional peers or academic institutions, are contrary to assurances given by Mr. Thomas L. Hughes, Director of the Bureau of Intelligence and Research, Department of State, to the President of the American Anthropological Association on November 9, 1965, and are incompatible with effective anthropological research.

4. Anthropologists employed or supported by the Government should be given the greatest possible opportunities to participate in planning research projects, to carry them out, and to publish their findings.

II. Support and Sponsorship

1. The most useful and effective governmental support of anthropology in recent years has come through such agencies as the National Science Foundation, the National Institutes of Health, and the Smithsonian

Institution. We welcome support for basic research and training through these and similar institutions.

2. The Fellows take this occasion to express their gratitude to those members of Congress, especially Senator Harris and Representative Fascell, who have so clearly demonstrated their interest in the social sciences, not only through enlarging governmental support for them, but also in establishing channels for social scientists to communicate their opinions to the Government regarding policies that affect the future of the social sciences and their utilization by Government.

3. When queried by individuals representing either host countries or groups being studied, anthropologists should willingly supply evidence of their professional qualifications and associations, their sponsorship and source of funds, and the nature and objectives of the research being undertaken.

4. Anthropologists engaged in research in foreign areas should be especially concerned with the possible effects of their sponsorship and sources of financial support. Although the Department of Defense and other mission-oriented branches of the Government support some basic research in the social sciences, their sponsorship may nevertheless create an extra hazard in the conduct of field work and jeopardize future access to research opportunities in the areas studied.

5. Anthropologists who are considering financial support from independent research organizations should ascertain the full nature of the proposed investigations, including sponsorship and arrangement for publication. It is the responsibility of anthropologists to maintain the highest professional standards and to decline to participate in or to accept support from organizations that permit misrepresentations of technical competence, excessive costs, or concealed sponsorship of activities. Such considerations are especially significant where grants or fellowships are offered by foundations or other organizations which do not publish balance sheets showing their sources of funds.

6. The international reputation of anthropology has been damaged by the activities of unqualified individuals who have falsely claimed to be anthropologists, or who have pretended to be engaged in anthropological research while in fact pursuing other ends. There also is good reason to believe that some anthropologists have used their professional standing and the names of their academic institutions as cloaks for the collection of intelligence information and for intelligence operations. Academic institutions and individual members of the academic community, including students, should scrupulously avoid both involvement in clandestine

intelligence activities and the use of the name of anthropology, or the title of anthropologist, as a cover for intelligence activities.

III. Anthropologists in U.S. Government Service

1. It is desirable that social science advice be made more readily available to the Executive Office of the President.

2. Where the services of anthropologists are needed in agencies of the Government, it is most desirable that professional anthropologists be involved at the project planning stage and in the actual recruitment of necessary personnel. Only in this manner is it possible to provide skilled and effective technical advice.

3. Anthropologists contemplating or accepting employment in governmental agencies in other than policy-making positions should recognize that they will be committed to agency missions and policies. They should seek in advance the clearest possible definition of their expected roles as well as the possibilities for maintaining professional contact, for continuing to contribute to the profession through publication, and for maintaining professional standards in protecting the privacy of individuals and groups they may study.

APPENDIX C

Institute for Defense Analyses Parable from Annual Report III (1958-1959)[1]

EXORDIUM: The Parable

The Minyans had had only bad luck ever since the Golden Fleece (a sheepskin altar cloth dyed purple and trimmed with gold fringe) was stolen from Zeus' shrine on Mt. Pelion. Their bronze weapons had proved no match for the iron blades of the barbarous Achaen spadassins who now ruled all of Northern Greece. Their ancient goddess had been deposed and her crude and greedy son Zeus raised to authority as supreme father god—a *father* god, mind you. Phthiotis was in the hands of King Peleas, as arrogant and crafty a tyrant as ever usurped a throne. And, to top it all, the barley crop had failed and food was scarce indeed.

Jason, rightful heir to the throne, came anonymously down to Iolcos to claim his kingdom. He taunted Peleas with a recital of Minyan misfortunes and accused him of cowardice for failing even to attempt to recover the Fleece from its sanctuary at the far end of the Black Sea. The upshot was that Peleas appointed him leader of a recovery expedition and agreed to relinquish the throne on successful completion of the mission.

In the first flush of enthusiasm many Minyans volunteered from throughout Greece—nobles, kings, established heroes and numerous potential ones, all eager to win honor and immortal fame.

But the initial 80-odd dwindled as the difficulties and hazards of the venture began to be understood: passing hostile Troy, plus a long voyage over a treacherous sea peopled with monsters and surrounded by strange and

---

[1] Reproduced by permission of the Institute for Defense Analyses. Illustrations from the original.

savage barbarians. Finally, as the Argo prepared to sail on the vernal equinox, the party was held together only by shame.

Then, three days before the event, with hardly a ship's complement left, with nothing but unhappy auguries visible, with dissension and suspicion in the residual ranks and morale at its nadir, Herakles of Tiryns joined the expedition.

This made the difference. Herakles (or Hercules, if you prefer) was a giant of a man, more than seven feet tall and of such prodigious strength that he had never been defeated in battle. He was in his fiftieth year, and had already performed six of his famous Labours. His coming put new heart into the group and the entire complexion of the undertaking changed rapidly.

Not that anybody really wanted him along. He was a difficult companion, of uncertain temper, a drunk, a brawler, and subject to unpredictable spells of madness during which he was upbraided by voices of past victims of his brass-bound olive club. But with him along there was a chance of success, if for no other reason that thereby he could not join the opposition. Thus the Argonauts satisfied one of the primary tenets of military strategy since the beginning of time: to lead from strength.

Their fortunes improved from that day, which was the 18th of March. They did wonderful things—great deeds of derring-do that historians and poets talk about to this day. As the Argosy unfolded, of course, the winning of the Fleece was, at the end, an accomplishment of diplomacy rather than a feat of arms. Nor was Herakles present then or on the difficult return voyage. But the point is, the Greeks could not have brought their sophistication and diplomacy to bear without the presence on their side of Herakles, the contemporary ultimate weapon, circa 1225 B.C. So March 18 was an important day for them and their cause.

March 18 is an important day for IDA too—the issue date of our Annual Reports of which this is the third. We hope we will be forgiven if we suggest that the search for superiority in weaponry in which the nation is engaged holds some parallel to the problems the Argonauts faced and solved.

Even if, today, war over a holy relic seems absurd, this truism of military science still prevails: force is a necessary element when bargaining with the fates on the lots they may offer.

APPENDIX D

Advanced Research Projects Agency
Village Security Pilot Study[1]

(original & revised)

[1]Reproduced by permission of the Defense Advanced Research Projects Agency.

VILLAGE SECURITY PILOT STUDY
NORTHEAST THAILAND
65-016

โครงการร่วม ไทย – สหรัฐ

ศูนย์วิจัยและพัฒนาการทหาร

JOINT THAI - U.S.

MILITARY RESEARCH AND DEVELOPMENT CENTER

ประเทศไทย
BANGKOK, THAILAND

VILLAGE SECURITY PILOT STUDY
NORTHEAST THAILAND

BY

D. J. Blakeslee
L. W. Huff
R. W. Kickert

T. W. BRUNDAGE
Director
OSD/ARPA R&D Field Unit

MANOB SURIYA
Air Vice Marshal
Commanding General MRDC

May 1965

Joint Thai - U.S.
Military Research and Development Center
Bangkok

APPENDIX I

ORIGINAL QUESTIONNAIRE

Rural Security
Physical Characteristics

I. GENERAL & LOCATIONAL

Data Source_____   Officials' Names

Village Name_____   Kamnan_____
                                          Headman_____
Population_____   Ass't Headman_____
                                          Head Teacher_____
Ethnic Groups_____   Abbot_____

_____

Coordinates UTM_____   Lat-Long_____

Elevation (MSL) Maximum_____   Distance_____ Direction_____

Nearest Police or Military Facility,
   Description and Distance_____

_____

Distances and Directions to Nearby Villages
   Village   _____ _____ _____ _____ _____
   Distance   _____ _____ _____ _____ _____
   Direction _____ _____ _____ _____ _____

II. DEFENSE PERIMETER

Nominal Defense Perimeter
   Major Axis   Description (Show on Sketch Keyed to
      Length_____   Photograph)
      Orientation_____   _____
   Minor Axis Length_____   _____
   Perimeter Length   _____
      Total   _____   _____
      Contiguous to Woods_____   _____

III. INTERNAL CHARACTERISTICS

Internal Configuration (Show on Sketch Keyed to Photograph)

                     Vehicle Roads   Cart Tracks

   Orientation   _____ _____ _____ _____ _____ _____
   Total Length _____ _____ _____ _____ _____ _____

Road (Motor Vehicle)
  Number, surface type_____ _____ _____
  Distance & Direction_____ _____ _____
  Orientation   _____ _____ _____

River, Stream, Canal
  Name   _____ _____ _____
  Distance & Direction_____ _____ _____
  Orientation   _____ _____ _____
  Navigability Best   _____ _____ _____
  Navigability Poorest_____ _____ _____

V. CHARACTERISTICS WITHIN ZONE OF VILLAGE INFLUENCE

Construction Materials (Show Limits on Sketch)
  Bamboo_____Approx. Area_____   Rock   Approx. Am't_____
  Other Wood   Laterite Approx. Am't_____
  _____Approx. Area_____

  _____Approx. Area_____

  _____Approx. Area_____

Cultivated Land Within Community Influence   Soil Types:
  (Show Limits on Sketch)   Sand_____
  Rice   Clay_____
    Paddy_____   Loam_____
    Hill _____
  Corn   _____
  Other   _____
          _____
          _____

Qualitative Description of Topography
_____
_____
_____
_____

<u>Fences</u>

Major:_____   Minor:_____
   Orientation ____ ____ ____
   Total Length____ ____ ____
                                     ____ ____ ____

     Ditches:_____   Other:_____
   Orientation ____ ____ ____
   Total Length____ ____ ____
                                       ____ ____ ____

Vehicle Population: Total_____
   Trucks >1 ton_____   <1 ton_____   Buses: Small_____   Large_____
   Sedans_____   Samlor_____   Bicycles_____   Oxcarts_____
   Vehicle Repair Facilities_____

  POL Consumption
   Gasoline: Storage_____   Consumption_____
   Kerosene: Storage_____   Consumption_____

Utilities
  Electricity_____

  Potable Water
    Wells Inside Perimeter_____   Pumps_____
    Wells Outside Perimeter_____   Pumps_____
    Reservoir Capacity_____   Location_____
    Water Quality_____

  Communications
   Telephones_____
   Receivers_____   Transmitters_____
      Broadcast Band_____   Power_____
      SW Band_____   Frequency_____

Buildings
  Dry Storage (number, volume)_____
  Wet Areas
    Buildings_____
    Compound Area_____
    Schools_____
  Public Shelter Areas_____
  Enclosed Mercantile: Number_____   Area_____
  Medical_____
  Machine Shops_____
  Woodworking_____

Dwellings
 Total_____
  Large: Good_____   Fair_____   Poor_____
  Medium: Good_____   Fair_____   Poor_____
  Small: Good_____   Fair_____   Poor_____

  Siding: Thatch_____   Wood_____
  Roof: Thatch_____   Wood_____   Metal_____

Staple Foodstuffs & Other Supplies: Rate of Supply (Consumption)

_____

_____

_____

Local Industries:_____

_____

Residents:

  Doctors_____   Carpenters_____   Police_____
  Local Healers_____ Smiths_____   Teachers_____
  Midwives_____   Cartwrights_____   Veterans:
  Spirit Mediums_____ Gun & Knifesmiths_____   RTA_____
                           Mechanics_____   RTN_____
                           Brickmakers_____   RTAF_____
                           Jar Makers_____   BPP_____

Weapons_____

_____

Animal Population
  Buffalo_____   Tools:_____
  Oxen_____   _____
  Cows_____   _____
  Horses_____   _____
  Pigs_____   _____
  Chickens_____   _____
  Ducks_____   _____

IV. EXTERNAL TRANSPORTATION

Railroad
  Designation_____
  Distance (Route)_____   Direction_____
  Means of Access_____

รูปลักษณะ เพื่อการ ป้องกันภัย
ในชนบท

๑. ทั่วไป และ สถานที่

แหล่งข้อมูล _____   ชื่อเจ้าหน้าที่
ชื่อหมู่บ้าน _____   กำนัน _____
จำนวนพลเมือง _____   ผู้ใหญ่บ้าน _____
กลุ่มชนเหล่าทาง ๆ _____   ผู้ช่วยผู้ใหญ่บ้าน _____
_____   ครูใหญ่ _____
จุดสัมพันธ์ _____   เจ้าอาวาส _____
ระกับความสูงสุด _____   แลก – ลองกิจุก
แหล่งกำลังตำรวจและทหารที่ใกล้ที่สุด   ระยะ _____ ทิศทาง
ลักษณะและระยะทาง _____

ระบุ ทางและทิศทางที่จะไปยังหมู่บ้านใกล้เคียง
หมู่บ้าน _____ _____   _____ _____
ระยะทาง _____ _____   _____ _____
ทิศทาง _____ _____   _____ _____

๒. เส้นรอบเขตป้องกัน

เส้นรูปอุบเขตป้องกันที่ทั้งขึ้น
  เสนยาศูนย์กลางตามยาว   รูปลักษณะ (แสดงในภาพ)
  ความยาว   _____
  แนววิถี _____   _____
  ระยะ เสนยาศูนย์กลางตามขวาง _____   _____
  ความยาวเสนรอบเขต   _____
  ทั้งหมด _____   _____
  ติดกับป่า _____   _____

๓. ลักษณะภายใน

รูปร่างภายใน (แสดงในภาพ)
          ถนนรถ   ทางเกวียน
แนววิถี   _____ _____ _____   _____ _____ _____
ระยะทั้งหมด _____ _____ _____   _____ _____ _____

๒

ถามยาว _____   ระยะทางชวาง _____
แนวถิ่ _____   _____   _____
ระยะทั้งหมด _____   _____   _____

  หลุม _____   อื่น ๆ _____
แนววิถิ _____   _____   _____
         _____   _____   _____

จำนวนยานพาหนะทั้งหมด _____
  รถบรรทุก ๑ ตัน _____ ๑ ตัน _____   รถเมล์ขนาดเล็ก _____ ขนาดใหญ่ _____
  รถนั่ง _____ สามล้อ _____   จักรยานสองล้อ _____ เกวียน _____
  บริการซอมรถ _____
การใช้น้ำมันเชื้อเพลิง
คลังน้ำมันเบ็นซิล _____   การใช้ _____
คลังน้ำมันกาส _____   การใช้ _____
สาธารณประโภค
  ไฟฟ้า _____

  น้ำ ,
  บอน้ำภายในบุเส่นรอบเขต _____   เครื่องสูบน้ำ _____
  บอน้ำนอกเสนเขต _____   เครื่องสูบน้ำ _____
  ขนาดอางเก็บน้ำ _____   ที่ทั้ง _____
  คุณภาพของน้ำ _____
         _____
         _____

การสื่อสาร
  โทรศัพท์ _____   เครื่องส่ง
  เครื่องรับ _____   กำลังสุง _____
  วิทยุกระจายเสียง _____   ความถี่ _____
  วิทยุคลื่นสั้น _____
สิ่งปลูกสราง
  ที่เก็บของแหง (จำนวน และขนาด) _____

บริเวณวัด
อาคาร _____ _____ _____
บริเวณวัด _____ _____ _____
โรงเรียน _____ _____ _____
บริเวณที่หลบภัยสาธารณะ

_____

จำนวนการค้า _____ บริเวณ _____
ยา _____ _____
ร้านเครื่องจักร์ _____ _____
ทำสินค้าไม้ _____ _____
บ้านเรือน
    จำนวนทั้งหมด _____
    ขนาดใหญ่ กี่ _____ ปานกลาง _____ เลว _____
    ขนาดกลาง กี่ _____ ปานกลาง _____ เลว _____
    ขนาดเล็ก กี่ _____ ปานกลาง _____ เลว _____
    ฝา   จาก _____ ไม้ _____
    หลังคา จาก _____ ไม้ _____ โลหะ _____
อาหารหลัก และ เครื่องอุปโภคบริโภคอื่น ๆ อัตราการส่ง (การบริโภค)

_____

_____
_____
_____

อุตสาหกรรมในท้องถิ่น _____

_____

ผู้อาศัย
    แพทย์ _____ ช่างไม้ _____ ตำรวจ _____
    หมอกลางบ้าน _____ ช่างเหล็ก _____ ครู _____
    หมอตำแย _____ ช่างประดิษฐ์ _____ ทหารยานศึก _____
    หมอยี _____ ช่างปืนและช่างทำมีด _____ ทหารบก _____
                         ช่างกุด _____ ทหารเรือ _____
                         ช่างกออิฐ _____ ทหารอากาศ _____
                         ช่างปั้นหม้อ _____ ตำรวจภูธรชายแดน _____
อาวุธ _____

_____

จำนวนสัตว์   เครื่องมือ

ควาย _____   _____

วัว _____   _____

วัวนม _____   _____

มา _____   _____

หมู _____

ไก _____

เป็ก _____

๘. การขนส่งภายนอก

รถไฟ

สถานีปลายทาง _____

ระยะทาง _____ ทิศ _____

ทางที่จะไปถึงไก _____

ถนน (สำหรับรถยนต์)

จำนวน ลักษณะผิวถนน _____ _____ _____

ระยะทาง ทิศ _____ _____ _____

แม่น้ำ ลำธาร คลอง

ชื่อ _____ _____ _____

ระยะทาง ทิศ _____ _____ _____

แนววิถี _____ _____ _____

เดินเรือไกที่ที่สุด _____ _____ _____

เดินเรือไกเถวที่สุก _____ _____ _____

๙. ลักษณะภายในเขตที่อยู่ภายใต่อิทธิพลของหมู่บ้าน

วัสดุในการก่อสร้าง (แสดงขอบเขตในภาพ)

ไม้ไผ _____ เนื้อที่ประมาณ _____ หิน จำนวนประมาณ _____

ไม้อื่น ๆ _____ เนื้อที่ประมาณ _____ หินลูกรัง จำนวนประมาณ _____

_____ เนื้อที่ประมาณ _____

เนื้อที่ทำการ เพาะปลูกภายใน เขตอิทธิพลของหมู่บ้าน   ลักษณะดิน
  (แสดงรอบ เขตบนภาพ)
    ราๆ   ทราย   _____
       ทุ่งนา _____   ดินเหนียว_____
   ภูเขา_____   ดินปนทราย_____
  ฐาวโภชน์_____
  อื่น ๆ_____
          _____
          _____

ลักษณะสูงต่ำของภูมิประเทศอย่างกว้าง ๆ

_____

_____

_____

_____

APPENDIX II

REVISED QUESTIONNAIRE

Rural Security
Physical Characteristics

I. GENERAL & LOCATIONAL

		Time In
Names of Officials:	Age	Office

Data Source(s)_____

Village Name_____
Village Age_____
  Origin of First Settlers_____

Origin of Subsequent Settlers____

Origin of Recent Settlers_____

Satellite Settlements and Year
Settled_____

Population_____Male _____
Houses_____Female_____
Families_____
Ethnic Groups: Lao _____
          Vietnamese_____
          Chinese _____
          Indian _____

Names of Officials: Age Office
Kamnan_____ ___ _____
Headman_____ ___ _____
1st Ass't Headman_____
_____ ___ _____
2nd Ass't Headman_____
_____ ___ _____
Head Teacher_____
_____ ___ _____
Abbot_____ ___ _____

Village Record Book: (Yes)(No)
Date of Last Entry_____
Coordinates UTM_____
Lat-Long_____
Elevation (MSL) Maximum_____
             Distance_____
             Direction_____

Nearest Police and/or Military Facility:
  Description and Distance_____

Police and/or Military Patrols to Village:
  Frequency, Size, Activities, Mode of Transport_____

Distances and Directions to Nearby Villages:
  Village _____ _____ _____ _____ _____
  Distance _____ _____ _____ _____ _____
  Direction_____ _____ _____ _____ _____

II. DEFENSE PERIMETER

Nominal Defense Perimeter
  Major Axis
    Length_____
    Orientation_____
  Minor Axis Length_____
  Perimeter Length
    Total_____
    Contiguous to Woods_____

Description (Show on Sketch Keyed to
    Photograph)_____
_____
_____
_____
_____
_____

III. INTERNAL CHARACTERISTICS

Internal Configuration (Show on Sketch Keyed to Photograph).

	Vehicle Roads			Cart Tracks	
Orientation	____	____	____	____	____
Total Length	____	____	____	____	____

Fences
  Major:

				Minor:		
Orientation	____	____	____		____	____
Total Length	____	____	____		____	____

Ditches

				Other		
Orientation	____	____	____		____	____
Total Length	____	____	____		____	____

Vehicle Population   Total:____
  Trucks: 4-Wheel____ 6-Wheel____ 10-Wheel____ Buses: Small____
  Sedans____ Samlor____ Bicycles____   Large____
  Motorbicycles____ Motorscooters____ Manufacturer(s):
  Motorcycles____ Ox/Buffalo Carts____

Vehicle Repair Facilities_____

POL Consumption:
  Gasoline   Storage_____ Consumption_____
  Kerosene   Storage_____ Consumption_____
  Diesel Fuel Storage_____ Consumption_____

Utilities:
  Electricity_____ Year Installed_____
  Small Rice Mill(s)_____ Year(s) Established_____
  Generator(s)_____ Year(s) Purchased_____ Uses____

  Privately/Communally Owned_____
  Owners_____

```
Water:
   Wells Inside Perimeter      Number_____  Location_____
                               Potable_____   _____
                               Not Potable_____   _____
                               Water Year Round____ _____
   Wells Outside Perimeter     Number_____  Location_____
                               Potable_____   _____
                               Not Potable_____   _____
                               Water Year Round____ _____
   Reservoirs_____  Location_____
                     _____  Privately/Communally Owned
                     _____  Contain Fish/Contain No Fish
                     _____  Water Year Round
   Ponds_____   Location_____
                     _____  Privately/Communally Owned
                     _____  Contain Fish/Contain No Fish
   Shared/Not Shared With (An)Other Village(s)_____  Water Year Round
   Pumps_____  Uses_____   Privately/Communally Owned

Communications:
   Telephones_____
   Radio Receivers_____   Brand Names_____
      Broadcast Band_____   _____
      SW Band_____
                               Stations Listened To_____
                               _____
                               Program Preferences_____
                               _____
   Radio Transmitters_____    Power_____  Frequency_____

Buildings:
   Rice Storehouses_____
   Wat Area(s)_____  Location(s)_____
      Age(s)_____   Shared/Not Shared With (An)Other Village(s)
      Buildings_____  _____  _____  _____
      Compound Area_____
   School(s)_____  Location(s)_____
      Age(s)_____   Shared/Not Shared With (An)Other Village(s)
   Public Shelter Area(s)_____
   Enclosed Mercantile_____
      Kinds_____
      (Inventory General Store Stocks)
   Medical_____
   Work Shops_____

Staple Foodstuffs and Other Supplies:_____
_____
Local Industries:_____
_____
```

Residents:
```
  Doctors             M_____   Retired Police_____
                      F_____   Veterans      _____  RTA____ RTN____ RTAF____ BBP____
  Health Officers  M_____   Priests       _____
                      F_____   Novices       _____
  Local Healers    M_____   Carpenters    _____        Ages of Youngest and
                      F_____   Smiths        _____        Oldest Veteran    _____
  Midwives          M_____   Gunsmiths     _____                          _____
                      F_____   Cartwrights   _____
  Spirit Mediums   M_____   Mechanics     _____        Current Draftees____
                      F_____   Brick Makers  _____
  Teachers          M_____   Potters       _____        Stationed At_____
                      F_____   Jar Makers    _____        _____
     Resident            _____   Wood Shingle Makers
     Nonresident         _____   Concrete Shingle Makers_____
     Village(s) of Residence_____
  Students          M_____   _____
                      F_____   _____
```

Weapons:
```
  Kind                         Number  Source                           Cost
  _____        _____   _____       _____  ___
  _____        _____   _____       _____  ___
  _____        _____   _____       _____  ___
```

Animals: Villagers Owning
```
  Buffalo   _____   _____
  Oxen      _____   _____
  Horses    _____   _____
  Pigs      _____   _____
  Chickens  _____   _____
  Ducks     _____   _____
```

IV. EXTERNAL TRANSPORTATION

Railroad:
  Designation_____
  Distance (Route)_____ Direction_____
  Means of Access_____

Road (Motor Vehicle):
  Surface Type_____
  Distance/Direction_____ _____ _____
  Orientation   _____ _____ _____

Bus Service to Village:
  Frequency_____ Cost_____

River/Stream/Canal
  Name   _____ _____ _____
  Distance/Direction   _____ _____ _____
  Orientation   _____ _____ _____
  Navigability (Best)   _____ _____ _____
  Navigability (Poorest)_____ _____ _____

V. CHARACTERISTICS WITHIN ZONE OF VILLAGE INFLUENCE

Construction Materials (Show Limits on Sketch)
  Bamboo Stem Size Approximate Number of Clumps
          _____ _____
          _____ _____
          _____ _____

  Other Wood (Kinds, By Name)   Forest Location/Distance:
          _____
          _____   Forest Size:
          _____
                                   Forest Use by Villagers:

  Rock   Approximate Amount:

  Laterite   Approximate Amount:

  Laterite Use by Villagers:

Cultivated Land Within Community Influence
  (Show Limits on Sketch)
  Rice   Soil Types (Sand/Clay/Loam):
    Paddy_____
    Hill _____
  Other Upland Crop Areas
         _____
  Gardens_____
  Orchards_____

Qualitative Description of Topography

_____
_____
_____
_____
_____
_____

APPENDIX III

OUTLINE GUIDE FOR SUBSEQUENT INFORMAL DISCUSSION

(1) Rice harvests this year compared with those of one year ago and two years ago

    (a) Suggested causes for any variations

(2) Quantities of rice currently stored in the village (estimate this by asking the number of households having harvested various quantities of rice during the last harvest)

    (a) Proportions of glutinous rice and nonglutinous rice harvested

(3) Range of amounts of rice harvested from one rai of village land

(4) Amount of rice needed by one (average) family (5-7 people) each year

    (a) Amount consumed

    (b) Amount kept for seed

    (c) Amount of surplus (if any) reserved for emergencies

(5) Amount of surplus rice sold, where, and for how much

(6) Surplus rice brought to market for sale by individual farmer and by what means, or by individual village buyer, or collected in the village by an urban rice mill owner

(7) Village products other than rice sold in town

(8) Earning activities of those villagers with insufficient land holdings and insufficient rice harvests

(9) Availability of paddy land for new families; amount in rai; cost per rai

(10) Availability of uncleared upland for new families; amount in rai; cost per rai

(11) Frequency of inter-village visits; by whom and their purpose

(12) Frequency of visits to town by villagers, and the purpose of these visits

(13) Frequency of visits to the village by townspeople (district officials, salesmen, buyers, relatives, police)

(14) Recent migrations to the village; number of families, their origins and reasons for moving

(15) Recent emigrations from the village; the number of families, to where, why

(16) The number of village children sutdying in a nearby urban center

(17)Trips by villagers to Bangkok; frequency, duration, and purpose

(18)Village history

(19)Remembered epidemics, floods, fires, murders

(20)Approximate number of births and deaths each year

    (a) Causes of death

(21)Frequency of thefts and incidents of banditry

    (a) Time of occurrency, number of individuals involved, weapons carried

    (b) Village losses (cattle, gold, cash, goods)

    (c) Response of the villagers; response of the police

    (d) Number of thieves and bandits apprehended

(22)Village night patrols; why they do or do not exist

    (a) Number of men and number of teams

    (b) Methods of patrolling

    (c) Duration of each nightly patrol

    (d) Frequency with which each village male adult must serve

    (e) Number and kinds of weapons carried

    (f) Seasonal variations in patrolling patterns

    (g) Estimates of patrol effectiveness

(23)Commune and village administration

    (a) Commune and village elections and appointments

(24)Relationships among the villages of a commune and between a single village and the district seat

APPENDIX E

American Anthropological Association
Principles of Professional Responsibility[1]

Adopted 1971; as amended through 1976.

Note: This statement of principles is not intended to supersede previous statements and resolutions of the Association. Its intent is to clarify professional responsibilities in the chief areas of professional concern to anthropologists.

Preamble

Anthropologists work in many parts of the world in close personal association with the peoples and situations they study. Their professional situation is, therefore, uniquely varied and complex. They are involved with their discipline, their colleagues, their students, their sponsors, their subjects, their own and host governments, the particular individuals and groups with whom they do their field work, other populations and interest groups in the nations within which they work, and the study of processes and issues affecting general human welfare. In a field of such complex involvements, misunderstandings, conflicts and the necessity to make choices among conflicting values are bound to arise and to generate ethical dilemmas. It is a prime responsibility of anthropologists to anticipate these and to plan to resolve them in such a way as to do damage neither to those whom they study nor, in so far as possible, to their scholarly community. Where these conditions cannot be met, the anthropologist would be well advised not to pursue the particular piece of research.

The following principles are deemed fundamental to the anthropologist's responsible, ethical pursuit of the profession.

I. Relations With Those Studied

In research, an anthropologist's paramount responsibility is to those they study. When there is a conflict of interest, these individuals must come first. Anthropologists must do everything in their power to protect the

---

[1] Reprinted by permission of the American Anthropological Association.

physical, social, and psychological welfare and to honor the dignity and privacy of those studied.

(a) Where research involves the acquisition of material and information transferred on the assumption of trust between persons, it is axiomatic that the rights, interests, and sensitivities of those studied must be safeguarded.

(b) The aims of the investigation should be communicated as well as possible to the informant.

(c) Informants have a right to remain anonymous. This right should be respected both where it has been promised explicitly and where no clear understanding to the contrary has been reached. These strictures apply to the collection of data by means of cameras, tape recorders, and other data-gathering devices, as well as to data collected in face-to-face interviews or in participant observations. Those being studied should understand the capacities of such devices, they should be free to reject them if they wish, and if they accept them, the results obtained should be consonant with the informant's right to welfare, dignity and privacy.

1. Despite every effort being made to preserve anonymity, it should be made clear to informants that such anonymity may be compromised unintentionally.

2. When professionals or others have used pseudonyms to maintain anonymity, others should respect this decision and the reasons for it by not revealing indiscriminately the true identities of such committees, persons, or other data [I. (c) 1. and 2. added 1975].

(d) There should be no exploitation of individual informants for personal gain. Fair return should be given them for all services.

(e) There is an obligation to reflect on the foreseeable repercussions of research and publication on the general population being studied.

(f) The anticipated consequences of research should be communicated as fully as possible to the individuals and groups likely to be affected.

(g) In accordance with the Association's general position on clandestine and secret research, no reports should be provided to sponsors that are not also available to the general public and, where practicable, to the population studied.

(h) Every effort should be exerted to cooperate with members of the host society in the planning and execution of research projects.

(i) All of the above points should be acted upon in full recognition of the social and cultural pluralism of host societies and the consequent plurality of values, interests and demands in those societies. This diversity complicates choice-making in research, but ignoring it leads to irresponsible decisions.

II. Responsibility to the Public

Anthropologists are also responsible to the public—all presumed consumers of their professional efforts. To them they owe a commitment to candor and to truth in the dissemination of their research results and in the statement of their opinions as students of humanity.

(a) Anthropologists should not communicate findings secretly to some and withhold them from others.

(b) Anthropologists should not knowingly falsify or color their findings.

(c) In providing professional opinions, anthropologists are responsible not only for their content but also for integrity in explaining both these opinions and their bases.

(d) As people who devote their professional lives to understanding people, anthropologists bear a positive responsibility to speak out publicly, both individually and collectively, on what they know and what they believe as a result of their professional expertise gained in the study of human beings. That is, they bear a professional responsibility to contribute to an "adequate definition of reality" upon which public opinion and public policy must be based.

(e) In public discourse anthropologists should be honest about their qualifications and cognizant of the limitations of anthropological expertise.

III. Responsibility to the Discipline

An anthropologist bears a responsibility for the good reputation of the discipline and its practitioners.

(a) Anthropologists should undertake no secret research or any research whose results cannot be freely derived and publicly reported.

(b) Anthropologists should avoid even the appearance of engaging in clandestine research, by fully and freely disclosing the aims and sponsorship of all research.

(c) Anthropologists should attempt to maintain such a level of integrity and a rapport in the field that, by their behavior and example, they will not jeopardize further research there. The responsibility is not to analyze and report so as to offend no one, but to collect research in a way consistent with a commitment to honesty open inquiry, clear communication of sponsorship and research aims, and concern for the welfare and privacy of informants.

(d) Anthropologists should not present as their own work, either in speaking or writing, materials directly taken from other sources [added 1974].

(e) When anthropologists participate in actions related to hiring, retention, and advancement, they should ensure that no exclusionary practices be perpetuated against colleagues on the basis of sex, marital status, color, social class, religion, ethnic background, national origin, or other nonacademic attributes. They should, furthermore, refrain from transmitting and resist the use of information irrelevant to professional performance in such personnel actions [added 1975].

IV. Responsibility to Students

In relations with students anthropologists should be candid, fair, nonexploitative and committed to the student's welfare and academic progress.

As Robert Lekachman has suggested, honesty is the essential quality of a good teacher, neutrality is not. Beyond honest teaching, anthropologists as teachers have ethical responsibilities in selection, instruction in ethics, career counseling, academic supervision, evaluation, compensation and placement.

(a) Anthropologists should select students in such a way as to preclude discrimination on the basis of sex, race, ethnic group, social class and other categories of people indistinguishable by their intellectual potential.

(b) Anthropologists should alert students to the ethical problems of research and discourage them from participation in projects employing questionable ethical standards. This should include providing them with information and discussions to protect them from unethical pressures and enticements emanating from possible sponsors, as well as helping them to find acceptable alternatives (see point (i) below).

(c) Anthropologists should be receptive and seriously responsible to students' interests, opinions and desires in all aspects of their academic work and relationships.

(d) Anthropologists should realistically counsel students regarding career opportunities.

(e) Anthropologists should conscientiously supervise, encourage and support students in their anthropological and other academic endeavors.

(f) Anthropologists should inform students of what is expected of them in their course of study; be fair in the evaluation of their performance; communicate evaluations to the students concerned.

(g) Anthropologists should acknowledge in print the student assistance used in their own publications; give appropriate credit (including co-authorship) when student research is used in publication, encourage and assist in publication of worthy student papers; and compensate students justly for the use of their time, energy and intelligence in research and teaching.

(h) Anthropologists should energetically assist students in securing legitimate research support and the necessary permissions to pursue research.

(i) Anthropologists should energetically assist students in securing professional employment upon completion of their studies.

(j) Anthropologists should strive to improve both our techniques of teaching and our techniques for evaluating the effectiveness of our methods of teaching.

V. Responsibility to Sponsors

In relations with sponsors of research, anthropologists should be honest about their qualifications, capabilities and aims. They thus face the obligation, prior to entering any commitment for research, to reflect sincerely upon the purposes of their sponsors in terms of their past behavior. Anthropologists should be especially careful not to promise or imply acceptance of conditions contrary to their professional ethics or competing commitments. This requires that they require of sponsors full disclosure of the sources of funds, personnel, aims of the institution and the research project, and disposition of research results. Anthropologists must retain the right to make all ethical decisions in their research. They should enter into no secret agreement with the sponsor regarding the research, results or reports.

VI. Responsibilities to One's Own Government and to Host Governments

In relation with their own governments and with host governments, the research anthropologist should be honest and candid. They should demand assurance that they will not be required to compromise their professional responsibilities and ethics as a condition of their permission to pursue the research. Specifically, no secret research, no secret reports or debriefings of any kind should be agreed to or given. If these matters are clearly understood in advance, serious complications and misunderstandings can generally be avoided.

Epilogue

In the final analysis, anthropological research is a human undertaking, depending upon choice for which the individual bears ethical as well as scientific responsibility. That responsibility is a human, not superhuman responsibility. To err is human, to forgive humane. This statement of principles of professional responsibility is not designed to punish, but to provide guidelines which can minimize the occasions upon which there is a need to forgive. When anthropologists, by their actions, jeopardize peoples studied, professional colleagues, students or others, or if they otherwise betray their professional commitments, their colleagues may legitimately inquire into the propriety of those actions, and take such measures as lie within the legitimate powers of their Association as the membership of the Association deems appropriate.

APPENDIX F

American Anthropological Association
Principles of Professional Responsibility[1]

Adopted by the Council of the American Anthropological Association
May 1971
(As amended through October 1990)

Note: *This statement enunciates general responsibilities for all anthropologists. Each of the units of the AAA may develop a more detailed statement of ethics specific to their particular professional responsibilities but in all cases consonant with the principles stated herewith.*

Preamble

Anthropologists' relations with their discipline, with the individuals and groups among whom they conduct research or to whom they provide services, with their employers and with their host governments, are varied, complex, sensitive, and sometimes difficult to reconcile. In a field of such complex involvements, misunderstandings, conflicts and the need to make choices among apparently incompatible values are constantly generated. The most fundamental responsibility of anthropologists is to anticipate such difficulties and to resolve them in ways that are compatible with the principles stated here. If such resolution is impossible, anthropological work should not be undertaken or continued.

Anthropologists must respect, protect and promote the rights and the welfare of all those affected by their work. The following general principles and guidelines are fundamental to ethical anthropological practice.

I. Responsibility to people whose lives and cultures anthropologists study

Anthropologists' first responsibility is to those whose lives and cultures they study. Should conflicts of interest arise, the interests of these people take precedence over other considerations. Anthropologists must do everything in their power to protect the dignity and privacy of the people

---

[1] Reprinted by permission of the American Anthropological Association.

with whom they work, conduct research or perform other professional activities. Their physical, social and emotional safety and welfare are the professional concerns of the anthropologists who have worked among them.

A. The rights, interests, safety, and sensitivities of those who entrust information to anthropologists must be safeguarded.

1. The right of those providing information to anthropologists either to remain anonymous or to receive recognition is to be respected and defended. It is the responsibility of anthropologists to make every effort to determine the preferences of those providing information and to comply with their wishes.

> a. It should be made clear to anyone providing information that despite the anthropologist's best intentions and effort anonymity may be compromised or recognition fail to materialize.

2. Anthropologists should not reveal the identity of groups or persons whose anonymity is protected through the use of pseudonyms.

3. The aims of all their professional activities should be clearly communicated by anthropologists to those among whom they work.

4. Anthropologists must not exploit individuals or groups for personal gain. They should give fair return for the help and services they receive. They must recognize their debt to the societies in which they work and their obligation to reciprocate in appropriate ways.

5. Anthropologists have an ongoing obligation to assess both the positive and negative consequences of their activities and the publications resulting from those activities. They should inform individuals and groups likely to be affected of any consequences relevant to them that they anticipate. In any case, however, their work must not violate these principles of professional responsibility. *If they anticipate the possibility that such violations might occur they should take steps, including, if necessary, discontinuance of work, to avoid such outcomes.*

6. Whether they are engaged in academic or nonacademic research, anthropologists must be candid about their professional identities. If the results of their activities are not to be made public, this should be made clear to all concerned from the outset.

7. Anthropologists must take into account and, where relevant, make explicit the extent to which their own personal and cultural values affect their professional activities. They must also recognize and deal candidly and

judiciously with the effects that the often conflicting demands and values of employers, sponsors, host governments and research publications may have upon their work.

II. Responsibility to the public

Anthropologists have responsibility to be truthful to the publics that read, hear, or view the products of their work.

A. In expressing professional opinions publicly, anthropologists are not only responsible for the factual content of their statements but also must consider carefully the social and political implications of the information they disseminate. They must do everything in their power to insure that such information is well-understood, properly contextualized and responsibly utilized.

B. Anthropologists bear a positive responsibility to speak out publicly, both individually and collectively, on issues about which they possess professional expertise. That is, they have a professional responsibility to contribute to the formation of informational grounds upon which public policy may be founded. Anthropologists should make clear the bases upon which their positions stand.

C. When engaging in public discourse anthropologists should be candid about their qualifications, and they should recognize and make clear the limits of anthropological expertise.

III. Responsibility to the discipline

Anthropologists bear responsibility for the good reputation of the discipline and its practitioners.

A. The integrity with which anthropologists conduct their affairs, and the rapport that they seek to maintain in the field and in other professional venues must be of an order that justifies trust and confidence. They must not behave in ways that jeopardize either their own or others' future research or professional employment. It is their responsibility to act in ways consistent with commitments to honesty, open inquiry, candor concerning sponsorship and research aims, and concern fro the welfare and privacy of all concerned parties. Anthropologists must address such conflicts as do arise among the interests of those parties and attempt to resolve them equitably.

B. Anthropologists must not represent as their own work, either in speaking or writing, materials or ideas directly taken from other sources. Anthropologists must give full credit in speaking or writing to all of their professional colleagues, anthropologists or non-anthropologists, who have contributed to their work.

C. When anthropologists participate in actions relating to hiring, retention and advancement, they should (except in the case of affirmative actions taken to redress historical imbalances) insure that no exclusionary practices should be perpetuated against colleagues on the basis of sex, marital status, color, social class, political convictions, religion, ethnic background, national origin, sexual orientation, age, or any other criterion irrelevant to academic performance. Nor should an otherwise qualified individual be excluded on the basis of physical disability. Anthropologists should, furthermore, refrain from transmitting, and resist the use of, information irrelevant to professional performance in personnel actions.

D. The cross-disciplinary nature of the activities of many anthropologists requires that they be informed of, and respect, the requirements of the nonanthropological colleagues with whom they work.

IV. Responsibility to students and trainees

Anthropologists should be candid, fair, and nonexploitative in their dealings with trainees and students, and committed to their welfare and progress. They have continuing responsibility to recognize the changing nature of the discipline, in both its content and its methodology, and further, in novel applications of anthropological knowledge and approaches. They have a further responsibility to convey current understandings to students and trainees.

A. Anthropologists should accept students into their programs in ways precluding and redressing discrimination on the basis of sex, marital status, color, social class, political convictions, religion, ethnic background, national origin, sexual orientation, age, or other criterion irrelevant to academic performance.

B. Anthropologists should strive to improve both their teaching techniques and the methods of evaluating their effectiveness as teachers.

C. Anthropologists should be receptive and genuinely responsive to students' interests, opinions, and needs.

D. Anthropologists should counsel students realistically regarding both academic and nonacademic career opportunities.

E. Anthropologists should be conscientious in supervising, encouraging, and supporting students in their studies, both anthropological and nonanthropological.

F. Anthropologists should inform students of what is expected of them, be fair in the evaluation of their performance, and prompt and reliable in communicating evaluations to them.

G. Anthropologists should impress upon students the ethical problems involved in anthropological work and discourage them from participating in ethically questionable projects.

H. Anthropologists should acknowledge orally and in print student assistance in research and preparation of their work; give appropriate credit for coauthorship or first authorship to students when their research is used in publications or lectures; encourage and assist in publication of worthy students papers and compensate students justly for the use of their time, energy, and ideas in research, teaching, and other professional activities.

I. Anthropologists should energetically assist students in securing legitimate research support and the necessary permission to pursue research and other professional activities.

J. Anthropologists should vigorously assist students in securing professional placement upon the completion of their studies.

K. Anthropologists should beware of the serious conflicts of interest and exploitation which may result if they engage in sexual relations with students. They must avoid sexual liaisons with students for whose professional training they are in any way responsible.

V. Responsibility to employers, clients, and sponsors

In all dealings with employers, clients, and sponsors anthropologists should be honest about their qualifications, capabilities, and aims. Prior to entering any professional commitment, anthropologists must review the purposes of sponsors, employers, or clients, taking into consideration their past activities and future goals. In working for governmental agencies or private businesses, anthropologists should be especially careful not to promise or imply acceptance of conditions contrary to professional ethics or competing commitments.

VI. Responsibilities to governments

Anthropologists should be honest and candid in all dealings with their own governments and with host governments. They should ascertain that they will not be required to compromise either their responsibilities or anthropological ethics as a condition of permission to engage in professional activities. Anthropologists are under no professional obligation to provide reports or debriefings of any kind to government officials or employees, unless they have individually and explicitly agreed to do so in the terms of employment.

Epilogue

Anthropological activity requires choices for which anthropologists individually and collectively bear ethical as well as scientific responsibility. This statement is designed to promote discussion and provide general guidelines for ethically responsible decisions. When anthropologists, by their actions, jeopardize peoples studied, professional colleagues, employers, employees, clients, students, or others, or if they otherwise betray their professional commitments, their colleagues may legitimately inquire into the propriety of such actions, and take such measures as lie with legitimate powers of the American Anthropological Association, as the membership of the Association deems appropriate.

Appendix G

Report of the Ad Hoc Committee
to Evaluate the Controversy Concerning
Anthropological Activities in Relation to Thailand

to the

Executive Board of the American
Anthropological Association

September 27, 1971

Part I: Anthropological Activities in Thailand

Part II: Guidelines on Future Policy

William Davenport
David Olmsted
Margaret Mead, Chairman
Ruth Freed, Executive Secretary

Anthropological Activities in Thailand[1]

Under instructions from the Executive Board the ad hoc committee examined all the documents previously collected by the Board or the Ethics Committee, correspondence in the Newsletter and other journals, and solicited further information from members, past and present, of the Executive Board and the Ethics Committee, from all individuals originally named in the controversy and all individuals named by any correspondent to the ad hoc committee, including members of other nation-states who were suggested as having relevant information. A special attempt was made to address letters to as many Thai social scientists and anthropologists as possible. In the case of communications that were not personally solicited, a request was sent to the author asking whether the communication could be used. The documentation for the ad hoc committee's work will be deposited in the archives of the American Anthropological Association. All members of the ad hoc committee and its Executive Secretary, Ruth Freed, have examined all of these materials in detail. We sent two form letters: 188 to anthropologists and other social scientists; we received 57 answers. The other form letter was sent to past and present members of the Executive Board and the Ethics Committee; in each case 12 letters were sent and 10 answers obtained.

The ad hoc committee also studied all of the documentation and correspondence originally a part of the Thailand controversy, including *The Student Mobilizer* (publication) of April 2, 1970. In addition, we collected and read published and unpublished papers, reports, manuscripts of parts of unpublished books, articles, and reviews in our attempt to carry out the charge from the Executive Board. Approximately 6,000 pages were read, and many reread, in order for the ad hoc committee to write this report.

Anthropological Research in Thailand: The Setting

The controversy over the activities of U.S. anthropologists in Thailand takes place during a period when U.S. society is grievously divided over the issue of the Indochina war. Many Americans, including all members of the ad hoc committee, consider the war to be unconstitutional, unwise, and unnecessary. News of atrocities perpetrated by the United States and its allies produces deep psychic disturbance among many people, because the incidents stem in part from racist attitudes which stain our social fabric and at the same time contravene our most revered ideals and cherished views of ourselves.

---

[1] Reprinted by permission of the American Anthropological Association.

Anthropologists of several nationalities have worked in Thailand in increasing numbers since the end of World War II. Americans have found it an especially congenial country in which to do research, and their numbers increased markedly as funds became abundant. From the correspondence received in response to the committee's request for information it is evident that anthropologists who have worked in Thailand have become a relatively close group of experts who share an uncommonly high regard for the peoples of the Thai nation and a deep concern for their political and social problems. Some anthropologists have concentrated on academic research exclusively; others have welcomed the opportunity to assist in a wide range of social development projects initiated by the Royal Thai Government.

In the early 1960's new U.S. missions were established in Thailand to assist in planned development. Prominent among them was USAID/USOM Thailand. Initially, these missions were concerned solely with development as proposed by the Thai themselves. Anthropologists were asked to participate and were given financial support from many U.S. Government sources for their work. It was a very favorable period for anthropologists who were already working there and new researchers were attracted by these opportunities.

However, this extremely favorable situation began to change as U.S. involvement in the Indochina war increased. The close political relationship between the United States and Thailand changed from that of partners in peace to allies in war. Large military bases were constructed. U.S. agencies began assisting the Thai government in strengthening its relationships to some of the peoples within the kingdom whose relationship to the central authority has been weak. There were incursions across Thai borders by neighboring groups and attempts to alienate some Thai citizens from their government. U.S. missions and Thai government agencies, formerly concerned mainly with social development, broadened their programs to include strategic and security matters. The change was gradual and subtle.

Most American anthropologists working in Thailand seem to have been incompletely aware of this merging of social and military objectives, and some may have chosen to ignore some of the more distasteful aspects of these shifts. Some of them, perhaps, seem to have been drawn along during these changes by their affection for the Thai and an optimistic belief that their professional advice and criticism of U.S. programs would, in the long run, secure the beneficial results that the Thai themselves desired. At the same time these same anthropologists continued to receive support from various U.S. sources—governmental and non-governmental—for their scholarly and scientific work as long as their projects appeared to conform to policy objectives.

It was in the same optimistic spirit that two advisory services were established in the United States. These were the Academic Advisory Council for Thailand, located at the University of California, Los Angeles, and the South East Asian Development Advisory Group, organized within the Asia

Society of New York. Both were backed by U.S. Government funds directed through the USAID. The ad hoc committee's investigations revealed that the operation and organization of AACT and SEADAG are greatly misunderstood. Both organizations have stated that they did not and do not engage in any secret or clandestine research.

Many of the anthropologists who became involved in mission-oriented work have become increasingly disillusioned over the slight effect their efforts had in shaping U.S. policies and have abandoned all their government connections. Some continue to believe that they can still moderate policies and continue to try to bring the programs in which they are involved into closer fit with Thai social and cultural aspirations. It is important to note in this connection that all U.S. Government programs with which anthropologists have been associated were carried out in conjunction and cooperation with the Royal Thai Government. Beginning with the formation of the National Research Council of Thailand (ca. 1964) it has been required that all anthropological research be approved by that body and progress reports be routinely submitted to it. So far as the committee could determine, all American anthropologists have complied with these requirements and no American anthropologist has come into serious conflict with any branches of the Royal Thai Government.

It is very likely that secret and clandestine intelligence work among Thai people has been conducted at the instigation of special U.S. military and government intelligence units. The ad hoc committee has no information about such covert work, nor could it be expected to have. The committee has been informed about some American anthropologists who have been approached with proposals that they engage in such intelligence activity, and who report that the proposals were refused. We mention this only in order clearly to distinguish such clandestine intelligence from the applied anthropology or mission-oriented research and consultation that American anthropologists, as well as anthropologists from other countries, have openly pursued.

From the beginning, the Thailand controversy was enveloped in an unwarranted conspiratorial atmosphere. The documents which were used by the Student Mobilization Committee in their so-called expose and published in their issue of *The Student Mobilizer* of April 2, 1970, were referred to as if they were secret. This suggested that copies could only be obtained by stealth. In fact, none of these documents was classified as secret. They were stolen from unlocked files in a university office, then reproduced and distributed in a manner which set the furtive tone for the subsequent accusations.

The accusations made by members of the Ethics Committee centered around the charge that many American anthropologists "were being used in programs of counterinsurgency." This is a grave charge, but was it in fact as sinister as it sounds? The answer, in the committee's view, requires a closer look at funding practices in the social sciences in the United States.

For some time, after a period in which projects had been accepted and funded generously and uncritically by government agencies, public funds have been difficult to obtain for research. Widespread anti-intellectualism, nurtured by faculty inflexibility and by remnants of the Joe McCarthy postulate that academic people are likely to be politically suspect, has been further aggravated recently by turmoil on university campuses. In such circumstances, research funds were not forthcoming from public sources unless the project could be made to appear directly pertinent to some "practical" end of high value to those holding the public purse strings. Thus the development of transformational grammar was largely financed out of the Department of Defense's interest in "communication"; at a later point, mathematics, engineering and physics came upon a bonanza in the wake of Sputnik; similarly, much social science, including anthropological, research was supported because it was described as related to health, in particular "mental health." For a long time, anthropologists, in Thailand and around the world, had enriched their various fields of "pure" science while at the same time contributing to the solution of problems requiring "applied anthropology." It happened that, during the Kennedy administration, the nation's military policy was changed from one of nuclear-confrontation-or-nothing to one including an alternative labeled "limited wars" or "counter-insurgency operations." The latter term—counterinsurgency—soon became the label under which funds were given, just as "communication" and "mental health" had been previously. The responses of individuals to the committee—and other relevant documents—list such activities as: construction of roads, schools, and organization of medical care, water supplies, cooperatives, and marketing facilities, as well as village security and mapping of trails, under the heading of counterinsurgency; these are much the same activities that were called "community development' at an earlier time. To attack a rural health research worker because his project is funded as counterinsurgency is to miss this fundamental point. While it is true that anyone helping to alleviate the lot of down-trodden or neglected people of a nation may lessen the changes of a revolution occurring—as Chou En-lai has pointed out in connection with Thailand—such activity is well within the traditional canons of acceptable behavior for the applied anthropologist, and is counterinsurgent only for present funding purposes; a decade ago it might have been "mental health."

In the committee's view, the point is not an unimportant one, however, since it testifies to a pervasive corruption of the life of the scholarly community in its relations with the government—our own and others. The mislabeling or redirecting of scientific projects in order to obtain funds may have seemed necessary; it may also have prepared anthropologists and other scholars to close their eyes to misuse of their data in practical situations and, in the long run, misuse of their talents vis-a-vis science.

Our reading of the documents convinces us that most of the criticism that developed from them relates to "counterinsurgency" in the above sense.

Many anthropologists working at various applied anthropological projects were judged guilty-by-association because their funds were procured in (perhaps) the only way they could have been in a Washington obsessed with the Cold War.

A New Responsibility Emerges

However, in attempting to analyze the great mass of contradictory and ambiguous statements, it became clear to the ad hoc committee that what lay back of the intensity of the present controversy was not only a genuine revulsion against events in Southeast Asia and different views of the relation between citizen and nation, but also that a new ethical dilemma, never envisaged before, and never stated clearly in any document submitted to the ad hoc committee, was evolving. This dilemma is so terrible in its possible consequence that neither side to the controversy seems able to articulate it.

It is clear that anthropologists now have to face the possibility that a publication of routine socio-cultural data about identified village communities, or the assemblage of unpublished data in centralized files, such as the Tribal Research Centre at Chieng Mai, might be used for the annihilation by bombing or other forms of warfare of whole communities, as such data lend themselves to computerization and mass depersonalization of communities marked for destruction.

There is no evidence that such use has been made of any such data in Thailand, and there have been repeated and competent denials that there is a computer in the Tribal Research Centre in Chieng Mai. But the documentation submitted to the committee, plus large amounts of information available in the press, testify to the practice in Southeast Asian conflicts of annihilating large numbers of villages suspected of providing aid and shelter to the enemy.

We believe it is this unarticulated but quite real danger that lies back of the extraordinary degree of emotion that has surrounded this whole controversy.

In the past anthropologists have been asked to take responsibility for individual informations, and for the integrity of cultures, but they have never been faced before in such a direct and appalling way with the possibility that normal community studies might be used so destructively. To our previously articulated ethical principles, we must now add, *anthropologists must not endanger identifiable villages or communities.*

Actions of the Ethics Committee and the Executive Board

The Executive Board. The actions of the Executive Board can be better understood if it is realized that the American Anthropological Association has undergone very rapid growth during the last 20 years. With only a membership of 500 to 750 in the last 1940's, there are now 7,000, of whom some 1,800 are Fellows, another 3,000 are Voting Members. The growth rate since 1965 has been approximately 55 percent.

Formerly the American Anthropological Association was a closely knit, small organization that conducted its affairs informally; the activities of the Executive Board have been and still are carried on within this tradition. The Board strives for friendly and harmonious relations and consensus in decisions. This was usually possible when the Association was small and relatively homogeneous; it no longer is. There are factions and blocs within the Association. Many of the problems come from reorganizing to meet new conditions; others are related to the internal politics of the Association and some to differences of opinion about U.S. foreign and domestic policies. Despite these difficulties, the Executive Board often achieves splendid, informal interaction.

In such a setting, the Board did not take sufficient care in setting up the two Ethics Committees (ad hoc and standing, 1969 and 1970); they should have been given detailed instructions for their procedures and activities. This is clear in hindsight; the actual series of decisions which created an ambiguous situation was characterized by compromise and failure of liaison between the Board and the committee and at least one oversight on the part of the Executive Secretary's office. The members of the Board and staff approached their duties conscientiously, from their several points of view. It is probably that their inability to deal more decisively with the developing problem of the controversy was in part a result of the pronounced differences of opinion among members of the Board. These differences were resolved by compromises that proved unsatisfactory to all. We commend the Board for finally taking action.

The Ethics Committee. Three members of the Ethics Committee, at least, engaged in public denunciation, based on stolen documents, which named several of their colleagues. The ad hoc committee concedes their right as citizens to take any political action they choose, and to receive approval from whatever groups may applaud such action. The ad hoc committee does, however, find reprehensible certain actions taken by various members of the Ethics Committee, viz. their unauthorized identification of themselves as members of said committee in connection with their public denunciations, thus involving the Association; their use of unethically-procured documents without public denunciation of the sources of such materials; accusations of colleagues ("hirelings," etc.) without opportunity for due process, or even proper notification of those concerned. (We reject their claim that they themselves named no names, in the light of the imminent publication of the documents in *The Student Mobilizer*, April 2, 1970.) The situation was both less sinister and more complicated than the press-releases by the Student Mobilization Committee and the Ethics Committee members seemed to indicate. While the Student Mobilization Committee might not be expected to ask for information from Thailand-based anthropologists, this ad hoc committee feels that a major opportunity was lost by the ethics Committee when some of its members spoke in haste and without so much as asking their colleagues for information on the situation regarding anthropological research in Thailand. At the least, it was unscholarly of them not to seek information where they must have known themselves to be ignorant, and the result was an unjustified, inaccurate, and unfair attack which has endangered research access for all anthropologists in Thailand and probably elsewhere as well.

The precipitation of this public dispute, without due and careful consideration of the repercussions upon our colleagues, both members of the American Anthropological Association and others, in contrary to the spirit of scholarly and scientific work and inimical to international cooperation.

We deeply regret any damage that has been done and we strongly urge that in comparable situations in the future the American Anthropological Association follow the principle enacted by the International Union of Anthropological and Ethnological Societies:

> "That the Permanent Council request national anthropological organizations to engage in the fullest possible consultation with colleagues in other countries before pronouncing judgment on the appropriateness or ethics of anthropological activity related to those countries."

This resolution should apply particularly to anthropologists in the host country and to other nationals involved in research in the host country.

Conclusions: Based on the whole body of written evidence considered by the committee.

1. No civilian member of the American Anthropological Association had contravened the principles laid down in the 1967 Statement on *Problems of Anthropological Research and Ethics* (Beals Report) in his or her work in Thailand.

2. United States aid to Thailand has changed in character during the last two decades. Evaluation of the performance of the anthropologists involved in such missions depends on the character of the particular agency or organization, the period at which the work was done, and the political views of the evaluator.

3. The U.S. anthropologists in Thailand have contributed in their capacity as field researchers much of value to anthropology.

4. The controversy within the American Anthropological Association is linked to wider political struggles in our society, but its vehemence is disproportionate to the acts of any anthropologist in Thailand.

5. *A new ethical imperative has emerged, the obligation to protect data on communities which might expose them to wholesale destruction.*

6. The Executive Board did not act with sufficient decisiveness.

7. Members of the Ethics Committee acted hastily, unfairly, and unwisely in making public statements—whether identifying themselves in their American Anthropological Association capacity or not—without first having consulted the anthropologists named in the purloined documents which formed the basis of their charges, and without having obtained authorization from the Board.

Part II

Guide Lines on Future Policy

In preparing this report the ad hoc committee has taken into account: the 1967 Statement on Problems of Anthropological Research and Ethics; Beals' *Politics of Social Research*, which gives background material on the preparation of that report; the two resolutions adopted by mail ballot in May 1971, on (1) *Role and Function of the Committee on Ethics*, and (2) *Principles of Professional Responsibility*; published and unpublished discussions of ethics submitted to the ad hoc committee between may 1971 and September 19, 1971 (when this report was completed). We have also taken particular cognizance of the issues and dilemmas that have been brought up in connection with research, applied anthropological work, and consultancies in Thailand since 1961.

Whenever an association has only one active and important committee in addition to an executive board, polarization may occur quite independently of the charge given the committee or the extent of polarization in the organization. The Ethics Committee was destined by its history, if not by the issues with which it also dealt, to be such a committee. We, therefore, recommend the establishment of two more standing committees: a committee to sift and weigh issues on which members of the Association have special competence, such as the mistreatment of isolated peoples, the destruction of hunting territories, military recruitment of segments of a population, etc.; and a committee on the relationship of anthropology and anthropologists to major contemporary issues of our time.

Specific Recommended Additions and Changes to the Present Statement on Ethics

Sanctions. The ad hoc committee does not recommend the use of such sanctions as expulsion without due process and changed membership procedure.

The ad hoc committee wishes to emphasize that the American Anthropological Association is a voluntary association of scholars and/or scientists for whom there is no entrance requirement except the completion of certain scholarly and/or scientific academic requirements; and no attempt is made to assess *competency* as a teacher, consultant, research worker, curator, etc., of those who are admitted to membership. If members are to be faced with the risk of expulsion for conduct deemed unethical by a majority of the current ethical board—which is what the present resolution recommends—then they should be most fully informed of the principles by which the Association expects them to guide their behavior, and warned that these principles will change, as the social situation changes. It is reasonable, if such a submission is required for membership, that public censorship or expulsion might be a sanction open to the Association, but as present membership requirements are set up, it is grossly illogical to censure a member for failure to follow principles that have never been used a condition of membership.

Issuance of Credentials. The committee regards the proposed credential as either a farce or a device to exercise differential punitive power on the order of the various oaths that were proposed during the Joe McCarthy era. As in the case of these oaths, those who are concealing their real purposes or intentions will have no hesitation in falsifying the record. The Association has no way of certifying to the truth of any such statements; such certification is, therefore grossly misleading to those to whom it would be presented. It would serve no purpose except to provide opportunities for the persecution of individuals whose activities may be personally or politically repugnant to temporary majorities in the shifting membership of successive executive boards.

Register of Organizations. This recommendation is much too vague and would be impossible to carry out even with a large investigatory staff. It should be revised to read, "to enhance the ability of Members and Fellows we suggest that the Association's Executive Office develop contacts and methods through which the status of any would-be sponsor could be ascertained, and also keep a roster of those organizations which have been demonstrated, in the course of enquiries, to have suspect sponsorship." It cannot be too strongly emphasized that such a list must be up-to-date, that organizations and agencies redefine their missions and programs, and that it was a frequent, and reprobated procedure of mccarthyism to attack individuals by associating them with organizations which had changed their orientation.

Secrecy and Withholding Research Data. The committee recommends a major departure from the Beals Report, and also from the May 1971 statements. Both those documents warn against secret research, pointing to classified government work as against the best interests of the peoples studied, and of anthropology. We agree, but wish to point out that there is no sure way to prevent misuse of data from "pure" research which is freely published. It is in the public domain and may be used for many purposes, malign as well as benign. We therefore suggest that each field-worker consider whether there is a possibility that his data could be misused, from the standpoint of his own ethical principles, and if so, that he not only change names of people and places but, in addition, consider delaying publication for a period—say five years—sufficient to make the data unusable by those planning annihilation, bombing or other atrocities. Actual names of persons and places could be made available, under conditions of secrecy, to qualified investigators, so that the scientific replicability of the research would be maintained. Thus, in order to protect the people studied—from persecution as well as annihilation—what may be required is more secrecy, not less secrecy. The new secrecy would have the advantage of being under the control of the investigator. In accepting such responsibility he would have to guard—in this day and age—against theft and xeroxing of his materials, preferably by coding them in such a manner that they could not be used by others to uncover what should remain hidden.

Area of Responsibility of the Ethics Committee. We believe that the Ethics Committee's activities should be confined to questions where anthropologists, as scholars and scientists, can be held responsible. It should not enter the field of applied anthropology, in which particular competence and acceptance of more specialized professional ethics are necessary. We recommend that any anthropologist doing applied work should become a member of the Society for Applied Anthropology and that the Society for Applied Anthropology, which was a pioneer in the development of a code of ethics, should work towards developing standards of competence and *professional* ethics which in time might evolve into professional board certifications (comparable to those used in medicine and law) and in licensing.

The Resolution of 1972 on "Principles of Professional Responsibility" has taken into account that some questions of professional ethics may be deemed more appropriate for action by the American Association of University Professors or the American Federation of Teachers. This is an inexplicit recognition that there is no profession of anthropology; that, professionally, members of the American Anthropological Association are teachers, administrators, research workers, applied practitioners in such fields as health, urbanization, and education; consultants, writers, editors, etc. Each of these is a profession with its own more or less well developed code. The Association cannot remain what it is, a voluntary association of such great diversity of fields of interest and specialization, unless it recognizes that it, as an association, can neither require nor certify to competence or specific ethical sensitivity in these various professional fields. Of the ethical admonishments under 4 in the 1971 Resolution, "Principles of Professional Responsibility" only *b* is strictly the responsibility of an anthropologist as a teacher. This should be more specific and read: "He should alert students to the special problems involved in anthropological research, particularly when such research is done in other countries, or among peoples who are politically vulnerable. He should also alert them to the special psychological hazards of field research and take pains to ascertain whether a student is in good health and able to stand the strain of his projected work." *h* should read: "Where field work is a requirement for degree completion, the anthropologist as teacher should make every effort to see that students under his supervision have a chance to obtain research funds."

There could well be a recommendation that anthropologists pay particular attention, as anthropologists, to the ethics of the professions they practice; the scholarly or scientific knowledge peculiar to their several disciplines—linguistics, cultural anthropology, archaeology, etc.—puts them in a position of responsibility which they cannot escape. In addition to their personal ethics as human beings and their political responsibilities as citizens, they also have special responsibilities because of their disciplinary knowledge.

We recommend that the Ethics Committee be renamed as *the Committee on Ethical Practices and Principles*.

Need for a New Standing Committee on Particularly Anthropological Responsibilities

There will inevitably be great diversity of opinion on major political issues and on the particular methods used to implement policies with political implications, but there are certain fields where anthropologists have special knowledge and special competencies and an obligation to speak out. These are such fields as: culture contact, enforced bilingualism, military recruitment of dependent minorities, invasion of an area by a mining operation, destruction of hunting and fishing territories, compulsory transplantation of villages or dispersal of population, and exposure of isolated groups to external agents of disease.

The American Anthropological Association should work out a procedure through which the whole Association can express an opinion on such issues, but the procedure should be such as to guarantee expertise, on the one hand, and protection for individuals and groups on the other. This may require a high level of confidentiality and secrecy.

The present controversy points up the need for such an orderly mechanism for translating the special expertise various anthropologists may possess into a factor in public policymaking. It is all too likely that the American Anthropological Association may be stampeded into taking public positions on such issues upon the basis of half-truths, hysteria, and powerful oratory. Each member should consider whether he/she want the American Anthropological Association to take a position he/she does NOT favor on such a basis. In order to avoid such ill-considered positions, it is suggested that a standing committee of the Association be set up for the purpose of screening such proposal and consulting with experts before reporting on them at the annual meetings. For example, in the country of X it is alleged that certain segments of the population are being mistreated. The Association's committee, in order to evaluate the charges, would conduct closed discussions with members who have had actual field experience in that country, preferably among the group in question. Anonymity for the consultants would make it possible for them to give their opinions frankly, secure in the assumption that their scientific work would not be ruined by a ban on access to the field, on account of publicly-attributed statements. The Association's committee would then report the case to the Executive Board for presentation to the membership, guaranteeing the competence of the consultants. The membership, with written evaluation of the facts before them, could then vote intelligently upon the proposed resolution. Thus the American Anthropological Association could benefit , in a way that it has not in the Thailand case, from the particular knowledge of the X-specialists, while the X-specialists would be immune from reprisal.

Need for New Standing Committee on Anthropological and Major Contemporary Issues

Through such a committee, members of the Association would be able to relate their different specialities and interests to such issues as: war, population control, social injustice to minorities, youth, women; problems of urbanization and the degradation of the environment, etc. This committee would be charged with bringing to the attention of the membership issues like these through forums and hearings. It would also respond to demands from the membership for various kinds of public airing of such issues. It would act as a screening committee for resolutions affecting its areas of concern and would hold public hearings at the beginning of the Annual Meeting and make recommendations to the Board on resolutions to be brought before the membership. In the past, the fate of resolutions on subjects as inclusive as war and disarmament has been determined by accidents of faulty phrasing, last-minute lobbying, or impassioned oratory. In some cases all three committees might be working on different aspects of the same problem.

Resolutions

Be it resolved:

A. That the Ethics Committee be reorganized as a standing Committee on Ethical Practices and principles and confine its attention to matters of scholarly and scientific ethics.

B. That a standing Committee on Particularly Anthropological Responsibilities be set up to prepare, with the help of confidential discussions with groups of specialist consultants, recommendations to the Board for presentation to the membership, on issues on which unprepared public discussion may be destructive.

C. That a standing Committee on Anthropology and Major Contemporary Issues be set up to provide for forums and hearings on such issues as war, population control, etc., in which anthropologists have a keen interest but no exclusive competence or responsibilities in terms of their specialized disciplines.

BIBLIOGRAPHY

Aberle, David F. Letter. *AAA Newsletter* 8:5 (May 1967):7.

_____. Letter. *AAA Newsletter* 11:7 (September 1970):19.

_____, and David M. Schneider. Letter. *AAA Newsletter* 11:9 (November 1970):7–8.

Agency for International Development. *Project Budget Submission Thailand FY [Fiscal Year] 1970.* n.p.: Department of State, September 1968.

American Anthropological Association. *Newsletter of the American Anthropological Association.* [Early issues published as *Fellow Newsletter*; cited as *AAA Newsletter*].

_____. "Background Information on Problems of Anthropological Research and Ethics" [the Beals report]. *AAA Newsletter* 8:1 (January 1967):1–13.

_____. "Statement on Problems of Anthropological Research and Ethics." n.p.: AAA, 1967.

_____. *Annual Report 1970 and Directory* (4:1). Washington, DC: AAA, April 1971.

_____. "Principles of Professional Responsibility." n.p.: AAA, 1971; amended through 1976; 1990 (revised).

Americas Watch. *Civil Patrols in Guatemala.* New York: Human Rights Watch, August 1986.

_____. *Closing the Space: Human Rights in Guatemala During President Cerezo's First Year.* New York: Human Rights Watch, February 1987.

_____. *Human Rights in Honduras: Central America's 'Sideshow.'* New York: Human Rights Watch, May 1987.

_____. *The Civilian Toll 1986–1987 (Ninth Supplement to the Report on Human Rights in El Salvador).* New York: Human Rights Watch, 30 August 1987.

_____. *A Certain Passivity: Failing to Curb Human Rights Abuses in Peru*. New York: Human Rights Watch, December 1987.

_____. *Tolerating Abuses: Violations of Human Rights in Peru*. New York: Human Rights Watch, October 1988.

_____. *Messengers of Death: Human Rights in Guatemala*. New York: Human Rights Watch, March 1990.

Anderson, Benedict R. O'G. "Withdrawal Symptoms: Social and Cultural Aspects of the October 6 Coup." *Bulletin of Concerned Asian Scholars* 9:3 (July–September 1977):13–29.

_____. "Studies of the Thai State: The State of Thai Studies" in *The Study of Thailand: Analyses of Knowledge, Approaches, and Prospects in Anthropology, Art History, Economics, History, and Political Science*, edited by Eliazer B. Ayal, 193-247. Athens, Ohio: Ohio University Center for International Studies, Southeast Asia Program, 1978.

Association for Asian Studies. "Program of the Twenty Second Annual Meeting." n.p., 1970.

Baldwin, Frank. "The Jason Project: Academic Freedom and Moral Responsibility." *Bulletin of Concerned Asian Scholars* 5:3 (November 1973):2–12.

Bangkok (Thailand) Post. "10,000 Share Soap Secrets." 24 August 1970.

_____. "Will the Message Wash Off?" 28 August 1970.

Beals, Alan R. Letter. *AAA Newsletter* 8:6 (July 1967):9.

Beals, Ralph L. *Politics of Social Research: An Inquiry into the Ethics and Responsibilities of Social Scientists*. Chicago: Aldine Publishing Company, 1969.

Behavior Today. "Outlook: Anthro Convention: Ethical Hassle." 29 November 1971.

Bell, Peter F. "Thailand's Northeast: Regional Underdevelopment, 'Insurgency,' and Official Response." *Pacific Affairs* 42:1 (Spring 1969):47–54.

Belshaw, Cyril. Letter. *AAA Newsletter* 11:8 (October 1970):2, 12.

Berreman, Gerald D. *The Politics of Truth: Essays in Critical Anthropology*. New Delhi: South Asian Publishers, 1981.

Binford, Sally R., and Lewis R. Binford. Letter. *AAA Newsletter* 8:6 (June 1967):9.

Blakeslee, D. J., L. W. Huff, and R. W. Kickert. *Village Security Pilot Study Northeast Thailand*. 3 vols. Bangkok: Joint Thai–U.S. Military Research and Development Center, 1965.

Blaufarb, Douglas S. *The Counterinsurgency Era: U.S. Doctrine and Performance 1950 to the Present*. New York: Free Press, 1977.

Blum, William. *The CIA: A Forgotten History*. London: Zed Books, 1986.

Braestrup, Peter. "Researchers Aid Thai Rebel Fight." *New York Times*, 20 March 1967.

Brant, Charles C. Letter. *AAA Newsletter* 10:5 (May 1969):4.

Brown, Richard. "Passages in the Life of a White Anthropologist: Max Gluckman in Northern Rhodesia." *Journal of African History* 20 (1979):525–41.

Buncher, Judith F., ed. *The CIA and the Security Debate, 1971–1975*. New York: Facts on File, 1976.

Carroll, Jerry. "A Question of Scholarship and Politics." *San Francisco Chronicle*, 6 April 1970.

Chilcote, Ronald H. *Theories of Comparative Politics: The Search for a Paradigm*. Boulder, Colorado: Westview Press, 1981.

_____. *Theories of Development and Underdevelopment*. Boulder, Colorado: Westview Press, 1984.

Chomsky, Noam. *American Power and the New Mandarins*. New York: Pantheon/Random House, 1967.

Columbia University CCAS [Committee of Concerned Asian Scholars]. "The American Asian Studies Establishment." *Bulletin of Concerned Asian Scholars* 3:3–4 (Summer–Fall 1971):92–103.

Cross, James E. *Conflict in the Shadows: The Nature and Politics of Guerilla War*. Garden City, NY: Doubleday, 1963.

Cunningham, Clark E. "Urgent Research in Northern Thailand." *Bulletin of the International Committee on Urgent Anthropological and Ethnological Research* 8 (1966):57–74.

_____. Letter. *AAA Newsletter* 8:4 (April 1967):10.

Darling, Frank C. *Thailand: New Challenges and the Struggle for a Political and Economic "Take–Off."* New York: American–Asian Educational Exchange, 1969.

Davenport, William. "The Thailand Controversy in Retrospect." In *Social Contexts of American Ethnology, 1840–1984* (1984 Proceedings of the American Ethnological Society), edited by June Helm, 65-72. Washington, DC: American Anthropological Association, 1985.

_____. David Olmsted, Margaret Mead, and Ruth Freed. *Report of the Ad Hoc Committee to Evaluate the Controversy Concerning Anthropological Activities in Relation to Thailand to the Executive Board of the American Anthropological Association* [Washington, DC: AAA], 27 September 1971.

Deitchman, Seymour J. *The Best–Laid Schemes: A Tale of Social Research and Bureaucracy.* Cambridge, Mass.: MIT Press, 1976.

de Sola Pool, Ithiel, et. al. *Social Science Research and National Security.* A Report Prepared by the Research Group in Psychology and the Social Sciences, Under Office of Naval Research Contract No. 1354(08), Task Number NR 170–379. Washington, DC: Smithsonian Institution, 5 March 1963.

Diaz, May N., and Lucile Newman. Letter. *AAA Newsletter* 13:1 (January 1972):3–4.

Dunn, Stephen P. Letter, *AAA Newsletter* 8:6 (June 1967):9.

Ehrich, Robert W. Letter. *AAA Newsletter* 8:2 (February 1967):7.

_____. Letter. *AAA Newsletter* 11:9 (November 1970):2.

Feldman, Jonathan. *Universities in the Business of Repression: The Academic–Military–Industrial Complex and Central America.* Boston: South End Press, 1989.

Feuchtwang, Stephan. "The Colonial Formation of British Social Anthropology." In *Anthropology and the Colonial Encounter*, edited by Talal Asad, 71-100. New York: Humanities Press, 1973.

Fortes, Meyer. "An Anthropologist's Point of View." In *Fabian Colonial Essays*, edited by Rita Hinden, 215-234. London: George Allen and Unwin, 1945.

Foster, George. Letter ("Anthropology on the Warpath: An Exchange"). *New York Review of Books*, 8 April 1971:43–44.

Garrett, Banning. "The Dominoization of Thailand." *Ramparts* 9:5 (November 1970):7–12.

Geddes, W. R. "Research and the Tribal Research Centre." In *Highlanders of Thailand*, edited by John McKinnon and Wanat Bhruksasri, 3-12. Kuala Lumpur: Oxford University Press, 1983.

Gillen, John P., George P. Murdock, and Alexander Spoehr. Letter. *AAA Newsletter* 8:2 (February 1967):7–8.

Girling, John L. S. *Thailand: Society and Politics*. Ithaca: Cornell University Press, 1981.

Gough Aberle, Kathleen. Letter. *AAA Newsletter* 8:6 (June 1967):11.

Gough, Kathleen. "Anthropology and Imperialism." *Monthly Review* (April 1968):12–24.

Gumperz, John J., et. al. Letter. *The (Berkeley) Daily Californian*, 13 April 1970.

Hailey, [The Right Honorable] Lord. "The Role of Anthropology in Colonial Development." *Man* 5 (1944):10–16.

Hanks, Lucien M., Jane R. Hanks, Lauriston Sharp, Ruth B. Sharp. *A Report on Tribal Peoples in Chiengrai Province North of the Mae Kok River (Bennington–Cornell Anthropological Survey of Hill Tribes in Thailand)*. Ithaca, NY: Cornell University, Department of Anthropology, Comparative Studies of Cultural Change, 1964.

Hinton, Peter. Letter. *AAA Newsletter* 12:3 (March 1971):11–13.

_____. Letter ("Anthropology on the Warpath: An Exchange"). *New York Review of Books*, 8 April 1971 [Abridged version of Hinton's March 1971 letter to the *AAA Newsletter*].

Horowitz, Irving Louis, ed. *The Rise and Fall of Project Camelot: Studies in the Relationship Between Social Sciences and Practical Politics.* Cambridge, Mass.: Massachusetts Institute of Technology, 1967.

Huff, Lee W. "The Thai Mobile Development Unit Program." In *Southeast Asian Tribes, Minorities, and Nations*, edited by Peter Kunstadter, 425–486. Princeton: Princeton University Press, 1967.

Huntington, Samuel P. *Instability at the Non–Strategic Level of Conflict* (Special Studies Group, Study Memorandum Number 2). Washington, DC: Institute for Defense Analyses, 6 October 1961.

_____. "Political Development and Political Decay." *World Politics* 17 (April 1965):386–430.

_____. *Political Order in Changing Societies.* New Haven: Yale University Press, 1968.

Institute for Defense Analyses. *Annual Report* [for 1956–57]. Washington, DC (the Pentagon): Institute for Defense Analyses, n.d.

_____. *Annual Report II* [for 1957–58]. Washington, DC: Institute for Defense Analyses, n.d.

_____. *Annual Report III* [for 1958–59]. Washington, DC: Institute for Defense Analyses, n.d.

_____. *Fourth Annual Report* [for 1959–60]. Washington, DC: Institute for Defense Analyses, n.d.

_____. *Annual Report Number Five* [for 1960–61]. Washington, DC: Institute for Defense Analyses, n.d.

_____. *Activities of the Institute for Defense Analyses 1961–1964.* Washington, DC: Institute for Defense Analyses, 22 April 1964.

_____. *The Tenth Year: March 1965 through February 1966.* Arlington, Virginia: Institute for Defense Analyses, n.d.

_____. *Report on the Activities of the Institute for Defense Analyses for the Fiscal Year Ending February 28, 1967.* Arlington, Virginia: Institute for Defense Analyses, n.d.

_____. *Annual Report 1968.* Arlington, Virginia: Institute for Defense Analyses, n.d.

_____. *Annual Report 1969.* Arlington, Virginia: Institute for Defense Analyses, n.d.

Isaacs, Stephen. "Asia Anthropology: Science or Spying?" *Washington Post*, 23 November 1971.

Jones, Delmos J. "Social Responsibility and the Belief in Basic Research: An Example from Thailand." *Current Anthropology* 12:3 (June 1971):347–350.

_____. Letter ("Anthropology on the Warpath: An Exchange"). *New York Review of Books*, 22 July 1971:37.

Jorgensen, Joseph. "On Ethics and Anthropology." *Current Anthropology* 12:3 (June 1971):321–334.

Kahin, George McT. *Intervention: How America Became Involved in Vietnam.* Garden City, NY: Anchor Books, 1987.

Kanok Wongtrangan. *Change and Persistence in Thai Counterinsurgency Policy.* (ISIS Occasional Paper No. 1.) Bangkok: Institute of Security and International Studies, Chulalongkorn University, September 1983.

Keesing, Felix M. "Applied Anthropology in Colonial Administration." *Science of Man* (1945):370–398.

Keyes, Charles F. "Security and Development in Thailand's Rural Areas." Bangkok: USOM/Thailand, October 1968.

Klare, Michael T. *War Without End: American Planning for the Next Vietnams.* New York: Alfred A. Knopf, 1972.

Kunstadter, Peter, ed. *Southeast Asian Tribes, Minorities, and Nations.* 2 vols. Princeton: Princeton University Press, 1967.

Leslie, Charles. Letter. *AAA Newsletter* 8:5 (May 1967):6.

Likhit Dhiravegin. *Postwar Thai Politics*. Bangkok: Faculty of Political Science, Thammasat University, 1986.

Lobe, Thomas. *United States National Security Policy and Aid to the Thailand Police*. Denver: University of Denver (Monograph Series in World Affairs, volume 14), 1977.

Lockwood, David E. "The U.S. Aid Program in Asia." *Current History* 49:291 (November 1965):257–261, 305–306.

Lomax, Louis. *Thailand: The War That Is, The War That Will Be*. New York: Vintage Books, 1967.

London School of Economics and Political Science. *Lectures and Classes in Colonial Administration and Anthropology*. London: University of London, 1934–1935, 1936–1937, 1937–1938, 1938–1939.

Malinowski, Bronislaw. *Dynamics of Culture Change: An Inquiry into Race Relations in Africa*. New Haven: Yale University Press, 1945.

Mallet, Marian. "Causes and Consequences of the October '76 Coup." *Journal of Contemporary Asia* 8:1 (1976):80–103.

Marchetti, Victor, and John D. Marks. *The CIA and the Cult of Intelligence*. New York: Alfred A. Knopf, 1974.

McCoy, Alfred. "Subcontracting Counterinsurgency." *Bulletin of Concerned Asian Scholars* (special issue: Vietnam Center at S.I.U. [Southern Illinois University], December 1970):56–70.

McGehee, Ralph W. *Deadly Deceits: My 25 Years in the CIA*. New York: Sheridan Square Publications, 1988.

Moerman, Michael. Letter. *AAA Newsletter* 12:1 (January 1971):9–11.

Morell, David, and Chai–anan Samudavanija. *Political Conflict in Thailand: Reform, Reaction, and Revolution*. Cambridge, Massachusetts: Oelgeschlager, Gunn & Hain, 1981.

Myers, Allen. "Scholars Join with US Gov't for Purposes of Counter-insurgency." *Student Mobilizer* 3:4 (2 April 1970):4–19.

NARMIC [National Action/Research on the Military Industrial Complex]. *Weapons for Counterinsurgency* (Local Action/Research Guide No. 1). Philadelphia: American Friends Service Committee, 15 January 1970.

New York Times. "Napalm Inventor Discounts 'Guilt.'" 21 December 1967:8.

_____. *The Pentagon Papers*. Toronto; New York: Bantam Books, 1971.

Okes, Imogene E. "Effective Communication by Americans with Thai." *Journalism Quarterly* 38 (1961):347–341. Reprinted in *Psychological Operations* 590-594. Department of the Army, 1976.

Pauker, Guy J. *Southeast Asia as a Problem Area in the Next Decade* [Tempo Report RM 58 TMP–34]. Santa Barbara, California: Technical Military Planning Operation, General Electric Company, 31 December 1958.

Phillips, Herbert. *Between the Tiger and the Crocodile: Scholarly Ethics and Government Research in Thailand*. Unpublished manuscript.

_____. Letter. *AAA Newsletter* 12:1 (January 1971):2, 7–9.

_____, and D. A. Wilson. *Certain Effects of Culture and Social Organization on International Security in Thailand*. Santa Monica, California: Rand Corporation, 1964.

Puey Ungphakorn. "Violence and the Military Coup in Thailand." *Bulletin of Concerned Asian Scholars* 9:3 (July–September 1977):4–12

Randolph, R. Sean. *The United States and Thailand: Alliance Dynamics, 1950–1985*. Berkeley: Institute of East Asian Studies, University of California, 1986.

Riggs, Fred W. *Thailand: The Modernization of a Bureaucratic Polity*. Honolulu: East–West Center Press, 1966.

Roseman, Alvin. "Thailand, Laos and Cambodia: A Decade of Aid." *Current History* 49:291 (November 1965):271–277, 305–306.

Rosenfeld, Henry. Letter. *AAA Newsletter* 8:4 (April 1967):9.

Rostow, Walt W. *The United States in the World Arena: An Essay in Recent History*. New York: Harper and Brothers, 1960.

_____. *The Stages of Economic Growth: A Non–Communist Manifesto*. Cambridge: Cambridge University Press, 1960.

Scoville, Orlin J., and James J. Dalton. "Rural Development in Thailand: The ARD Program." *Journal of Developing Areas* 9 (October 1974): 53–68.

Shenker, Israel. "Anthropologists Clash Over Their Colleagues' Ethics in Thailand." *New York Times*, 21 November 1971.

Siffin, William J. *The Thai Bureaucracy: Institutional Change and Development*. Honolulu: East–West Center Press, 1966.

_____, and Charles F. Keyes. "Concerning Local Government in Thailand: A Brief Selective Biography of Materials." In *Local Authority and Administration in Thailand*, edited by Fred von der Mehden and David A. Wilson, 170–191. Los Angeles: United States Operations Mission Thailand/Academic Advisory Council for Thailand, 1970.

Southeast Asia Development Advisory Group. *Directory 1966/67*. New York: Asia Society, [1967?].

_____. *Ad–Hoc Seminar on Employment*. New York: Asia Society, 1972.

_____. *Ad–Hoc Seminar on Labor Strategies*. New York: Asia Society, 1973.

_____. *Tenth Panel Seminar on Southeast Asian Development Goals— 1980*. New York: Asia Society, 1973.

_____. *Ad–Hoc Seminar on Communist Movements and Regimes in Indochina*. New York: Asia Society, 1974.

_____. *Ad–Hoc Seminar on Development and Finance of Local Government in Thailand*. New York: Asia Society, 1976.

The Student Mobilizer, 3:4 (2 April 1970) [Published by the Student Mobilization Committee to End the War in Vietnam, Washington, DC.].

Tanham, George K. *Trial in Thailand*. New York: Crane, Russak & Co., 1974.

[Thai] Department of Police, Department of Local Administration (DOLA), and Communist Suppression Operations Command (CSOC), *Evaluation Report: VSO [Village Security Officer] Training Project*. [Bangkok?:] n.p., n.d. [post–July 1967 seems likely].

[Thai Land Development Department.] "Seminar on Shifting Cultivation and Economic Development in Northern Thailand, Draft Programme—January 18 to 24, 2513 [1970]." n.d. [December 1969]. (Eric Wolf, private papers.)

Thinapan Nakata. *The Problems of Democracy in Thailand: A Study of Political Culture and Socialization of College Students*. Bangkok: Praepittaya International, 1975.

Tribal Data Center. "List of Consultants and Interested Persons, Attending the Consultants' Meeting," n.d. [December 1969 or January 1970]. (Eric Wolf, private papers.)

_____. "Proposal for Village Data Card," n.d. [January 1970.] (Eric Wolf, private papers.)

_____. "Meeting of Consultants and Interested Persons," 14 January 1970. (Eric Wolf, private papers.)

Tribal Research Center. "Six Years Later: An Interview with Peter Hinton." n.p.: 20 May 1976 (mimeo). (Alfred McCoy, private papers.)

Trombley, William. "UCLA Advisors Work with AID Unit in Thailand." *Los Angeles Times*, 2 April 1970.

Tugby, Donald J. "Ethnological and Allied Research Problems of Southeast Asia." *Current Anthropology* 11:1 (February 1970):49–54.

United States Department of the Army. *Minority Groups in Thailand* (Ethnographic Study Series). [Department of the Army Pamphlet No. 550–107.] Washington, DC.: Department of the Army, 1970. [Prepared by the Cultural Information Analysis Center (CINFAC) of the Center for Research in Social Systems (CRESS) of American University.]

_____. *The Art and Science of Psychological Operations: Case Studies of Military Applications*. 2 vols. [Department of the Army pamphlet No. 525–527.] n.p.: Headquarters, Department of the Army, 1976. [Prepared by the American Institutes for Research (AIR), Washington, DC., under Army contract.]

United States Congress. House of Representatives. *Behavioral Sciences and the National Security*. Report No. 4 Together with Part IX of the Hearings on Winning the Cold War: The U.S. Ideological Offensive by the Subcommittee on International Organizations and Movements

(Dante B. Fascell, Chairman) of the Committee on Foreign Affairs. Washington, DC: U.S. Government Printing Office, 1966.

United States Congress. House of Representatives. Committee on Appropriations, Subcommittee. *Department of Defense Appropriations for 1963, Hearings* (part 5), 87th Congress, 2nd session. Washington, DC: U.S. Government Printing Office, 1962.

_____. *Department of Defense Appropriations for 1965, Hearings* (part 5), 88th Congress, 2nd session. Washington, DC: U.S. Government Printing Office, 1964.

_____. *Department of Defense Appropriations for 1966, Hearings* (part 5), 89th Congress, 1st session. Washington, DC: U.S. Government Printing Office, 1965.

_____. *Department of Defense Appropriations for 1968, Hearings* (part 3), 90th Congress, 1st session. Washington, DC: U.S. Government Printing Office, 1967.

_____. *Department of Defense Appropriations for 1969, Hearings* (part 2), 90th Congress, 2nd session. Washington, DC: U.S. Government Printing Office, 1968.

_____. *Department of Defense Appropriations for 1970, Hearings* (part 5), 91st Congress, 1st session. Washington, DC: U.S. Government Printing Office, 1969.

U.S. Information Agency. "Attitudes, Communications and Communist Propaganda: Factors in Insurgency in Southeast Asia—1962" [R–76–62 (A)]. n.p: U.S. Information Agency, 1962. Reprinted in *Psychological Operations*, 553-572. Department of the Army, 1976.

United States Operations Mission/Thailand. *Thai–American Economic and Technical Cooperation.* [Bangkok:]: USOM/T, March 1965.

_____. *Evaluation Report: Joint Thai–USOM Evaluation of the Accelerated Rural Development Project.* Bangkok: [USOM/T], 30 May 1965.

_____. *Evaluation Report: Second Joint Thai–USOM Evaluation of the Accelerated Rural Development Project.* 2 vols. Bangkok: [USOM/T], July 1966.

_____. *Impact of USOM–Supported Programs in Changwad Sakon Nakorn*. [Bangkok:]: Research Division, USOM/T, 22 May 1967.

USOM/Thailand, Research Division. "Current Research Projects in Thailand." [Bangkok:] USOM/T, 23 March 1966.

_____. "Economic and Social Benefits of Roads in the North and Northeast." [Bangkok]: USOM/T, 18 July 1966.

_____. "Election of a Phuyaiban [village leader] in a Highly Security–Sensitive Village in the Northeast" [by Toshio Yatsushiro]. Bangkok: USOM/T, August 1966.

_____. "The Role of Cultural Factors in Worker–Client Relationships: A Two Way Process" [by Toshio Yatsushiro]. Bangkok: USOM/T, August 1966.

_____. "Advanced Overall Summary (revised): Village Attitudes and Conditions in Relation to Rural Security in Northeast Thailand, An Intensive Resident Study of 17 Villages in Sakon Nakorn and Mahasarakham Provinces" [by Toshio Yatsushiro]. Bangkok: USOM/T, May 1967.

_____. *Village Changes and Problems: Meeting with Village Leaders and Residents of Ban Don–Du, Tambon Khwao, Amphur Muang, Mahasarakam Province, February 10, 1967*. Bangkok: USOM/T, Research Division, July 1967.

_____. "*Khao Teung Prachachon* or Reaching the People" [by Liang Jayakal]. Bangkok: USOM/T, August 1967.

_____. "Local Indigenous Security Unit (Homeguard): Preliminary Tables." [Bangkok:] USOM/T, 16 November 1967.

_____. "Local Indigenous Security Unit (Homeguard): Preliminary Tables (Villagers)." [Bangkok:] USOM/T, 28 November 1967.

_____. "Local Indigenous Security Unit (Homeguard): Preliminary Tables" (Kamman and Phuyaiban [leader of group of villages and village leader]). [Bangkok:] USOM/T, 8 December 1967.

_____. "An Evaluation of the Home Guard by Local Officials, Members of the Guard and Villagers." [Bangkok:] USOM/T, 3 January 1968.

_____. "The Home Guard, A General Summary." [Bangkok:] USOM/T, 7 January 1968.

_____. "Field Interviews with Amphoe, Tambon, and Muban [district, subdistrict, and village] Officials and Villagers about Local Administration and Local Problems in Changwat [Province] Udorn Thani. [Bangkok:] USOM/T, 25 January 1968.

_____. "Attitude Survey of Rural Northeast Thailand." [Bangkok:] USOM/T, October 1968.

von der Mehden, Fred R., and David A. Wilson, eds. *Local Authority and Administration in Thailand.* (Report No. 1.) Los Angeles: United States Operations Mission Thailand/Academic Advisory Council for Thailand, 1970.

Watanachay Winitjakul, ed. *Samut Phap Duan Tula* [*October Photograph Notebook*]. Bangkok: National Student Union of Thailand, Thammasat University, 1988.

Weiner, Jeff. "Thailand Counterinsurgency." *UCLA Daily Bruin*, 6 April 1970.

Werner, Oswald. Letter. *AAA Newsletter* 11:9 (November 1970):2, 7.

Wilson, David. *The United States and the Future of Thailand.* New York and London: Praeger Publishers, 1970.

Wolf, Eric R., and Joseph G. Jorgensen. "Anthropology on the Warpath in Thailand." *New York Review of Books*, 19 November 1970.

_____. Letter. *AAA Newsletter* 11:7 (September 1970):2–3, 19.

_____. Letter ("Anthropology on the Warpath: An Exchange"). *New York Review of Books*, 8 April 1971:45–6.

_____. Letter ("Anthropology on the Warpath: An Exchange"). *New York Review of Books*, 22 July 1971:38.

_____. Letter. *AAA Newsletter* 13:1 (January 1972):3.

Yarborough, LTG (Ret.) William P. "Civil Assistance in Laos." In *Psychological Operations*, 458-459. Department of the Army, 1976.

Yatsushiro, Toshio. Memorandum, "Reports Resulting from Intensive Village Studies Focussed on Rural Security and Related Conditions." n.d. [post-February 1967 is most likely]. (Delmos Jones, private papers).

_____, and USOM/Thailand Research Division. *Village Organization and Leadership in Northeast Thailand: A Study of the Villagers' Approach to Their Problems and Needs*. Bangkok: n.p. [Department of Community Development and USOM/Thailand], May 1966

Young, Stephen B. "The Northeastern Village:A Non–Participatory Democracy." Bangkok: n.p [most likely part of a USOM/Thailand series of documents], September 1966.

ARCHIVAL SOURCES

National Anthropology Archives of the Smithsonian Institution, National Museum of Natural History, Washington, D.C. American Anthropological Society Archives 1979B, Boxes 7 and 8.

Aberle, David F. Memos to "The President, President Elect, Executive Board, Executive Director, and Secretary of the AAA," 10, 11 May 1970.

Academic Advisory Council for Thailand. *AACT Subcommittees*, n.d.

_____. *People Seen on AACT Trip: November 10 to December 22 1970.* [On the document "1970" has been crossed out and replaced with "1969 (?)"], n.d.

_____. *Meeting of the Academic Advisory Council for Thailand*, 19 October 1968; 24, 25 January 1969; 10, 11 June 1969; and 23, 24 July 1969.

Agency for International Development. *Amendment No. 3 to the Contract Between the United States of America and the Regents of the University of California* (PIO/T 493–190–3– 60152–A1; PIO/T 493–000.2–3– 90050), 1 September 1968 (mimeograph).

American Anthropological Association. *Charge to the Ad Hoc Committee to Evaluate the Controversy Concerning Anthropological Activity in Thailand*, n.d.

_____, Committee on Ethics. Letters to President, et. al. of the American Anthropological Association, 2 May 1970.

_____, [Wayne Shuttles, Acting Chairman]. *Annual Report of the Committee on Ethics*, September 1970.

American Institutes for Research. *Counterinsurgency in Thailand: The Impact of Economic, Social, and Political Action Programs.* Pittsburgh, PA: American Institutes for Research, December 1967.

_____. "Trip Report: Visit to Amphoe Nong Han, Changwad Udon, 28 May–6 June 1969."

_____. "Advisory Panel Meeting, 30 June–4 July 1969, Agenda."

_____. [Statement of Expenses/Bill from Michael Moerman], 5 July 1969.

Association for Asian Studies. "1970 Academic Panels on Thailand," n.d.

_____. "Program of the Twenty-Second Annual Meeting," 1970.

Beals, Ralph L. Letter to George Foster, 1 May 1970.

Berreman, Gerald D. *Statement by Professor Gerald D. Berreman*, 3 April 1970.

_____. Letter to George Foster, 10 April 1970.

_____. Letter to Lauriston Sharp, 22 April 1970.

_____. Letter to President, et. al. of the American Anthropological Association, 30 April 1970.

_____. Letter to President, et. al. of the American Anthropological Association, 11 August 1970.

Cunningham, Clark E. Letter to the Editor, *New York Times*, 16 May 1967. [I am unaware whether or not this was published.]

Ehrich, Robert W. Memorandum to members of the Ethics Committee of the American Anthropological Association, 22 January 1970.

_____. Letter to the Executive Board of the American Anthropological Association, 10 May 1970.

Institute for Defense Analyses. *Consultant Security Briefing*. Arlington, Virginia: IDA, October 1965.

_____. "The Thailand Study Group." [Minutes from a "Jason Summer Study" at Falmouth Intermediate School, Falmouth, Massachusetts] 20, 21, 22, 27 [?], 28, 29, 30 June; 3, 4, 5, 6, July 1967.

_____. "Insurgency in Thailand" [apparently a working paper from "The Thailand Study Group"], 3 July 1967.

Jayawardena, Chandra. Letter. *New York Review of Books*, 21 January 1971 (unpublished).

Keyes, Charles F., and Peter Kunstadter. Letter to George Foster, 29 April 1970.

Moerman, Michael. Letter to Dr. Paul A. Schwarz, 13 February 1970.

_____. Letter to Eric Wolf, 8 April 1970.

_____. Letters to George M. Foster, 24, 30 April 1970.

_____, and Charles Keyes. *Memo to AACT Members and Ad Hoc Committee on ARPA [Advanced Research Projects Agency] Northeastern Thailand Project*, n.d. [January–March 1967].

_____, and University of California at Los Angeles. [Abstract of a report titled "Analysis of Lue Conversation: Providing Accounts, Finding Breaches, Taking Sides" on a form labeled "Document Control Data—R & D."], 12 August 1968.

Nibhond Sasidhorn. Letter [of invitation to Tribal Data Centre Project Meeting of Consultants and Interested Persons], 23 December 1969.

Olmsted, David. Letter to [Margaret] Mead, [William] Davenport and [Ruth] Freed, n.d. [1971]

Oughton, G. [Gary] A. Letter to Eric Wolf, 15 December 1970.

Phillips, Herbert. Letter to Gerald Berreman, Joseph Fischer, Frederic Wakeman, 4 April 1970.

_____. Letters to Eric Wolf, 5, 6, 16 April 1970.

_____. Letter to William Rittenberg, et. al., 1 May 1967.

_____. Letter to M.R. Khukrit Pramoj, 6 May 1970.

_____. Letter to George Foster, 9 May 1970.

_____. Letter to members of the Committee on Ethics of the American Anthropological Association, 19 May 1970.

_____. Letter to Margaret Mead, 24 April 1971.

_____. Letter to James F. Gibbs, 29 December 1971.

_____. Letter to Seymour Deitchman, 24 September 1978.

Piker, Steven. Letter to Eric Wolf, 6 April 1970.

Poats, Rutherford. Letter to Senator J. W. Fulbright, n.d. [first page missing].

Rabinow, Paul. et. al. Letter to Dr. H[erbert]. Phillips, 24 April 1967.

Sahlins, Marshall and Eric Wolf. *Statement of Marshall Sahlins and Eric Wolf*, [30 March-2April 1970].

Schneider, D.M. Letter to the President, et. al. of the American Anthropological Association, 30 June 1970.

Sharp, Lauriston. *Statement of Lauriston Sharp*, 1 April 1970 and, with minor alterations, 3 April 1970.

_____. Letter to Officers of Cornell University, 8 April 1970.

_____. Letter to Anthropology Colleagues, 9 April 1970.

_____. Letter to the Academic Community, 10 April 1970.

_____. Letter to Eric Wolf, 17 April 1970.

_____. Letter to George Foster, 8 May 1970.

_____, and David A. Wilson. Letter to Rey Hill, et. al., 18 March 1970.

Spiro, Melford. Letter to George Foster, 24 April 1970.

_____. Letter to Eric Wolf, 27 April, 21 May 1970.

_____. Letter to Robert Ehrich, 21 May 1970.

Suttles, Wayne. Letter to the Executive Board and Members of the Ethics Committee [of the AAA], 14 September 1970.

U.S. Congress, Committee on Government Operations, Foreign Operations and Government Information Subcommittee. *Hearing on Thailand and the Philippines* (John E. Moss, chairman), 16 June 1969 (mimeograph).

Wilson, David A. *Statement by David A. Wilson*, 3 April 1970.

Wolf, Eric R. Letter to Michael Moerman, 14 April 1970.

_____. Letters to Herbert Phillips, 3, 12 April 1970.

_____. Letters to Steven Piker, 3, 12 April 1970

_____. Letter to Lauriston Sharp, 3 April 1970.

_____. Letter to Mr. Lehman, 25 May 1970.

_____, and Joseph Jorgensen. Statement, 30 March 1970.

_____, and Joseph Jorgensen. Letter to Lauriston Sharp. 22 April 1970.

_____, and Joseph Jorgensen. Letter to the president, et. al. of the American Anthropological Association, 25 May 1970.

Yatsushiro, Toshio. Memorandum, "Reports Resulting from Intensive Village Studies Focussed on Rural Security and Related Conditions," n.d. [post–February 1967 is most likely].

The Margaret Mead papers in the U.S. Library of Congress, Washington, D.C. The Manuscripts Division: Margaret Mead Papers. Organizations File E-12, Folders 1-3; Scheduling File, 1970-1972.

[AAA, Ad Hoc Committee to Evaluate the Controversy Concerning Anthropological Activities in Thailand.] "AAA–CTC [Committee on Thailand Controversy] Bibliography," 25 August 1971.

Freed, Ruth. Letter to Margaret Mead, 14 June 1971.

_____. Letter to Margaret Mead, 27 August 1971.

_____. Letter to Margaret Mead, 12 October 1971

_____. Letter to Margaret Mead, 16 November 1971.

Geddes, W. R. Letter to Margaret Mead, 27 May 1971.

"Itinerary for Dr. Margaret Mead: June 19, 1971–September 4, 1971." Margaret Mead papers, U.S. Library of Congress.

Lehman, Edward. Letter to Margaret Mead, 28 March 1972.

Mead, Margaret. Letter to Edward Lehman, 10 April 1972.

_____. Letter to Ruth Freed, 20 September 1971.

_____. Letter to Edward Lehman, 24 September 1971.

Wagley, Charles. Letter to Margaret Mead, 20 October 1971.

Interviews and Correspondence

Aberle, David F. Telephone interview with author, 8 May 1991.

_____. Letter to author, 8 May 1991.

Beals, Alan R. Letter to author, 23 April 1991.

Berreman, Gerald. Telephone interview with author, 14 May 1991.

Chance, Norman. Telephone interview with author, 30 April 1991.

Davenport, William. Letter to author, 2 April 1991.

_____. Telephone interview with author, 18 June 1991.

Ehrich, Robert. Telephone interview with author, 24 April 1991.

Foster, George M. Letter to author, 28 March 1991.

_____. Telephone interview with author, 30 May 1991.

Huff, Lee W. Telephone interview with author, 21 May 1991.

Jones, Delmos J. Personal interview with author, 2 May 1991.

Jorgensen, Joseph G. Letter to author, 15 April 1991.

_____. Telephone interview with author, 10 May 1991.

Marr, David. Letter to author, 16 April 1991.

McCoy, Alfred W. Letter to author, 13 February 1991.

Moerman, Michael. Letter to author, 6 April 1991.

Neher, Clark. Telephone interview with author, 24 April 1991.

Olmsted, David. Telephone interviews with author, 29 April, 21 May 1991.

Phillips, Herbert. Telephone interviews with author, 1 May, 21 May 1991.

Piker, Steven. Letter to author, 27 March 1991.

_____. Telephone interview with author, 5 April 1991.

Sahlins, Marshall. Telephone interview with author, 24 April 1991.

Sharp, Lauriston. Telephone interview with author, 29 April 1991.

Turner, Terence. Telephone interview with author, 6 May 1991.

Wilson, David A. Telephone interview with author, 2 May 1991.

Wolf, Eric. Personal interview with author, 4 April 1991.

_____. Telephone interview with author, 21 May 1991.

Wyatt, David. Telephone interview with author, 24 April 1991.

_____. Letter to author, 25 April 1991.